Fine WoodWorking on Woodshop Specialties

Fine WoodWorking® *on* Woodshop Specialties

27 articles selected by the editors of *Fine Woodworking* magazine

The Taunton Press

Cover photo by Deborah Fillion

©1987 by The Taunton Press, Inc.

First printing: January 1987
Second printing: October 1990
International Standard Book Number: 0-918804-75-2
Library of Congress Catalog Card Number: 86-51292
Printed in the United States of America

A FINE WOODWORKING Book

FINE WOODWORKING® is a trademark of The Taunton Press, Inc.,
registered in the U.S. Patent and Trademark Office.

The Taunton Press, Inc.
63 South Main Street
Box 5506
Newtown, Connecticut 06470-5506

Contents

Introduction

In an earlier era, wood was primary among materials, it was what there was, and if you wanted to make a thing, wood was what you'd use. Today if a person works in wood, it's by choice, for we also have plastic and cement and glass, and myriad techniques for joining and shaping metals. Even so, I'm always astonished by the diversity of the complex things people make of it—fishing rods, beehives, clocks, microscopes and airplanes—as well as by the intricacy of the commonplace things people tend to take for granted—panel doors, barrels, picture frames, staircases. This volume, the 20th and last in the *Fine Woodworking on* . . . series of reprinted articles, explores such wooden specialties.

John Kelsey, editor

Wooden Clockworks

Design and construction require ingenuity, care

by John R. Lord

Clock designed and made by author ticks off the seconds but has no hands. Frame and pendulum are bird's-eye maple; large wheels are laminated from strips of various hardwoods with wooden teeth set into slots sawn in rims. Original wooden escapement has been replaced by experimental version of acrylic plastic (top center); base is Formica-covered plywood on hardwood framework. Pendulum has effective length of one meter and beats once a second; escape wheel has 30 teeth; center wheel (extreme right) rotates once in 144 minutes.

Clocks—old and new—are a subject of very personal interest to me, not only from the standpoint of historical value but also from one of design. It follows that the approach by which I design and construct my clocks is also personal. I hasten to mention that clock design and construction have been thoroughly documented down through history (further reading, page 9) and I make no claim as to the classical propriety of my designs or means of executing them. As an artist I formulate a careful plan at the outset. But then, within certain parameters of scale, strength and function, I may do almost anything, even violate all rules of horology, to pursue my vision. That confession out of the way, let us proceed.

I shall endeavor here to explain how clocks work, how to design a clock mechanism from scratch, and how to make it out of wood. The designing is not very difficult once the principles of escapements and gears are understood, and the manufacture is within the reach of an amateur craftsman with average facilities. A clock could be made entirely by hand, tediously. But there is no complete plan in this article, for I want most of all to encourage original design. Although a clock can be made to tell accurate time, it is a mistake to be constrained by this historically recent requirement. With the works exposed, face and hands can be absent, allowing greater appreciation of the marvelous machine called clock.

A clockwork is a transmission ma-

John R. Lord, of Waterloo, N.Y., has designed and built several wildly different clock-like mechanisms. He has an M.F.A. from Syracuse University. All prices throughout as of 1978.

chine, a train of intermeshed gears and pinions, set in rotary motion by the kinetic energy of a falling weight. An escapement mechanism divides the weight's long fall to the floor into tiny increments. A swinging pendulum regulates the rate at which the weight is allowed to fall, eking out its energy in brief, uniform and countable bits.

My romance with clockworks and timepieces (the term clock, strictly, denotes an hour-striking device as well) overtook me in London when I visited the National Science Museum. Some of the oldest running tower clocks are there, iron machines of great complexity and beauty, dating from the 14th century. I spent hours studying them as they beat the inexorable seconds.

Clockwork is not the product of a linear evolution, nor did it spring whole from any single source. It represents the convergence since the Middle Ages of several diverse technologies. Toothed wheels as a means of transmitting power were described by Archimedes, and ancient Greek artisans used them in complicated devices for computing the relative positions of the sun, moon and planets. This technology was preserved by Arab civilization and transmitted to Europe in the 12th century. The escapement was invented in China in the 9th century and reached Europe 500 years later, when monks developed weight-driven clockworks regulated by an inertial escapement called "verge and foliot." These clocks had no dials—they were used to automatically strike the prayer bells. In the 16th century, when faces were added to tower clocks, most had only an hour hand. A minute hand, while technically possible, would have been pointless. The mechanisms were too inaccurate to give

meaning to the minutes, and anyway, few cared.

Clocks did not become accurate until the pendulum regulator replaced the verge and foliot. For a pendulum of any given length from suspension to bob, the period of oscillation is constant, regardless of the amount of swing or weight of bob. This was noticed in the middle of the 17th century by several observers, among them Galileo and Christian Huygens. Although Galileo made the first drawings of a pendulum clock, the Dutch astronomer Huygens first built one.

Most early clocks were hand-forged of iron, by blacksmiths. Not far into the 15th century, brass became more widely available and was quickly

From *Fine Woodworking* magazine (Spring 1978) 10:44-51

Starting from the Thomas plans and using a Shopsmith with hand tools, Richard Heine of Santa Monica, Calif., built four clocks like this. Now he has formed a company, The Finest Hour, and is tooling up to produce about 20 a month to retail at $2,000. The clock stands 65 in. high. Case and works are Brazilian rosewood; hands and pendulum bob are cocobolo. The wheels for the prototypes were made by pasting paper patterns on the wood and bandsawing. Now Heine uses a metalworker's gear-cutting machine. These clocks use a watch-type escapement, a close cousin of the recoil anchor. The lever spans only three teeth, minimizing expansion problems, but the price is a complex escape wheel with fragile short grain across many of its teeth.

Crutch — Suspension
Back plate
Bob
Escape lever
Escape wheel - 30
Escape pinion - 8
Spacer
Thomas with clock
Front plate
Latch
Timing nut
Weight arbor
Ratchet
Shaft cover
Second wheel - 60
Seconds
Minute wheel - 30
Second pinion - 8
Minute pinion - 8
Center wheel - 64
Hours
Figures represent number of teeth
Pawl
Minutes
Crown wheel
Cannon pinion - 10
Hour wheel - 32

This exploded view of an all-wooden clock is taken from an 8-sheet set of plans developed and sold by Ralph D. Thomas, shown at right with his prototype. Thomas, a Western Electric executive, got interested in clocks 15 years ago, after helping his son make a gear-driven gizmo for science class. He found that although many old clocks use wooden wheel trains, none was made entirely of wood, so he made one. It takes 40 hours to build and comes apart.

Thomas sells his wooden-clock plans from his home at 1412 Drumcliffe Rd., Winston-Salem, N.C. 27103; the plans are also available from Constantine, 2065 Eastchester Rd., Bronx, N.Y. 10461.

adopted because it is much easier than iron to shape. A simultaneous interest in watches and smaller clocks demanded increased use of brass, although supply continued to be scarce until the Industrial Revolution because of the tortuous process by which it was made. A melt of copper and tin was poured from a crucible into a flat puddle and hammered by hand to workharden it. The brass was reheated red, cooled and hammered some more, then cut to shape and filed smooth.

Wooden patterns were probably necessary for making these early clocks, and some enormous mechanisms were made entirely of wood, in the tradition of grist mills. Smaller wooden clockworks were made in backwaters such as the Black Forest of Germany, and in Colonial America. The American tradition of wooden wheel trains, using scarce metal only for arbors and escape wheels, continued during the development of mass production after 1800, but by the middle of the century the

same Industrial Revolution had made brass readily available and wood was replaced. Many factory-made wooden clocks of 150 years ago are keeping good time today.

How clocks work

People usually don't understand just what it is that drives and regulates a pendulum clock. The most common questions are, "Where's the motor?" and "How does the pendulum make it go?" Although the swinging pendulum is the eye-catching part of most clocks, it is simply a regulator. All the energy comes from the gravity-induced fall of the suspended weight (which can be replaced by a coiled spring or an electric motor). The wheel train transmits this kinetic energy to the time-computing motion works for display by the hands, and also to the escape mechanism. The escapement's release-relock sequence passes tiny impulses on to the pendulum, making up for frictional losses and keeping it swinging. In turn,

each beat of the pendulum allows the escapement to unwind, thereby emitting a tick or a tock.

All this time-computing and power-transmitting wheelwork could be removed, reducing the clock to its bare minimum: A weight hung from a cord wrapped directly around the arbor of an escape wheel with escape lever, crutch and pendulum (diagram on next page). This clock would run, but that's all. If it had a 30-tooth escape wheel and a one-meter pendulum, it would count the seconds. The weight acts through a lever arm whose length is the radius of the arbor, thus exerting force to turn the escape wheel. Unlike a spring or even an electric motor, this force never fluctuates and it needs no care other than periodic rewinding.

Instead of an escape wheel with 30 teeth, which would rotate once a minute, the minimum clock might be made with a single wheel of 1,800 teeth. Connected to the same one-meter pendulum, the wheel would ro-

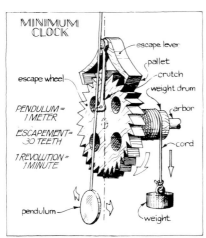

escape lever
pallet
escape wheel
crutch
weight drum

PENDULUM =
1 METER

arbor

ESCAPEMENT =
30 TEETH

cord

1 REVOLUTION =
1 MINUTE

pendulum

weight

Minimum clock would tick off the seconds, but that's all.

'Clock IV', by Lawrence B. Hunter of San Diego; 86 in. high, 36 in. wide, 19 in. deep; made of walnut with ⅛-in. birch dowel in an edition of six, $3,500 each. Hunter, a sculptor, writes that he is 'trying to eliminate the nonessential and distill down to the very essence of the clock and its skeletal structure, then organize the parts into a visual whole.' The great wheel has 160 pin-type teeth, the escape wheel has 72 teeth, the lantern pinion has eight leaves. The pendulum beats once in 1¼ seconds, and the single hand turns once an hour.

tate once an hour, still counting every second. But an 1,800-tooth wheel is hardly practical. This is why clockmakers use a train of wheels and pinions. The essential tick-tock mechanism remains the same.

Tick, tock

The diagram at left on the next page breaks the release-relock sequence of the escape mechanism into the stages that produce a tick and a tock—two seconds in the life of the clock. This is a recoil-anchor escapement, so called because the lever is shaped like an anchor, and because there is a small backward motion at the end of each beat.

Aside from the precise shape of the wheel and lever, which I will discuss shortly, the physical requirement here is that their arbors be mounted below the suspension point of the pendulum. The crutch, which transmits the impulse to the pendulum, is an extension of the arbor that carries the escape lever and embraces the pendulum rod without being attached to it. This ensures that the pendulum will beat freely without hindrance of friction. Note that the escape lever may be below the wheel or alongside it, as long as it is balanced to rock freely.

Without the governing influence of the pendulum, the escape mechanism would oscillate rapidly and irregularly, expending the energy of the system in a whirring clickety-clack. Thus the pendulum is the soul of the system, forcing it to eke out its store of power, second by second. It accomplishes this by virtue of the physical laws innate to it: A pendulum of given length, unhindered by frictional drag, will swing from side to side in a given time and that time will be constant no matter how wide the arc of swing. (This is not strictly true when the arc is very wide, but it is true when the arc is only a couple of degrees.) Further, a pendulum one meter long will always take one second to swing. Since each swing of the pendulum releases one-half tooth of the escape wheel, a 30-tooth wheel will rotate once a minute, and tick each second.

The time of the swing depends upon the length of the pendulum and the acceleration of gravity, which varies minutely according to latitude and elevation above sea level. The time of swing has nothing to do with the weight of the bob, as long as the bob is heavy compared to the weight of the arm

from which it hangs. The formula is:

$$t = \pi \sqrt{\frac{l}{g}} \quad \text{or} \quad l = \frac{t^2 g}{\pi^2}$$

where t is the time of one swing from left to right in seconds, the familiar π equals 3.1416, l is the length of the pendulum and g is the acceleration of gravity, 32.17 ft/sec² or 9.81 meters/sec².

If the beat is to be 2 seconds, the pendulum will be 13 ft. ½ in. (or 4 meters) long; if the time is 1½ sec., the pendulum is 7 ft. 4 in. (or 2.25 meters) long; if it is one second, the pendulum is 39.14 in. (or 1 meter) long; if the time is a half-second, the pendulum is 9.8 in. (or 25 centimeters) long. A clock is adjusted by minutely changing the length of the pendulum, usually by means of a thread and nut at the suspension point or under the bob.

The escapement

Whether the aim is a timepiece or a kinetic sculpture, the design process should begin with the pendulum and escapement. There are many types of escapement; the traditional workhorse is the recoil anchor shown here. It is a simple yet eminently workable design. The escape wheel and the escape lever (the anchor) are laid out together, as in the diagrams at right. The one shown is right-handed and turns clockwise. A left-handed wheel will also work. The most difficult procedure is spacing the 30 points around the circumference of the wheel. No matter how careful you are with an adjustable drafting triangle, there's always something left over at the end. I treasure an old 60-tooth ratchet wheel I found at a scrap yard. I can draw the wheel the size I want, plunk the master down on it, and extend lines from its points to the wheel's circumference.

The configuration shown, where the back of each tooth drops directly to the base of the next at the root circle, is sturdy enough for wooden construction. Wear will be least when the wheel is lightest, however, and narrower teeth are best for fabrication in brass or plastic. To draw them, construct a second circle tangent to a 20° angle from a radius, its vertex at one of the points on the rim. Draw the backs of all the teeth tangent to this circle, just as the fronts are tangent to a 10° circle. I have made escapements of solid and laminated wood, iron, and acrylic plastic, and

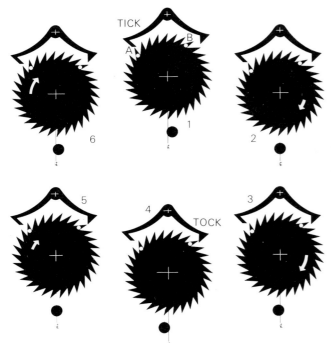

TICK

6   1   2

5   4   3

TOCK

A   B

Two seconds in the life of an escapement, told in six steps reading clockwise. Sequence begins with a tick (1) as the tooth A smacks the entry pallet and the pendulum swings toward its rightmost point. The turning escape wheel pushes the entry pallet (2), rocking the lever and sending an impulse via the crutch to the pendulum as it begins to swing leftward. Tooth A escapes (3) and the wheel turns, but immediately tooth B is caught by the exit pallet, tock, stopping the motion (4). Tooth B pushes the exit pallet (5), rocking the lever and prodding the pendulum toward the right. Tooth B escapes (6) and the cycle repeats.

To lay out an escape wheel of 30 teeth: Draw circles of outside and root diameter, i.e. 6 in. and 4½ in. Divide circumference into 30 equal parts (12°). From one of these points, draw a radius and a line making an angle of 10° with it. Draw a circle tangent to the 10° line. Draw lines from each point tangent to the 10° circle. These lines define the front faces of the teeth. Connect each point to the root of the previous point. This defines the back face of each tooth. For a wheel of brass or plastic, draw a second circle at 20° to a radius and make the back face of each tooth tangent to it.

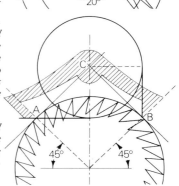

12°   10°   20°

To lay out an escape lever spanning 7½ teeth: Draw a vertical line through the center of the wheel. Since the lever is to span ¼ of the teeth (7½), draw two lines at 45° to the vertical. This locates A and B, the tips of the entry and exit pallets.

Draw tangents to the wheel through A and B. They intersect at C, the center of the escape lever axle. A tangent is perpendicular to a radius.

C   A   B   45°   45°

Draw a circle at C whose radius is one-half the distance between centers. Draw tangents to this circle through A and B. These tangents define the faces of the entry and exit pallets. The remainder of the escape lever may be any shape.

have settled on plastic.

The escape lever shown embraces one-quarter of the wheel's circumference, or 7½ teeth. This is the most common configuration, and (if you have no taste for geometric construction) the distance between arbors is 1.41 times the diameter of the wheel. The number of teeth embraced can be up to one fewer than half the total, and as few as two or three. The layout procedure is the same. The difference is the distance between arbors—the more teeth, the farther they are apart; the fewer, the closer together.

This construction locates the active faces of the entry and exit pallets, and the distance between arbors. These are the only absolutes—the form of the rest of the lever is left to the designer. But absolute precision is essential in locating and fabricating the active surfaces, else the clock won't run. The tips of the teeth and the pallets must be as smooth and hard as possible, allowing no irregularity in their motion. Some makers saw out the bearing surfaces and replace them with a denser material, a watchmaking practice whereby tiny,

flat jewels are cemented to the pallets. They do not wear and they are absolutely smooth.

The importance of the pendulum in all this contrasts with the relative simplicity with which it can be made—the Thomas clock uses a croquet ball on the end of a dowel. It must be suspended above the escapement, on a vertical line with the wheel arbor. The suspension may be as simple as a strap of leather or a steel shim stock, a point set in a dimple (Thomas), a knife edge in a groove—anything that allows the pendulum to swing freely in a flat, smooth arc.

The exact location of the crutch is a function of the arc or swing and of the amount of rock designed into the escape lever, and is best found by experiment and observation. The exact shape of the crutch may range from a flat stick with two protruding dowels that embrace the arm, to wherever your imagination takes you. One caution: Not more than 1/32 in. of space should exist between the crutch forks and the arm, or the impulse won't be of sufficient duration ever to catch up.

'Clock III' by Lawrence Hunter uses a verge-and-foliot escapement. The horns atop the clock swivel majestically back and forth, taking two seconds each way, releasing a tooth of escape wheel each time. Wheel has 15 contrate teeth—that is, teeth are parallel to arbor rather than perpendicular to it.

'Inventor Released,' escapement-mechanism sculpture by David and Marji Roy of South Woodstock, Conn. Powered by the hanging weight, the L-shaped arm rises to kick escape lever, releasing a tooth and allowing large wheel to rotate a full turn clockwise or counterclockwise. The Roys produce a variety of escapement sculptures in limited editions that retail in the $100 to $250-range.

The time train

In the diagram below, the time train of a typical clock is spread out on a line. It proceeds in two directions from the center wheel: To the right, it energizes the pendulum and is regulated by it; to the left, it computes and displays the hour. The weight's energy is transmitted via the center wheel, which drives the pinion of the second wheel (so called because of its position in the train, not because it counts the sec-

onds); the second wheel drives the pinion of the escape wheel. Proceeding the other way, the pinion of the center wheel (the cannon pinion) drives the minute wheel, whose pinion drives the hour wheel. The figures are the tooth counts of each wheel and pinion.

If you should somehow have access to a computer and plotter, it can be used to lay out very accurate wheels. It can also lay out elliptical wheels, square wheels and star-shaped wheels. They must run in identical pairs, and always turn end-to-side. They do not turn at a constant speed, but rather at double speed half-way around, and half-speed the rest of the way, averaging out where they ought. They seem to gallop.

The wheels are generally arranged—but needn't be—to run the minute and hour hands from a common center, which requires a hollow arbor called a cannon tube concentric with the arbor of the center wheel.

For convenience, the weight drum may also be on a hollow arbor concentric with the center wheel. Note that the weight drum may be connected to another whole train of wheels. These have nothing to do with computing the time, but rather with how often one must rewind the clock. Thirty-day movements are common in brass clocks, but in wood old friend gravity takes his vengeance in the form of friction and inertia at each connection. When the time is told, most of the weight's energy is lost. The longer the movement, the more slowly the weight must fall, and the more freely the mechanism must turn. Eight days is about the limit in wooden clockworks.

The ratios in the diagram are used in many grandfather clocks, but they aren't sacred. The point is to make the minute hand rotate once for 60 turns of the second hand, and the hour hand once for 12 turns of the minute hand. Many different wheel ratios, a few specified in the chart opposite, will do the same thing. These combinations will be most useful to the maker of wooden works, but others can be figured from the logic below. For practical purposes, begin with a one-meter pendulum and a 30-tooth escape wheel.

This pendulum beats once a second, and each beat releases half a tooth on the escape wheel (each tooth acts twice, once on each pallet of the escape lever). Thus the 30-tooth escape wheel rotates once a minute, or 60 times an hour. Its arbor is therefore a good place to mount the second hand. Since the escape wheel and its pinion are fastened to the same arbor, the pinion must also rotate 60 times an hour. In one hour the pinion's eight leaves will engage 60×8 or 480 teeth on the second wheel, thus turning it eight times. The second wheel pinion also turns eight times, engaging $8 \times 8 = 64$ teeth on the center wheel. The center wheel has exactly 64 teeth, so it will rotate once an hour. Put the minute hand here.

Turn now to the motion work to the left of the center wheel. The cannon pinion, 10 teeth, is fastened to the center wheel arbor and therefore rotates once an hour or 12 times in 12 hours, thereby engaging 120 teeth on the minute wheel. Since it has 30 teeth, it will have to rotate four times in 12 hours. The minute pinion also rotates four times, so in 12 hours its eight teeth will engage 32 teeth on the hour wheel, which happens to have exactly 32 teeth. It will rotate once in 12 hours. The hour hand goes here.

Notice that in 12 hours, while the hour wheel rotates only once, the pendulum beats once a second—an astonishing 43,200 times. In any gear train, the number of rotations of the last pinion to one rotation of the first wheel will be equal to the product of all teeth in the wheels divided by the product of all the leaves in the pinions. In a clock, the teeth in the escape wheel are multiplied by two because each acts twice. The pendulum itself is the last pinion, one beat being one "rotation." Thus,

$$\frac{32 \times 30 \times 64 \times 60 \times 30 \times 2}{8 \times 10 \times 8 \times 8} = 43,200$$

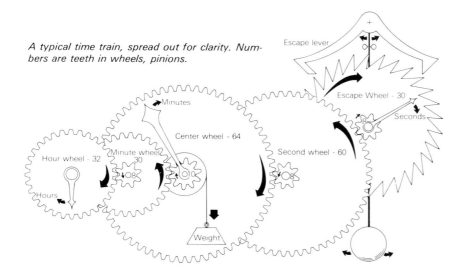

A typical time train, spread out for clarity. Numbers are teeth in wheels, pinions.

Escape lever

Escape Wheel - 30

Minutes

Center wheel - 64

Seconds

Hour wheel - 32

Minute wheel 30

Second wheel - 60

08

010

8

Hours

Weight

Chiming clock train made by M.C. Hall of Austin, Tex., right, is alongside a 19th-century Eli Terry movement. Hall, 74, a retired aircraft tool engineer, adds an extra wheel, a deadbeat anchor and brass bushings to get a 30-day movement. Front and back plates are quartersawn white oak, wheels are quartersawn black cherry, one-piece arbors and pinions are maple. Terry's pinions are holly.

Wheels and pinions

A complete discussion of the geometry of wheels and pinions would fill a book. For clockwork purposes, consider two rollers pressed tightly together, one driving the other. The smaller, the pinion, is the driven; the larger, the wheel, is the driver. The relative speed of each would depend on their diameters, and if slippage could be prevented, rollers would drive a clock. In practice, teeth are necessary and teeth must mesh just as smoothly as if the wheels were plain rollers. The effective size of intermeshed gears is the size of the imaginary rollers, and is called the pitch circle. The teeth must be shaped so that the transmitted motion is absolutely uniform, or the clock will stop.

In engineering practice, for a wheel with N teeth, the relationship between the pitch diameter PD and the outside diameter OD has been standardized:

$$PD = OD \frac{N}{N+2}$$

For gears to mesh at all, the number of teeth in the wheel and the leaves in the pinion must be directly proportional to the diameters of their pitch circles. Engineers call this the pitch of the gear, and specify it by the number of teeth per inch of diameter of the pitch circle. Thus a 7½ in. wheel with 60 teeth is 8-pitch. So is a 1-in. pinion with eight leaves. The wheels in the Thomas clock are 8-pitch.

The Thomas clock uses the type of gears engineers use to transmit power. The teeth of the wheels and pinions have the shape of involute curves. Historically, clockmakers settled upon cycloidal teeth, a shape that is easier to make and equally efficient, since a clock doesn't transmit great amounts of torque. Cycloids generated by circles come in pairs, and one pair matches a straight line with an epicycloid that is so close to circular that the difference doesn't matter. The mating teeth are shaped as in the diagram below. When they are made of brass, the faces of the pinion leaves are radial; when made of wood, they are made parallel. The small circle that defines the profile of the wheel teeth is half the diameter of the pinion's pitch circle, and the arc is struck from midway between two teeth, on the pitch circle of the wheel.

While it would be convenient to design pinions with very few leaves, the practical lower limit is eight. This is because friction is markedly higher when gears begin to interact before the meshing teeth pass an imaginary line connecting the center of the wheel and pinion, compared to when they mesh after this line. With a pinion of fewer than eight teeth, the interaction begins before the line of centers; with eight, at the line; with more than eight, after the line. The situation is improved with the lantern pinion—even with as few as six pins, the action begins well after the line of centers. A lantern pinion will mesh well enough with both cycloidal and involute wheels, and also with tinker-toy style teeth made of dowel.

Wheel construction

Most woodworking shops aren't equipped for the specifics of gear cutting, so it becomes necessary to invent. An index wheel is the handiest tool, in

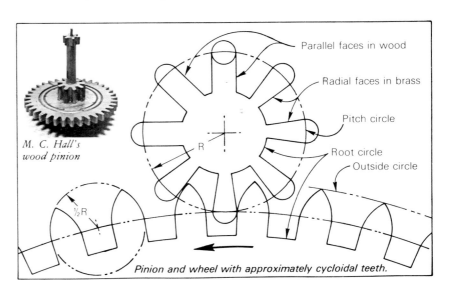

M. C. Hall's wood pinion

Parallel faces in wood
Radial faces in brass
Pitch circle
Root circle
Outside circle

Pinion and wheel with approximately cycloidal teeth.

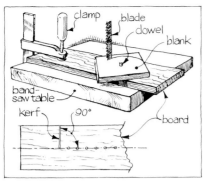

A piece of plywood can quickly become a circle-cutting jig for the band saw. Space holes for a dummy arbor along a line perpendicular to the blade. Carefully adjust guides, rotate blank into the blade.

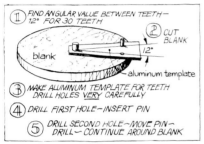

An aluminum or brass template, carefully made, will space holes around a blank.

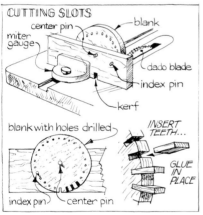

Use the table saw to turn the holes into slots. The trick is aligning the first hole with the dado blade, so the slot will be perfectly radial. Then drill through a hole for the index pin, and all the slots will be radial.

Lantern pinion from Lawrence Hunter's 'Clock IV' engages pin wheel laminated of seven veneer layers, five of them running around the rim and two running crosswise.

terms of accuracy gained and time saved, but it is rarely available. Fortunately there are ready substitutes. I urge constant surveillance of junkyards and scrap machinery for any gears of reasonable size and some number of teeth which will divide into usable numbers and provide a pattern for tracing. Two of the best to own have 60 teeth and 96 teeth. Between them they yield 2, 3, 4, 5, 6, 8, 10, 12, 15, 20, 24, 30, 32, and 48 teeth. The next best alternative is a protractor and an adjustable triangle.

Another home remedy is a jig for cutting round wheel blanks, as in the diagram at left. Much cut and try goes into clockwork and the ability to generate wheels easily and quickly is a big help. With well-adjusted saw guides, a sharp blade and care in alignment, this jig will deliver a very accurate blank.

There are several alternatives regarding the actual fabrication of clock wheels. At its most basic, a wheel is no more than a single, solid disc of wood with teeth cut into its circumference. The easiest way to make one is to draw a full-size paper pattern, glue it onto the wood, and cut around the profile with a jigsaw, band saw or coping saw. The problem with this type of wheel is seasonal movement of the wood, short-grain fragility and difficulty of replacing a broken tooth in case of disaster.

As a hedge against the wood's tendency to warp with the weather, I laminate wheels of several narrow strips, or of pie-shaped wedges. I usually mismatch each strip with respect to the next according to the annual rings; veneers can be inserted between pieces for further visual interest. I've seen wheels cut of birch plywood, very stable.

I use inserted teeth because if one becomes damaged, it can be replaced singly. This necessitates sawing a series of radial slots in the rim of the wheel. I do this by first drilling a ring of properly spaced holes, using the template shown in the diagram. If the template layout and initial drilling are not absolutely accurate, the last hole will have a very strange relationship to the first. But the job can be done with care.

Thus far we have a set of holes evenly spaced around the wheel. We could press dowels into them and use them as pin wheels, which also allows interesting variations such as right-angle drives. To cut the holes into slots to accept inserted teeth, I use the table-saw

Close-up of author's clock shows laminated wheel construction with inset teeth and lantern pinions. Crutch is bandsawn from laminated veneers, pendulum rod is bird's-eye maple, suspension is a piece of leather caught in a saw kerf.

jig shown in the diagram. The difficult part comes only once, in aligning the blade with the first hole to be cut. Once this position is ascertained the locating pin is fixed and the rest of the slots follow like clockwork.

Such a simple jig is bound to chip the wood as the blade exits, but I find chipping minimal and anyway it is later negated by turning each wheel on a lathe. I do this both for esthetic reasons and to reduce the weight of the train. The result is a flat-bottomed radial slot ready for the inset tooth. I thickness a straight board and rip it to width, then slice the teeth to length and glue them in place. Once mounted, I file the faces of each tooth by hand to a close fit.

Pinions can be made just like small wheels, of solid or laminated wood. But they are tricky and I prefer the lantern pinion. It consists of two circular plates of wood, plastic or metal, with the necessary number of holes spaced around the pitch diameter. Leaves are simply short lengths of dowel or acrylic rod pressed into the holes. One of the circular plates can be eliminated and its holes drilled directly into the wheel.

The distance between centers of two mating gears ought to be the sum of the radii of their pitch circles. In practice, this is a good place to start. But it is best to put each pair of wheel and pinion on dummy arbors and adjust the distance until they turn most freely.

Most clock problems come from improperly depthed wheels. There must always be some clearance between the outside diameter and root diameter of mating wheels, and enough clearance between tooth faces to allow a little backlash. The remedies usually involve careful sanding. A stick the shape of the space between two teeth, with sandpaper glued to it, is a useful file. Sometimes the sanding goes too far and a tooth must be built up with a slip of veneer, or be replaced.

I've used dowel for the arbors on which the wheels ride, and I've turned my own dowel to try and avoid warping and swelling. But dowel vacillates between squeaky tight in the bushings to such looseness that the clock becomes a locked-up woodpile. I therefore switched to aluminum—I like the juxtaposition of color and texture, and it just plain works. However, many makers find dowel entirely satisfactory.

The arbors turn in bushings in the frame that keeps the clock together. The Thomas clock doesn't use bushings, merely countersunk holes lubricated with graphite to keep friction down. Others drill oversize holes and press bearings into them. In my effort to maintain high tolerances, I machined bushings of a very dense and stable monomer-impregnated maple. It is made by putting the wood in a vacuum to remove the air from the cells, then flooding it with plastic resin, which fills the voids in the wood and hardens. I machined the bushings several thousandths of an inch oversize and pressed them into the frames. They

A clockmaker's depthing tool, this one designed by M.C. Hall. Upright arms pivot at baseplate, allowing large wheel (foreground) to mesh with pinion (concealed by smaller wheel). When teeth mesh perfectly, points (left) may be used to strike arcs, on which arbor centers must lie.

probably aren't necessary.

Once I've settled the layout of the holes, I tape the front and back frame pieces together and clamp them to the drill-press table. I drill one hole most of the way through, then turn the whole thing over and come back the other way, to avoid a bad chip-out. Then I press in a bushing or a dummy arbor and proceed to the next hole.

Because I want to emphasize the personal nature of design, I won't dwell on the details of the frame. It can be full front and back plates, or very skeletal supports just where they are needed for the wheel arbors, as long as they are absolutely rigid and parallel.

A ratchet-and-pawl system is the most direct way to wind up the weight and couple it to the wheelwork, as in the diagram below. The pawls may be attached directly to the center wheel, as in the Thomas clock, and the weight suspended by a pulley system to increase the time between windings. Or the pulleys may be eliminated by fixing the pawls to a separate great wheel, coupled by a pinion to the center wheel.

As the weight drum is wound up (by hand in my clock, but most use a couple more wheels and a key), the pawls back over the ratchet. When the weight is fully wound, the pawls move forward and engage the ratchet. I chose not to display the weight and so hung it from a fine cable inside the base of the clock. You may want it to be an integral part of the design. I've used a 7-Up can full of lead—since it is hidden, its lack of charm is not noticed. After the clock is running, tinkering and wear will eliminate some friction, and the beast will of its own accord run more easily and require less weight. I suggest avoiding cast lead weights and using a container full of sand, lead shot or ball bearings—some easily divisible material. □

Further Reading

[Editor's note: Of the four books listed, only Britten's is still in print. For the others, check libraries and used bookstores.]

Britten, Frederick James, *Old Clocks and Watches and Their Makers*. 8th edition. Edited by Cecil Clutton et al. New York: E.P. Dutton, 1973, $40. The 7th edition, published in 1956, is more complete.

Gordon, G.F.C., *Clockmaking, Past and Present*. 2nd edition. London: Technical Press, 1949.

Grimthorpe, Edmund Beckett, *Rudimentary Treatise on Clocks and Watches and Bells*. London: J. Weale, 1850.

Milham, Willis I., *Time and Timekeepers*. New York: Macmillan, 1923.

Wheel-cutting machine designed and built by M.C. Hall is indexed by interchangeable aluminum wheels mounted on the same shaft as chuck that holds the work. Assembly is lowered into saw-type cutter which is shaped to remove the space between two teeth at a single pass.

'Clock II' by Lawrence Hunter is regulated by dowel-pin escapement, above, with tinker-toy motion works, below.

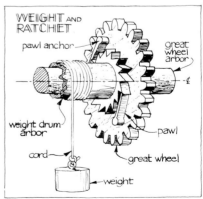

WEIGHT AND RATCHET

pawl anchor

weight drum arbor

cord

great wheel arbor

pawl

great wheel

weight

Weights hang from pulleys on cord wrapped around arbor, and ratchet engages pawls on great wheel, which couples to time train via pinion on center wheel arbor. Or, pawls may be attached to center wheel itself.

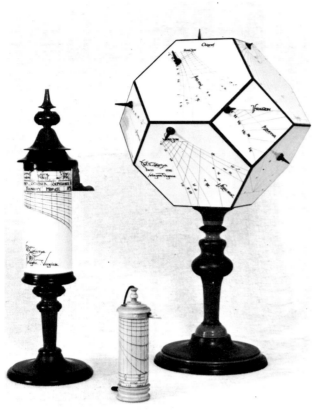

These sundials tell local apparent time. They are accurate to about 10 minutes. Cap of cylindrical dial, left, is twisted to align projecting gnomon with month or astrological house, then whole instrument is rotated until gnomon's shadow is vertical. Shadow's tip crosses graph at the hour. Small shepherd's dial, center, works the same way except it is portable and rotates suspended from a cord. Fourteen-sided polyhedron is a demonstration sundial—each face is laid out according to a different formula. It is oriented by being rotated until all the shadows tell the same time, and it incidentally will then have found true north. Cylindrical dials are cherry and boxwood; polyhedron is plywood covered in paper, 15 coats of gesso and 10 coats of varnish. All the markings are hand-drawn.

Marshall-type microscope, 18 in. high, $900, is made of boxwood, cocobolo and cherry. It magnifies about 100 times, although best resolution is at somewhat lower power. Its parts are disassembled at the top of the next page.

Scientific Instruments of Wood
Simple hand tools, old methods, and ingenuity

by Stanley N. Wellborn

After a brief encounter with M.U. ("Zak") Zakariya, 36, of Arlington, Va., it quickly becomes obvious that he is no ordinary woodworker. In fact, most observers look on him and his methods as throwbacks—to the 19th if not the 17th century.

Consider first the items he makes: wooden microscopes, medieval sundials, astrolabes and cross staffs, elaborately turned chess sets and candelabra, early musical instruments and a wide variety of traditional tools seldom seen in modern workshops. Add to that his work as a calligrapher of Arabic, a cabinetmaker and metalcrafter, a designer of art objects based on antique patterns and an accomplished painter of still lifes and Islamic murals. Then note that he is virtually self-taught, prefers hand tools to power equipment and does most of his work by eye, using his own sense of proportion and line rather than measurements. Yet in a compact, tightly-organized shop, he produces articles that meet industrial tolerances.

His philosophy of woodworking bears examination because of the historical perspective it gives to craftsmen who welcome the sophisticated devices, conveniences and shortcuts that are available today. "I had no tools when I started out—not even a wood saw," he says. "I had to hacksaw each piece and then use small files to get a proper fit. So much of woodworking is mental discipline and patience. If you become single-minded enough, you will find a way to get it done, even if you don't have tools or training." He observes that "the one crucial thing that early woodworkers realized was that even simple tools would do an enormous amount of work if they were sharp. Unfortunately, sharpening is the most neglected aspect of woodworking."

Many of Zakariya's designs are based on research he has done in European libraries and museums, particularly on

From *Fine Woodworking* magazine (November 1978) 13:40-43

Parts of the Marshall microscope. Specimen stage, right, carries mirror for reflecting light, spring-retained slide mounting and small specimen tweezer. Drawer in base contains several objective lenses.

Left, low-power Nuremburg-type microscope was commonly made for students until about 1850. Zakariya's reproduction, mahogany and coco-bolo, is 14 in. high and sells for $600. Above, French Directoire-style chess set, in natural and stained boxwood, was the standard pattern of the 18th and early 19th centuries. Malayan-style set, in tray, is made of ebony and boxwood, as is the playing board. Pine box is decorated with precise knife-cut lines given emphasis by the finish. Zakariya resaws stock for chessboards and boxes with a homemade 30-in. frame saw, made of hickory for its strength and mass, with an ordinary bowsaw blade refiled for ripping. Right, Zakariya at his pedal-powered machinist's lathe.

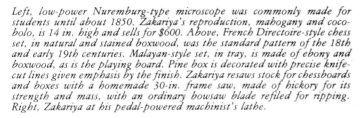

work done in the 18th and 19th centuries by the French artisans Charles Plumier and Louis-Eloy Bergeron and the Italian turner Filippo Senger, who worked in the Court of Florence from 1675 to 1704. He has also undertaken extensive study of the five volumes by John Jacob Holtzapffel, the 19th-century British expert on materials, toolmaking and turning. "These artisans were fascinated with mechanics and invention. They pushed tools to the limit just to prove that something could be done," Zakariya says. "Sometimes, the results were perfectly god-awful, things that made a mockery of the craft. But they also produced profound and incredible works of art, things that are difficult to believe could be done on a lathe. I try to incorporate the best of what they did in my work." Although Zakariya doesn't advocate throwing out all the modern devices in the world, he does feel that woodworkers should begin with nothing but simple hand tools. "There is no question that when you put a chisel or saw into a piece of wood by hand, you understand the nature of the wood better than if you use a power mortiser or a table saw. And it's a lot less noisy, which for me is an important consideration."

As a teenager, Zakariya worked in a machine shop and a clock works in his native California, then traveled through Europe and North Africa, where he observed old-world wood and metal crafters. He returned to California to work five years for an antique dealer, where he made a number of instruments and reproductions. "That was where I learned the value of research." he says. "I'd be asked to produce a caliper or a sundial and I'd go to a book or museum and study it. Usually, it would include a number of my own variations or improvements, because I'm not interested in exact

reproductions. But making a copy was a great way for me as a beginner to see how medieval craftsmen got things done."

Now settled in Arlington, he divides his time between Islamic calligraphy and producing instruments for scientific and academic research. The bulk of his instrument-making is done on a Barnes machinist's lathe built in Rockford, Ill., and patented in 1886. He found it in a Washington, D.C., junk store. Powered by a bicycle-style

Zakariya's Islamic calligraphy in the Muhaqqaq script. The text is the Koranic verse, 'We have created you male and female.'

foot pedal, it is similar to a lathe that Zakariya trained with in the early 1960s.

"This machine, though simple, is quite superior for my kind of work, since it has instant and variable control of speeds and a quick reverse. I think the best lathe work is frequently done at slow speeds and with extremely sharp tools," Zakariya says. The reason? "Fast speeds encourage scraping, and slow speeds encourage cutting. Scraping is necessary sometimes, but too often it is simply a lazy habit. It vibrates the work, it tears up the surface, and it simply is not as gentle a technique as cutting. In his books, Holtzapffel often said that excellent turning did not require high speeds." Zakariya advises many turners to reduce the speeds of power lathes through use of electronic controls on the motor.

The microscopes that Zakariya builds require finely cut wood threads to hold the lenses in place, and he has refined the technique of lathe threading using special hand-guided cutters he adapts from Holtzapffel. The lathe, using combi-

The bow drill, shown in a working drawing below, is accurate and easy to control. Its loose string wraps around the hand-held wooden pivot, which rotates as the bow is moved back and forth. Two pulleys increase the speed range. It has enough torque to drill steel. Zakariya has also made an auxiliary pivot that fits into the lathe tool post.

Handmade planes. The jointer, left, 23 in. long, is of sycamore—an unfortunate choice, because it moves too much and must be resurfaced seasonally. The 14-in. rabbet plane, center, is a traditional pattern, with a full range of stops and fences. Molding plane, right, is made of maple.

nations of gears and a blade-holding carriage that traverses the stock, is capable of cutting from 5 to 28 threads per inch in wood, and more than 150 per inch in metal. In addition, it can thread up to within ⅛ in. of an exterior or internal shoulder. "The threads are very clean and free of breakouts and rough edges, because the operator can make many passes, with a particularly fine cleanup pass," Zakariya says. He feels that chasers—chisels that have teeth for making threads—weaken the surface fibers, resulting in a less attractive thread.

The best woods to thread, in Zakariya's view, are boxwood, lignum vitae, cocobolo, maple and most of the fruitwoods. Although many of his instruments use woods that are dark and heavy, Zakariya is partial to lighter woods with a minimum of grain pattern. Boxwood, he feels, is the "best wood

that ever grew," and most of his smaller items are made of it. He also turns ivory and brass for miniature fittings.

Zakariya is fascinated by instruments because one encounters a variety of disciplines in producing them. A microscope, for example, requires precise optics and lens placement. A sundial must be calibrated to a particular latitude and involves complex geometrical configurations and astronomical calculations. Musical instruments offer problems of tone and proportion. "What is really amazing is that the people who figured all this out had none of the resources that we do today, and yet they produced sundials and optical devices that were as sophisticated and precise in their time as modern computers and electron microscopes are today," he says.

Many instruments require finishing with a variety of coatings to ensure stability. For example, one sundial required

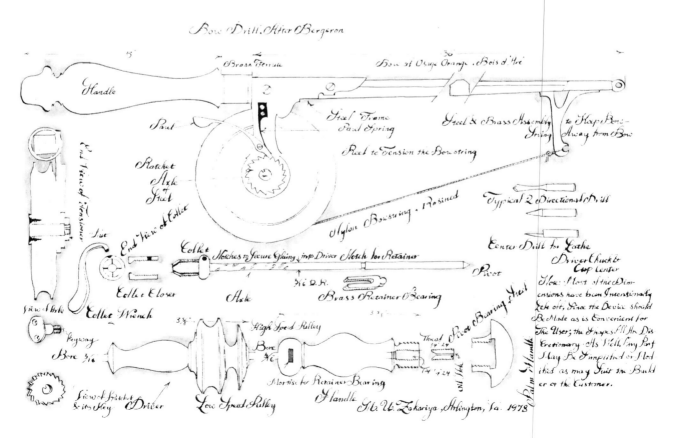

the following: The cherry wood was stained with leather-shoe dye mixed with alcohol, soaked in linseed oil, then restained with butcher's wax and lampblack using oil-wet sandpaper on the lathe. The calibrated portion was given fifteen coats of gesso, then a coat of rabbitskin glue, after which the time indicators were drawn in pen and ink. This was followed by eight coats of polyurethane varnish, then wet sandpaper from 230 to 600 grit using liquid detergent on the lathe, and finally a combination of steel wool, rottenstone and light oil.

One of Zakariya's recent instruments is a geometrical chuck he designed from a Holtzapffel drawing to cut continuous designs in the surface of flat wood and metal. The chuck, made with hand tools of sheet steel and brass, fits on the headstock of the lathe. A flat piece of stock is mounted on the instrument and is rotated by the chuck against a spinning cut-ter bit mounted in the tool rest. By changing gear ratios, a multitude of variations on five, six, seven and eight-pointed rosettes is possible, as well as many other designs.

Few woodworkers would attempt to emulate the kind of work done in his shop, a fact that Zakariya acknowledges. But he is convinced that woodworkers who take the time to relate what they are doing to the origins of modern woodcrafting will find the results rewarding. "These old 18th and 19th-century craftsmen were professionals in every sense. We can't hold a candle to the kinds of work they produced then," he says. "If we can keep that in mind while we work, it can't help but inspire our own production." □

Stan Wellborn, a Washington journalist, is a frequent contributor to Fine Woodworking. *1978 prices throughout.*

Making a Microscope
by M.U. Zakariya

Building historical scientific instruments is essentially a toolmaking process, because every instrument requires special tools and jigs. In their day, these tools were ingenious technological breakthroughs. We must often reinvent them now, occasionally with improvements, and it can be done at little expense with only a modestly equipped shop. Once made, many of these tools can be used in other projects. Hardly ever is there one correct procedure that excludes other approaches. With good improvisations you can get some tools to do the work of the ones you don't have.

The functional aspects of an instrument must be figured out before beginning the actual work. This may require research and often takes longer than making the piece. This means the geometry of sundials and scales, the optics of microscopes, as well as the working parts, how they must fit, and the special scales and divisions on altitude and navigational instruments. A choice of woods must be made, keeping in mind the use to which the piece will be put and how various woods shrink and expand. I never make accurate plans, but do make plenty of working sketches for features like threads, dimensions, details and positions. Examining old instruments can give you important clues on how to achieve your ends. An instrument should never be copied without knowing its principles of operation. You should always sign and date your work, since there are folks abounding who would pass an instrument off as antique, and in the end cause havoc among collectors and historians of early science.

Let me run through some typical steps in making the little microscope. First, the lenses are selected, measured and set aside, and the best distance between them noted on your plan. Select the wood and rough-saw it oversize. It has nine individual wooden parts, and we find that three parts (the barrel, the eye-piece barrel and the eye-piece rim) are all of similar size and will eventually go together—so they are in one piece of wood. The legs are similar, so one piece of wood is cut. Next, all this wood is turned cylindrical and the ends faced off square. Then the legs are separated into three, as are the barrels, their parted edges then being faced square.

Here you will need some wooden chucks, which are easy to

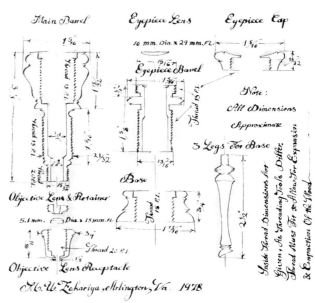

Wooden cup chucks.

Small boxwood microscope, disassembled above, is a feasible introduction to making historical scientific instruments.

make and are described in Holtzapffel. It is a good idea to make several, for many sizes. They can be used over and over and resized as desired. Maple is a good wood. Tap one end to fit on your nose spindle thread. Put it on the nose, turn it, then saw it laterally and run a bolt through it to clamp it by squeezing the kerf. In the end of this chuck, turn the receptacle to hold whatever part you wish. You fasten the work in and release it by means of the bolt.

Figure out internal and external dimensions of threads and fits. Wood threads should fit slightly on the loose side, so when the wood's dimensions change or the roundness gets oval, the threads will still work. You will need some kind of steady rest for your lathe, to support the end of a piece you are boring or threading internally. You could start first by preparing the wooden chuck to take the barrel blank, then

In the 16th and 17th centuries, the cross staff was the standard navigator's instrument for measuring celestial elevations and thus finding latitude. The navigator first estimated the elevation of the sun or a star, then selected the appropriate vane from the four shown here. He planted one end of the staff in his eye socket, slid the vane until its ends touched the star and the horizon, and locked it in place. He then read the elevation from the appropriate scale on the staff.

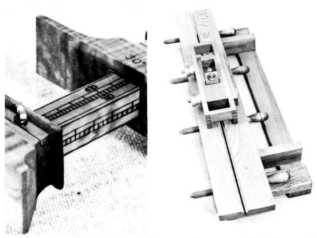

A navigator could get a fix on the sun without going blind by standing with his back to it and measuring the shadow cast by one of the larger vanes. The small vane would be set at the end of the staff and aligned with the horizon. Zakariya hand-cut a set of 51 stamps for setting the numbers and letters into the wood (detail, left). He also had to make a special fine-line cutting gauge and a center-finding box. The curly maple beam of the cross staff must be absolutely straight and square, so the vanes can slide freely and accurately. Zakariya made a 5-ft. shooting board, right, to plane it. The stock is set in the groove and clamped by the four wooden screws. The plane is carried by a beechwood box that straddles the stock, so its height above the board can be set precisely. The plane iron is sharpened to a 45° bevel and sits at a 60° angle in its osage body. Holtzapffel recommends such steep angles for difficult woods, and Zakariya gets a flawless surface—although the iron must be ¼ in. thick to eliminate chatter, and its cap must be set very fine.

support it on the end with the steady rest, bore it to size, and thread it internally. (If your lathe doesn't have a lead screw and change-gear threading carriage, you will have to find another way, such as chasers, or taps and thread boxes, or even building a lathe with a traversing mandrel.)

Next turn the barrel around, remove the steady rest and support the objective end by putting into it a tight plug with a center hole in it, and hold that end with your tailstock center. Turn it to dimensions and do the threads. Next, bore the eye-piece barrel. It can then be placed on a wooden arbor with a little powdered rosin on it to give a grip; the driven end of the arbor can be held in a wooden chuck or by a four-prong driver chuck, or whatever is convenient. Turn the long end, thread it, then reverse the barrel and turn and thread the short section onto which the eye-piece rim will be screwed. At this point, turn a depression on the end of this barrel into which the eye-piece lens will fit. Be sure the barrel and eye-piece barrel screw together nicely before breaking down the setup.

Again, using the wooden chuck, thread the eye-piece rim and bore its hole equal to the bore at the top of the eye-piece barrel. Turn the blank rim around in the wooden chuck, and turn the face detail. Screw the two barrels together, and screw on the eye-piece rim. Now you have an assembly, ready to finish. The quick way to do this is while they are all together. The rosined mandrel is driven by the headstock, and the objective end is supported by its plug with the tailstock center. Proceed to turn all outside contours. Think ahead to avoid making mistakes, like turning into a bore and ruining the piece. You may have to do this a couple of times just to learn caution. Bore and thread the base in the wooden chuck, as well as the face details of both sides. Drill the holes for the three legs. I made a division plate for this and used a bow drill fixed into the cross-slide. Then thread the base back onto the completed barrel assembly, and turn its contours. Turn the legs and glue them in. The objective-lens capsule is also done in a wooden chuck, but because it is so small, you have to be very careful. It is now ready to finish. I like to soak this kind of work in warm linseed oil.

Instead of turning the pieces assembled together, plugs to be held in a wooden chuck can be made, each plug threaded to fit each piece. Then the pieces can be turned on these plugs. The plugs can also act as sizing gauges. Eventually you may accumulate a box of these plugs and mandrels which can be fitted to other jigs.

For anyone interested in instrument-making or precision woodworking, the five volumes of John Jacob Holtzapffel—a compendium of over a century of toolmaking experience—are required reading. What isn't covered in these books can be gotten elsewhere, but the clarity of the explanations makes them the finest how-to books ever written. Volumes four and five, on plain and ornamental turning, have been reprinted by Dover (180 Varick St., New York, N.Y. 10014). The first three volumes, covering materials, cutting methods and abrasives, have not yet been reprinted. They are available in some libraries and are a key to basic hand and machine production techniques—very resourceful stuff.

The 1749 edition of *L'Arte de Tourner* by Charles Plumier is available in French and Latin text from Woodcraft, 41 Atlantic Avenue, Box 4000, Woburn, Mass. 01888. An English translation, by Dr. Paul L. Ferraglio, can usually be obtained through inter-library loan. □

The Miniature Shipwright
After a while, you *feel* ⅜ inch tall

by Lloyd McCaffery

When people ask me where I get the patience to build model ships, I tell them that no job was ever more exciting or so full of challenges. A good model is an exact replica, in miniature, of a specific ship on a particular day in its history, and the modelmaker must cope with the same sorts of problems the original builders contended with. Scale to them meant that each part of the ship had to be strong enough to do its job without being overbuilt. This economy of material, a sort of "form follows function," generates a beauty that gives ships a universal appeal. The modelmaker must recapture this essential rightness in the taper of each mast and spar, in the run of each plank, and even in the way each piece of rigging responds to gravity. Absolute fidelity to visual scale is the key. No piece of thread, for instance, will hang in the

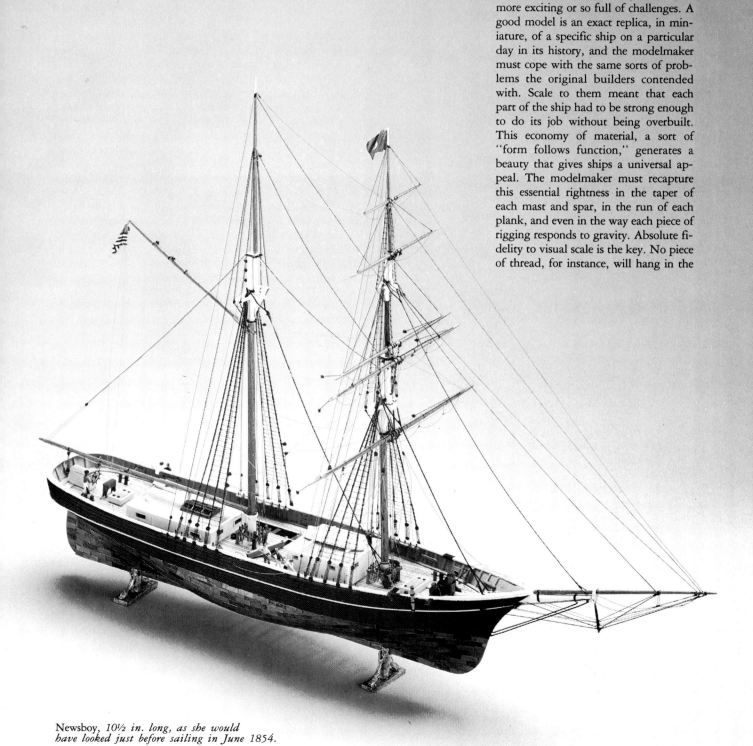

Newsboy, *10½ in. long, as she would have looked just before sailing in June 1854.*

McCaffery showcases his miniatures on a mirrored base.

same curve as a full-size rope on the actual vessel, so rigging must not only be the right thickness, it must be twisted from wire, so that its curve can be precisely shaped. That job is, however, one of the easy ones—you simply attach some strands to a lathe, then allow them to twist up, just as workers did in the old, quarter-mile-long ropewalks.

As much as possible, I build a ship the same way that it was constructed in the shipyard. In plank-on-frame construction, the keel is laid, ribs (called frames) are attached to it, and the framework is planked, with each plank pinned down by wooden spikes called treenails. I research the original plans, scale them down photographically, then seek ways to match each part.

A modelmaker's main tool is ingenuity, and with each model new challenges arise. Some of my early models had solid hulls, but I wanted to recreate the hull's actual construction. I came across a trick for making the frames. All you do is lay up the blank for the hull as a stack of thin pieces of wood, so that it resembles a sliced loaf of bread. After the exterior of the hull has been shaped, every other slice becomes the blank for a frame, and the rest of them are thrown away. The inside curve can be easily cut with a knife.

I recently returned from a trip to some European maritime museums, where I had the opportunity to search out original drawings and to see many fine old models. In my own models, ¹⁄₁₆ in. usually equals 1 ft. The old models were made to a much larger scale, and some 100-gun ships-of-the-line are almost 6 ft. long. They were made for the Admiralty in advance of construction, so that politicians—who couldn't understand construction drawings—could pre-judge the ship's lines and accommodations. In those days it wasn't necessary to show the masts and rigging, because they were standardized. Models today have a different purpose. They recapture, in jewel-like form, the nostalgia of bygone beauty, and as educational tools they serve to put us in touch with the past. A tour through an exhibition hall in Mystic Seaport, Conn.—where models, artifacts, paintings and dioramas make the past almost palpable—leaves one so entranced that, on emerging, daylight and the 20th century seem remote.

Modelmaking captures the spirit in the same way. On my European tour I had the good fortune to be allowed to take the measurements of a full-size English Royal Barge built in the early 18th century. As I climbed aboard and started measuring oars and planks, I had the feeling that I had done all this before. Then I recognized the sensation—it was the way I feel when working on a model. After a few hours of miniature work, parts no longer seem small, a sixteenth of an inch actually *becomes* a foot, and you yourself end up less than ⅜ in. tall.

Scale applies to wood grain as well as to surface textures. The best wood I've found for masts and spars is South American lancewood, which is also called lemonwood and degame. It can be planed and sanded down to a needle point, and is a pleasant, yellow color, with no objectionable figure. For planking and carving, boxwood is an excellent choice, if you can find some that is really slow-grown. Holly is superb for its workability and clear, light color. Aromatic red cedar is somewhat perverse—much too soft and brittle—but it holds a crisp edge and its color is incomparable. Fruitwoods in general are good for miniatures, being diffuse-porous and hard enough to not dent easily. They offer a nice range of darker woods for visual contrast. Ring-porous woods such as oak and ash are out of the question, of course, due to the large, open-grain patterns. And many otherwise beautiful woods, for example mahogany, are just not tight-grained enough. For some applications, such as cutting intricate parts that will have areas of fragile end grain, I make up miniature sheets of plywood from plane shavings. These are easy to work without splitting.

Glue can be troublesome because it is not to scale, and anything not to scale is noticed by the eye and destroys the magic. White and yellow glues are good for large wood joints. These must fit tight, and any squeeze-out must be pared away. I use cyanoacrylate for small, detailed fittings, such as a ⅛-in. dia. ships' wheel, built up from wire.

Scrapers and planes leave a better surface than sandpaper. My favorite cutting tool is a single-edge razor blade, but used dental probes can be honed into a full line of tools that will rival any woodcarver's. I do most of my milling on the tablesaw attachment for a Unimat lathe, and the jointer attachment comes in handy, too. Otherwise, hand tools work best for most jobs. One exception is power-carving small details. For this, dental burs provide a wide range of shapes. I find it best to use them in an old-style dentists' drilling machine rather than a flexible-shaft machine or a hand-held motor tool. The dental engine is powered by belts, and its handpiece doesn't whip.

In making a model, precision and attention to detail are a must. But these factors must be considered in relation to the whole work, including the case. The model must be a unified whole. It serves nothing to master one part of the job at the expense of another, and artistic impact must take precedence over mere fussiness. A model is a sculpture. A successful sculpture can have any degree of finish, but if it lacks unity, it will be a failure as a work of art.

I've seen many models that I consider failures because they don't hang together. Some fail because of scale, some because of workmanship. Some are simply doomed from the start—a lovely model can hardly be inspired by an ugly ship. Historical inaccuracy is another major flaw. Some modelmakers seem to believe that their imagination can take the place of research. Yet a single historical flaw can undo all their effort. The design problems were worked out by seamen long ago, and their solutions have a beauty tested by use. No old ship ever sailed on whimsy, and sooner or later, truth will out. □

Lloyd McCaffery, of Madison, Conn., has been making miniature ship models for over a quarter of a century.

From *Fine Woodworking* magazine (September 1983) 42:79-81

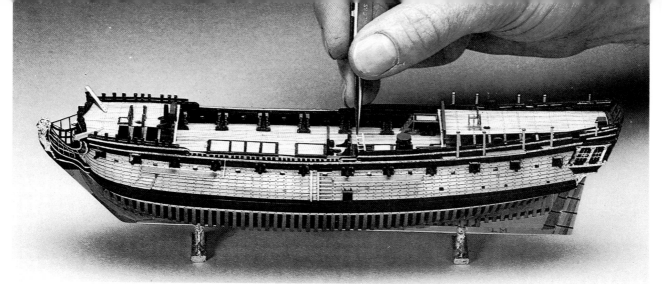

Miniature ships can be as challenging as the modelmaker dares. Above is a hull model of Boston, *a 24-gun frigate launched in 1747. McCaffery uses tweezers to put the ladder to the hold in place. The boxwood deck planks, right, are individually fastened to the cherry timbers with treenails (wooden pegs, here made from toothpick points). Cannons are turned and bored, then painted.*

In the photo below, painting is well under way on the port quarter of the brigantine Newsboy. *McCaffery often leaves one side of his miniature ships open to show the interior framing. Newsboy's copper-plated bottom, sheathed with 0.002-in. foil, is shown on p. 15. Her deck is holly.*

Photos: White Light

The Patternmaker's Trade
From sculpted wood to metal castings

by Paul Suwijn

Having become a respectable cabinetmaker by the usual hit-or-miss methods, I found myself in the typical quandary—how to earn a decent living working wood. One day I dropped in unannounced at the shop of an established designer/craftsman, showed him my portfolio and asked him for advice. While I rhapsodized about my interest in design, his emphasis was squarely on craftsmanship. Since he did all the design work himself, he was interested in hiring skilled craftsmen who could take a set of drawings and build a piece from start to finish without asking questions. For this reason, he had just hired a journeyman patternmaker.

I left this fellow's shop determined to find out about patternmakers and what makes them a special species of woodworker. Checking through the phone directory, I found several pattern jobbers listed and proceeded to investigate. Repeatedly I was told by foremen at small shops that if I wanted to land an apprenticeship in patternmaking, I would have better luck applying at a large, industrial outfit with an in-house pattern shop. I did just that, and the fates must have favored me that day, for about a week later I was hired.

In retrospect, I can fairly say that I entered a world of abstract woodworking unlike anything the average cabinetmaker is likely to encounter. The point of wood patternmaking is a very practical one—to produce the forms that create molds for metal castings—but the work is scarcely less than elegant in its best expressions. For the first time I had the pleasure of working with full-scale machine tools maintained in top condition, and was introduced to several woodworking tools and machines I had never run into before. I am grateful to have experienced, bit by bit, the meaning of master craftsmanship, and to have had the opportunity to watch and learn from the real practitioners.

Modelmaking—Patternwork starts in the engineering office. Designers reach a point where it becomes difficult to fine-tune their conceptions without reference to a three-

Working on a complicated model for a machine part, like this compound-action cutter-holding device, requires precision and broad experience in the trade. Such models as these are built from engineers' drawings.

Author installs the gating (which will produce the pouring channels) on the core-print area of a complex wooden pattern for a machinery casting. The job of the pattern is to define the exterior portions of the cast-metal object by making an impression in a sand mold.

Photos: Mike Wampler, courtesy of the Gleason Works, Rochester, N.Y.

From *Fine Woodworking* magazine (January 1981) 26:82-87

dimensional model. In many pattern shops some tradesmen satisfy this need by doubling as machine-modelmakers. The modelmaker constructs a scale assembly, frequently of wood, from the engineers' layout drawings. The usual sequence for large machinery begins with an explicit ¼-scale model, which can be shuttled back and forth from the pattern shop to the engineering office as improvements are made.

When most of the bugs have been worked out of the reduced-scale model, a full-scale model is made. It incorporates the machine's most important moving elements and represents its troublesome features in detail. All the major electrical cables and hydraulic lines are fitted to the model as are dummy switches, controls, loading apparatus and guarding. The thinking in many firms runs thus: The machine model, whatever its cost, justifies its expense in revealing problems before they prove really costly, and the model can be used to demonstrate a new concept in machine design to prospective customers. Models also acquaint the sales staff with a new machine, rendering it more tangibly than blueprints.

The modelmaker scales his work directly from the layout prints, which are preliminary, often incomplete drawings of the machine. Working within tolerances of about 0.050 in. on large work, he must be patient and diplomatic, as he will be required to tear down and rebuild the model as the design evolves. Modelmakers must have a talent for deciphering complex drawings and for discerning inconsistencies in design as the model progresses. Engineers value the services of a good modelmaker, for he's the one who first gives solid shape to their concepts. The information he provides as the model progresses can be an active contribution to the final product.

Patternmaking—Once the final model has been made and its design perfected as much as possible, the machine is broken down into its component elements and detailed blueprints are made for each of these parts. Wooden patterns—precise replicas of the cast parts—are made from these prints. The pattern leaves its shape in a sand mold, which when filled with molten metal yields the finished casting. For more information on how patterns are used, see box, p. 86, on foundry practices. Preliminary prints of the cast parts are sent to the pattern shop for study and comments. Throughout the modelmaking and detailing stages, the engineers consult with the most experienced patternmakers and the foundry metallurgist to avoid designing a part that isn't practical to cast. Difficult castings are debated at length before the collective talent arrives at the best solution.

Patternwork is used for a wide range of casting, from a jack plane to a complex industrial machine frame weighing many tons. Patterns are not always made of wood. High-production foundries use metal patterns cast from wooden masters or built up and machined from standard metal stock. Wax, plaster, clay, Styrofoam, fiberglass and castable urethanes and epoxies (suitably wood-cored) are common pattern materials—each suited to a particular need. Wood patterns, however, are most useful for producing one to several hundred castings because it is difficult to surpass wood for economy, its ratio of strength to weight, and easy tooling.

Patternwork consists mainly of two parts—making the pattern, which defines the exterior form of the casting, and making the core box, which defines the interior shape of the casting, the thickness of its walls, and, in some cases, difficult external features. The combination of external mold halves and the internal and external sand cores describes all the features of a complex casting, inside and out. Patternwork for small and moderate-sized castings is usually assigned to a single craftsman. Blueprints show the parting-line and coring layout marked out plainly by the shop supervisor, with notes about material and machine finish allowances.

To simplify the print and to account for draft and machine finish enlargements, the patternmaker makes a precise, knife-scribed layout of the job on a separate board or sheet of plywood. If he needs layout sticks for core-box or pattern construction, he makes them at this point. The layout process helps eliminate making careless omissions as the patternmaker builds the pattern, and it helps clarify his picture of what he must construct. Separating layout and construction is a very satisfactory arrangement in practice. Calculations that are made during the building process are a source of error and can waste much good effort—as in the common case of too much stock removed.

If a pattern assignment is particularly time-consuming or rushed, several patternmakers may work together under the supervision of a master craftsman, who is responsible for coordinating their work, checking the layout and determining the clearances between the parts. He may prepare a set of templates in advance which will guarantee the fit of all the parts. Every dimension is measured and recalculated by the

In a sand-match pattern, the projecting male half of the pattern will become the female part of the mold, and the female pattern half will form the male half of the mold. This method eliminates the need for separate sand cores. Dark areas represent cast metal.

AUTHOR'S NOTE: For a comprehensive treatment of this subject, see Ed Hamilton's *Patternmaker's Guide* (American Foundrymen's Society, Cast Metals Series, Des Plaines, Ill. 60016).

Patternmakers use wood lathes with screw-driven crossfeed tool posts, like those on metalworking lathes, to achieve maximum accuracy when turning. Pattern being turned here is made from stacked, segmented rings, glued one atop another.

Patternmakers apply leather fillets to a completed core box. Fillets create radii at sharp junctures of a casting's elements, adding considerably to the strength of the metal at these points and helping to prevent cracked castings.

pattern checker. He uses an independently made layout to reduce further the chance for error. If any features need rework, he reports these to the patternmaker. When the pattern equipment meets with his approval, it is dispatched to the foundry for molding and coremaking.

Since it is very costly to scrap castings, great pains are taken to deliver strong, dimensionally perfect wood patterns to the foundry. Patterns are built durably, and their accuracy is within 0.015 in. on new work, and sometimes closer on light patternwork for non-ferrous casting. The relative position of all the features must also fall within this tolerance. Good joinery and clean appearances are not, in themselves, sufficient. Patternmaking is thus excellent training for any precision woodworking, though it is also rewarding in itself.

Tooling costs for quality wood patternwork are very high indeed, and are written off against long, successful casting runs. Pattern commissions in the $5,000 to $50,000 range are common for heavily-cored patterns, which often resemble exact and foolproof puzzles with marginal clearances provided between the pieces to ease assembly of the mold, built-in markers to clear up the relation between the parts and anchoring and gas-venting devices and pouring systems.

Materials—Top-grade lumber is used in wood patternmaking—clear South American mahogany, cherry, yellow poplar, white or sugar pine, and sometimes basswood, with hard maple used for reinforcement. Pattern lumber is sorted for absence of defects and straightness of grain (figure is unwelcome), and it arrives roughsawn at the shop, since a full spectrum of thicknesses is needed. Our shop stocks from 10,000 to 15,000 board feet, and we consume a great deal of ¾-in. and 1-in. A/B fir plywood for large core-box walls and floors, and for concealed headers in hollow constructions. We also use tempered Masonite, sheet aluminum, brass and band iron for templates and local surface buildups. Frequently, we cast aluminum elements from wooden master patterns for features

that would be too fragile if constructed from wood.

Common pine is satisfactory for one-shot work and in stacked constructions (common in wood patternmaking) when capped with more durable material. Massive, stacked work, requiring lots of pneumatic and hand carving or overhead milling—patterns for turbine and pump housings are good examples—is made up from prelaminated sugar pine or mahogany blocks. But where tolerances may be as close as 0.003 in., we use cherry or Spanish cedar because of their excellent tooling qualities and dimensional stability.

Methods of construction—The patternwork in our shop is classified in three grades. First-class means we use the best hardwood with elements spot-glued, doweled and heavily screwed together. Flat-head screws (#14, from 1 in. to 6 in. long, or #10 and #8 for light work) stiffen the pattern against the weight of the molding sand. Screw heads are set in counterbores, capped with tapered hardwood plugs that are pared flush to the pattern surface, and set cross-grain to the surrounding material so they can be spotted quickly. Core boxes have separable interior assemblies, screwed to the box walls and floor from outside so that no section prevents the independent removal of the others. This permits fairly easy breakdown in case of a design change.

Less durable but more easily worked materials, like pine or poplar, are acceptable for second-class work. Nails replace screws in third-class construction, and quicker assembly practices are used so long as flimsiness is avoided and dimensions are correct. Common pine and basswood are suitable for some third-class constructions.

Small patterns are usually built in blocked-up fashion, solid throughout, while larger work begins with a reinforced frame of clear pine or poplar. The frame is then sheathed with vertical planking (mahogany for first-class work) to achieve the finished dimensions. The top planking is housed within the projecting upper tips of the wall sheathing, and care is taken to avoid telegraphing of joints, which causes mold damage, and warpage, which fouls dimension.

It is common practice to saw relief kerfs into the backside of wider planks, or to rip them into narrow strips and glue them up to the required width, reversing (or bucking) the grain of each successive strip to combat warpage. Most such work is glued-up oversize to permit rapid stacking, then scraped and planed to thickness. Finish nails, tacked in at an angle, align the ends of stacked material and prevent the strips or planks from swimming out of position when being clamped.

For developing a cylindrical form we use the stacked-ring approach. Full rings of four, five or six segments are prepared on a perfectly flat surface from an accurate segment template, then glued to height with joints in adjacent rings staggered. The four and six-segment formulas are especially easy to lay out, but we use eight or ten segments per ring for large work to minimize waste. Using the template, we nest the segments on a wide section of plank, allowing just enough room between for bandsawing and cleanup. Stave constructions, reinforced by concealed header/backbone systems, are also common in large cylindrical patterns. Stavework can be adapted also to accomplish transitions in regular contours, or in truncated cones by tapering each stave over its length.

In order to maintain accuracy on turned work, wood lathes with crossfeed tool posts are preferred over those with ordinary tool rests. Where large, regular contours are needed, we employ overhead wood-milling equipment. Large circles are accurately cut on the pattern mill, which has a rotating cutter that reaches down from above at any given angle, while the work is secured on a table that can travel along two horizontal axes or rotate full-circle.

Hand tools, rules and gauges—Most cabinetmaker's hand tools apply readily to patternmaking. Because accuracy in layout and construction is essential, patternmakers use machinist's combination squares and calipers (Starrett Tools, Athol, Mass. 01331, is the best producer). Braces and pneumatic guns are used for driving screws. A good set of trammels, rapid-action dividers and top-quality marking and panel gauges are indispensable for layout (Freeman Supply Co., 1152 E. Broadway, Toledo, Ohio 43604 sells a bronze panel gauge that has no peer). Patternmakers prefer to use bent-shank (also called crank-handled) chisels and in-cannel gouges for flush or contour paring. Recently I counted about 20 special-function tools in our shop, including bent-shank chisels, scrapers, marking and scribing instruments, planes and accessories to standard machine-tools—all shop made— that fill the gaps left by standard cabinet tools.

Pattern assembly is typically done on polished granite or machined-iron surface plates to ensure a true reference surface at all stages of the work. Surface gauges are more reliable than ordinary rules for establishing precise locations on pattern sidewalls. The finer side of wood patternmaking sets aside the ruler, replacing it with the micrometer, the dial-indicator calipers and the vernier height gauge. Some tool-and-die training is helpful in this refined corner of the trade.

Most cast metals shrink fractionally as they solidify. Shrinkage varies according to the metal. It's about $\frac{1}{10}$ in. per foot for cast irons, $\frac{3}{16}$ in. for aluminum, $\frac{5}{32}$ in. for brass and bronze, and $\frac{1}{4}$ in. to the foot for lead. Wood patterns must therefore be proportionately larger than the object they re to produce, and every pattern is scaled to a particular casting alloy. Thus

patternmakers work with expanded rules (called shrink rules). They're made in one or two-foot lengths and read in fiftieths of an inch, with a given shrinkage factor stamped on the face. In the finest patternwork, shrinkage for each dimension is calculated in advance, on the blueprint, because the finest measuring instruments read to standard rulings.

Because rough treatment in the foundry eventually ruins a wooden pattern, a run of thousands of castings starts with a very fine wooden master. Its impression is taken, then a new working pattern is cast from wood-cored epoxy or urethane plastic, or from cast aluminum or nickle-plated cast iron. The castable plastics have negligible shrinkage. But if the working pattern is to be aluminum or iron, the wood master will have to account for double shrinkage.

Apprentices, journeymen and masters—Pattern shops take on apprentices when business is good. The period of training runs from four to five years and may include direct experience in the foundry or machine shop to broaden the apprentice's knowledge of the trade. High-precision shops sometimes require, and may pay for, classroom study at a local tool-and-die institute. Some programs are state-mandated and lead to journeyman's certification. New apprentices are sometimes granted a moderate tool allowance.

Patternmakers in our shop are classified C, B, A or Master, according to proven ability to do jobs of increasing difficulty. It's not uncommon for a class-A patternmaker to make $20,000 yearly (1981), and a master may earn appreciably more. The foreman bids on outside work and decides questions about design in cooperation with the project engineer, metallurgist and foundry manager, while the patternmaking staff is usually left to concentrate on the good practice of the trade.

The work atmosphere in a pattern shop is disciplined and studious. An industrial-methods approach doesn't work well because the work is one-of-a-kind. Instead, the traditional wisdom, the experience and the intelligence of the individual patternmakers are relied upon. Thus, you'll find in a pattern shop a high level of work motivation and a fairly keen competition for the best jobs.

It takes a couple of years for a good apprentice to find his pace and produce consistent results. The advice given to a new apprentice in our shop is, "Take your time, just make sure you do it right." Expectations increase with experience, but seldom to the point of pressure in a good working situation, since this eventually fouls concentration (and blackens the heart). Proverbial wisdom has it that there are only two times when a patternmaker rushes—when he's making a mistake, or when he's fixing one.

Neither age nor gender is any real barrier to the trade, though I've never met a woman patternmaker. I trust that any determined woman cabinetmaker could open that door. When I began in our shop, I had the pleasure of working next to a 75-year-old retired master who had come in temporarily to help us through a heavy period. He was still a keen and productive tradesman, with a wonderfully light heart and an eagerness about his work. He made a point before he left to encourage each of the apprentices to stick with the trade, and expressed the undiminished sense of enjoyment that he still found in the work.

Paul Suwijn is a draftsman at the Gleason Works, Rochester, N.Y. He is also studying machine design.

What Foundries Do

Foundryman pours a medium-size casting. Encased in a metal flask, the drag mold in the foreground is filled with cores that will form the internal ribwork of a machine frame.

Wood patternmaking came into being in answer to the needs of Renaissance bell and ordnance founders, then further developed during the Industrial Revolution in response to the rapid growth in the demand for machinery castings. These days, we're surrounded by tools, machines and other objects made of cast metal, and each of them begins as a precise pattern, usually made of wood. Patternmaking has always reflected the state of foundry technology and makes sense only in light of casting practice. I'll discuss the basic concepts of shrinkage, draft, core boxes, core prints, patterns and parting lines with reference to sand-casting technique, the most common method of producing large metal castings.

A wooden **pattern** is used in the foundry to create a void in packed sand. The pattern is withdrawn and molten metal is poured into the void—the shape of the pattern thus translates directly into the shape of the casting. Many patterns are split into upper and lower halves. Sand cores are often secured within the mold cavity to define difficult features and to create chambers inside the casting. But since the pattern itself never contacts the molten metal, once made, it can be re-used indefinitely, though the time comes when it is cheaper to rebuild patterns than to refurbish them.

Casting sand is a fine, uniform sand mixed with water and clay or a resin-catalyst mixture; when packed against the pattern, it holds its shape, forming a **mold**. Initially brick hard, the mold is chemically constituted so that as the molten metal cools, its heat degrades the binders in the sand, making it easy to remove the mold from the cooled casting and to recycle the sand. Patterns are delivered to the foundry mounted on flat metal plates or wooden decks called **foundry boards**. An open-ended box, called a **flask**, is set down on the board, allowing room all around the pattern for the sand, which is mechanically cast down onto the pattern until the flask is full. Excess sand is raked off, and a sturdy metal plate is clamped atop the flask. The whole affair is now rolled over so that the foundry board, carrying the pattern with it, can be drawn off on a true perpendicular. This operation completes the lower half of the mold, known as the **drag**.

The upper half of the mold, the **cope**, is made in the same way, but without the heavy metal plate. The sand is secured in the cope flask by iron bars wedged across the width, and by twisted *L*-shaped rods of wrought iron, called **gaggers**, buried in the sand. This allows a pouring dish (connected by tunnels to the main mold cavity) to be built up on its top surface, along with the venting system. An overhead crane and a sand pit are required for rolling the larger variety.

Because the pattern must be pulled out of the sand, leaving its image intact behind, all its vertical walls must have taper, or **draft**. On a typical pattern the walls slope outward to the base, with the uppermost surface buried deepest in the sand. Because pattern features start at different levels, degrees of draft vary from point to point, and will have to be blended between high and low elements. Thanks to draft, most patterns may be drawn off cleanly, although some trowel repair is acceptable on non-critical mold surfaces.

Since the cope and the drag have to match exactly, the pattern halves must be precisely located when mounted on their foundry boards, but mirror-wise to one another. A locater frame is pinned to the first board; then blocks of wood that contact all the critical edges of the pattern half are dogged and glued to the frame. The pattern half is secured from be-

low by screws, dowels and lags. Now the frame with blocks of wood attached is flipped over onto the companion board, where it will correctly locate the other pattern half. Split elements of the pouring system are mounted the same way.

For short runs, patterns may be sent to the foundry unboarded. The two loose halves are doweled together with parting-line profiles matched exactly. They can be molded directly by first placing the drag pattern on a foundry board and filling its flask. When the flask is rolled over, the drag pattern is left in place. The alignment dowels allow the cope pattern to be placed on top, then a thin layer of washed sand, mixed with a parting agent, is spread on the parting line. Now a second flask is pinned on top of the first and filled with sand. The two mold halves are then separated at the parting line, and both pattern halves removed, leaving a complete mold.

A simple, unsplit pattern can be cast entirely in the drag by enclosing the cavity with a solid cope mold, unfeatured except for its pouring tunnel, called a **sprue**. But patterns, like their molds, are usually split along a horizontal parting line. And because a pattern half is molded on a foundry board, the parting line continues from the pattern's edges out to the rim of the flask. Although this parting plane is typically flat all across, it may be made irregular at the edges of the pattern in order to define recesses or projections that fall near the logical parting line. This device is a **sand match**.

A classic use of the sand match is seen in the cast-iron frying pan. The wooden form of the pan's exterior is mounted upside-down on one foundry board, while a recess routed in the other board is sized and located to cancel all of the mold impression but the uniform thickness of the pan itself. If the pan pattern were 2.25 in. high, the recess might be 2.13 in. deep, leaving a vacant .12-in. shell for the metal when the two mold halves are put together. If you check the one in your kitchen, you'll see that the pan's handle was split between the two boards and that it fits the hand better than if it were contoured on one side and flat on the other.

Parting-line orientation affects pattern costs and casting success, particularly when a casting has a number of external

Mahogany pattern, left, with projecting core prints is made in halves (cope and drag) split along a parting line. The accompanying core box, above, molds half of the sand core that will define the interior cavity in the casting.

Making molds from patterns

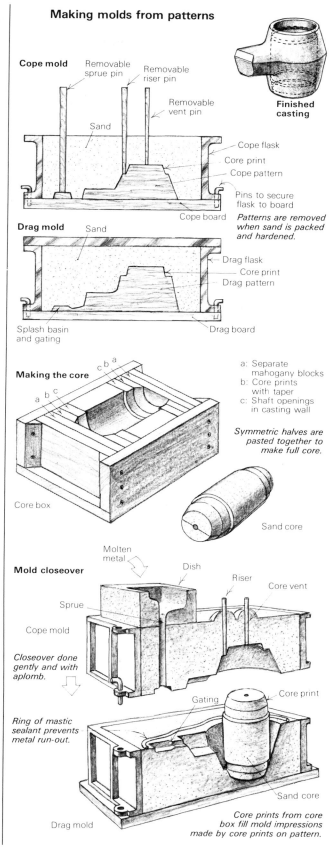

Cope mold · Removable sprue pin · Removable riser pin · Removable vent pin · Sand · Cope flask · Core print · Cope pattern · Pins to secure flask to board · Cope board

Patterns are removed when sand is packed and hardened.

Drag mold · Sand · Drag flask · Core print · Drag pattern · Splash basin and gating · Drag board

Finished casting

Making the core · c b a · a b c · Core box

a: Separate mahogany blocks
b: Core prints with taper
c: Shaft openings in casting wall

Symmetric halves are pasted together to make full core.

Sand core

Mold closeover · Molten metal · Dish · Riser · Core vent · Sprue · Cope mold

Closeover done gently and with aplomb.

Ring of mastic sealant prevents metal run-out.

Gating · Core print · Drag mold · Sand core

Core prints from core box fill mold impressions made by core prints on pattern.

projections or recesses, or when its hollow and internal sand cores must be supported. Patterns are also split to minimize their height, and to locate in the drag half of the mold the most critical surfaces to be machine-finished. Sand inclusions and gas bubbles tend to migrate upward to the cope, so casting flaws are liable to be concentrated there. Because of this, a generous machine-finishing allowance will be added to cope finish surfaces. Finish allowances vary from ⅛ in. to 1 in., depending on scale and complexity. This excess is built onto the pattern to provide that excess metal.

Castings often call for projections or recesses on their outer walls that are too far up on the pattern half to be defined by the sand-match method. Pockets or undercuts in the outer cast walls would lock the pattern in the sand. Most interior cavities cannot be defined directly from the pattern. This problem is solved by providing the mold with a **sand core**, which when suspended from pockets in the mold wall defines a hollow in the casting. The core itself is molded in a **core box**, containing a specially shaped, tapered cavity into which casting sand is packed. The box is then inverted and drawn off. A block of wood, called a **core print**, is attached to the pattern covering the troublesome external area, or as an extension of an opening in the casting's wall. The core print leaves a pocket in the mold wall when the pattern is molded. Part of the sand core will fit exactly in the mold-wall pocket, cancelling that space. The rest of the core defines the difficult feature or cavity. Cores must be vented by a tunnel system leading to the upper mold surface. The intense heat of pouring that decomposes mold binders produces flammable gas, which is burned off at the top of the vents.

Pouring systems, called **gating**, are also built onto the patterns so they'll make an impression in the sand. They're designed to minimize sand inclusions, porosity and shrinkage voids in the cast metal, and thus the patternmaker finds himself in regular contact with the foundry metallurgist. Patternmaking apprentices in foundry-associated shops spend considerable time constructing foundry boards, mounting patterns and building gating systems. In addition to gas vents, the cope halves of large molds need vertical channels called flow-offs or **risers** to lead off excess metal and dross, and to shrink-feed thick sections of the casting. Running from the highest surface of the mold cavity to the uppermost mold surface, risers signal the foundry crew that the pour is complete.

After the mold cools—large work may take a day or two—the rough casting is shaken out of the mold. Extraneous parts (pouring channels, risers, fins around cored areas and along the parting line) must be cut or chipped off. The casting is washed, sand-blasted or shot-blasted clean, and the parting ridge and surface scale are ground away. If no defects turn up, it is painted and sent to the machine shop.   —*P.S.*

WOOD TYPE

Minding your p's and q's

by Simon Watts

hen a modern department store uses movable type to print a poster, it's continuing a tradition that goes back to Johannes Gutenberg, his wooden press and his famous Bible. Gutenberg developed the small, reusable cast-metal letter that first made book printing economical. But for poster-size type, letter blocks of hardwood are still as practical today as they have been for centuries.

One factory in Wisconsin, Hamiltons, turns out wood type to the tune of a million dollars a year. They slice maple logs like loaves of bread, then painstakingly dry and finish them to type-height tolerances of 0.002 in. The elaborate processing makes the wood so valuable that the factory even weighs offcuts to monitor the waste.

On a much smaller scale, a museum in Old Town, San Diego's historical district, demonstrates how wood type was manufactured in an 1868 newspaper office. I spent two days with the museum's curator, Richard Yale, a cheery, unpretentious man of 73 who sports a black string tie and looks like a small-town lawyer or editor of 50 years ago—an appearance he cultivates to the point of being frequently mistaken for a reincarnation of Colonel Sanders. Yale, a master typographer, has patterns for 36 different type faces, and can produce an astonishing variety of letter designs and sizes—all with fairly simple equipment and in a very small space.

Demonstrating the process in his garage workshop, Yale pulled out a 6-in. high letter pattern, a mirror image of the actual letter (the blocks are reversed in printing). I'd always thought that the expression "mind your *p*'s and *q*'s" meant watching your pints and quarts when making merry. Yale, however, interprets it as a warning to apprentice printers—a lower-case *p* is a backwards *q*. Yale also told me that for hundreds of years all wood type was carved by hand. It wasn't until 1834 that a new invention, the router, was combined with an old device, the pantograph, to allow large-scale production.

To produce a letter, Yale mounted the pattern in the pantograph and traced the stylus around its outline. At the other end of the machine, the router's high-speed cutter exactly duplicated the design on a smaller scale. By changing the mechanical link-age of the pantograph, Yale can use the same pattern to cut letters from ½ in. to 4 in. high. The style we chose for the block letters shown here is named after circus magnate P.T. Barnum.

Yale then took a homemade trimming knife and deftly cleaned the inside corners of each letter, the tight spots where the router bit couldn't reach. As he worked, he explained that all wood type in the smaller and medium sizes, 1 in. to 7 in. high, is made from blocks of end-grain hardwood. This is because flat grain wears unevenly, summer wood being denser than spring wood, and also because fine details such as serifs (the small lines that finish off the main stroke of a letter) are fragile and tend to break off. End grain has high compression strength, and since shrinkage along the grain is negligible, the blocks, and therefore the heights of the letters, do not vary with changes in humidity.

Pear, maple, alder, cherry and applewood all make strong, durable type. Letters more than 2 in. high are known as "Second Coming" type—used only for drastic news. Although it's feasible to make large end-grain type, it's impractical to make these letters much more than 7 in. high because perfect stock this big is hard to find. Instead, large type is made from flat grain, which often is mounted on plywood or particleboard to reduce shrinkage and warping. An alternative to routing out the letters is to cut them from heavy veneer and then mount them on particleboard. The only tools needed are a fretsaw or jigsaw and wood files to clean up the rough edges.

Every day, all over the country, small businesses print posters and ads on modern presses that accept combinations of wood, metal and plastic type. These usually work by rolling the paper over the inked type. Yale's 1841 press, in contrast, works by forcing a flat platen down onto the type, more like Gutenberg's original model. As I watched Yale prepare to pull a proof, he locked the letter blocks in a metal frame called a chase, inked them with a roller, and laid paper on top. Then he slid the chase into the press and pulled the action lever. At the first attempt, some of the letters printed fainter than others. These he shimmed up with slips of paper, then ran a second proof. This time it was letter-perfect. □

Simon Watts teaches wooden boatbuilding and is the author of Building a Houseful of Furniture *(Taunton Press, 1983). Photos by the author.*

From *Fine Woodworking* magazine (January 1985) 50:52-53

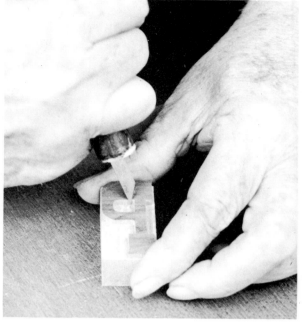

Richard Yale, who runs a newspaper-office museum in San Diego, guides the stylus on a pantograph/router around the outlines of a 6-in. pattern to cut a fancy letter A (above). To trim places where the router bit can't reach, such as the inside corners of a P (top right), he uses homemade knives. Yale made the letters used for the headline on the facing page, then pulled a proof on an 1841 Washington press, a working exhibit at the museum (center and bottom right). Shown below are samples of wooden type styles still used for posters by supermarkets and other small businesses.

Wooden Puzzles
Easy to make, but tough to solve

by Stewart T. Coffin

Many years ago, while engaged in the home enterprise of making canoe paddles, I found myself with the problem of what to do with piles of odd-shaped wood scraps. What emerged from this (with some help from my three children) was an intriguing little puzzle of 12 notched sticks. This in turn led to other ideas for new and unusual geometric puzzles—some 70-odd at the latest count—which soon grew into a thriving family business. Recently, with my labor force gone thither and shop space crowded out by other projects, I've been encouraging others to try their hand at this fascinating craft. This article should be enough to get any woodworker started—those who become addicted will find more of the same in my book, *Puzzle Craft*.

Puzzles don't have to be especially complicated or difficult to make to be absorbing. We found that the one that consistently brought the most amusement at craft fairs was our buttonhole puzzle, also known as the "idiot stick." (We used to make them from scraps of exotic wood, but a popsicle stick would do instead.) It's no more than a short length of hardwood with a loop of string that's just slightly too short to pass over the end of the stick. It ties through a buttonhole, just like a price tag, and the idea is to get it off in one piece. I know of a few of these sticks that are still attached to the same jacket or

Photo: White Light

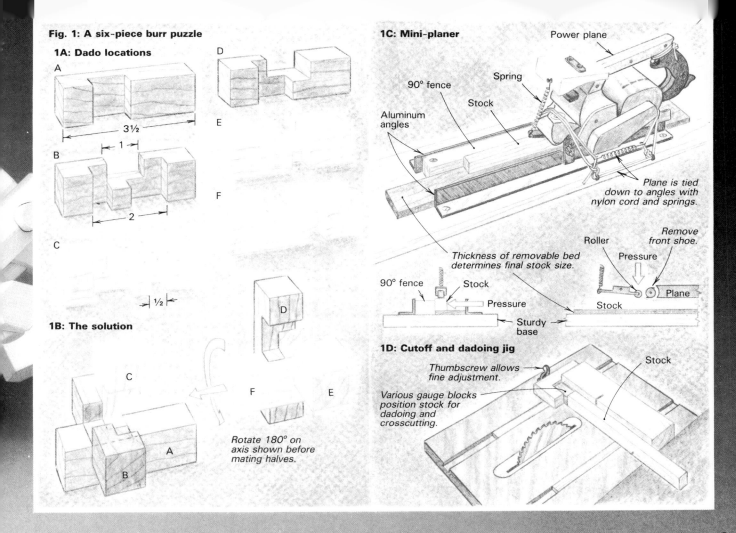

Fig. 1: A six-piece burr puzzle

1A: Dado locations

A

B

C

D

E

F

$3\frac{1}{2}$

1

2

$\frac{1}{2}$

1B: The solution

C

A

B

D

F

E

Rotate 180° on axis shown before mating halves.

1C: Mini-planer

Power plane

Spring

90° fence

Stock

Aluminum angles

Plane is tied down to angles with nylon cord and springs.

Thickness of removable bed determines final stock size.

Remove front shoe.

Roller

Pressure

90° fence

Stock

Pressure

Stock

Plane

Sturdy base

1D: Cutoff and dadoing jig

Stock

Thumbscrew allows fine adjustment.

Various gauge blocks position stock for dadoing and crosscutting.

sweater we put them on ten years ago, but whether the clothing's owners are still working out the solution or not, I can't say. (I have to admit that the first time somebody tied one on me, I had to cut the cord.) For readers who find such teasers more frustrating than interesting, the solution is given at the end of this article.

Some of my puzzles have been licensed to manufacturers, but most were engineered so I could make them in limited production in my small shop. I started with only an 8-in. tablesaw and a belt sander. Later I found a thickness planer to be indispensable, but because of the small scale of the work, I made mine from a portable power plane mounted over a fixed bed, as shown in figure 1C. Eventually I added two more tablesaws—one just for ripping and one for making notches—and, finally, a bandsaw.

Among all interlocking puzzles, the six-piece burr (the center puzzle on the facing page) is one of the most ancient. Many people are apt to dismiss it on sight as being too trivial, but while some variations of the burr puzzle have numerous solutions and are therefore fairly easy to solve, others such as the one shown in figure 1, which has just one solution, can be quite taxing.

When making a burr, as with most other puzzles, the woodworking is simple and straightforward, but all cuts must be extremely accurate or the puzzle will be sloppy. To check measurements, you'll want at the very least a good set of vernier calipers, or, better yet, a micrometer. Keep in mind that wood shrinks

and swells with changes in humidity. Don't aim for too tight a fit on a dry winter day or the puzzle will lock solid in summer. Saws must be set up square and true and kept very sharp—a hollow-ground (no-set) plywood blade will do fine.

Domestic woods such as cherry, walnut and white oak can be used, but my preference is Honduras mahogany because it's more stable. Among the more exotic tropical woods, Brazilian rosewood is my first choice.

Thickness the sticks to exactly 1 in. square. I first rip the stock to $1\frac{1}{16}$ in. square. To bring the sticks down to final dimension, I set the planer to skim off the sawmarks on two adjacent faces, then reset it to final size and skim the other two.

Next I cut the sticks to their 3½-in. finished length. I never mark sizes on the stock, because that would be a time-wasting and inaccurate step when such close tolerances are required. Instead, I rely on a jig to ensure accuracy and speed. The setup shown in figure 1D holds the stick exactly square to the blade, and positions it to length by means of a removable gauge block. The same setup, with different gauge blocks, ensures that the notches are in the right place. I cut them with a dado set shimmed out with paper to 0.002 in. oversize.

When I've cut the pieces, I test the fit and give them a very light sanding to ease the corners, making the parts much more inviting to handle. To keep the appearance crisp, I lightly chamfer the ends of the sticks with a flat file. Then I dunk each piece

Coffin's 'Octahedral Cluster' puzzle, apart and assembled. The basic 12-sided block is made on the tablesaw jig shown below.

in thinned lacquer and immediately wipe it off with a clean rag. With oily woods such as rosewood, no lacquer is necessary.

The burr puzzle is an *orthogonal* puzzle—its geometry is based on the cube. Another sort of puzzle is the *rhombic-dodecahedral* type ("R-D," for short), whose geometry is based on a figure with 12 sides. The jig shown in the photo below easily makes 12-sided blocks. It's simply a V-cradle set at 45° to the sawblade. Place a 1½-in. square stick in the cradle, with its end against the stop at the far end of the V. Push the jig

This V-cradle jig makes solid 12-sided blocks as described in the text. Such blocks can be glued together to make the author's 'Octahedral Cluster' puzzle, shown at the top of the page. The clamp is necessary only for the final cut.

through the sawblade, rotating the stick after each pass, to cut off its four corners. Then advance the stick by means of a gauge block. (The length of the block depends partly on the width of your sawblade's kerf—try 2⁵⁄₁₆ in., and adjust to suit.) Cut about halfway through the stick from all four sides; at the last cut, a 12-sided block will result. Then trim the stick's corners, advance it with another gauge block and repeat the process.

You can glue these little rhombic dodecahedrons together to make various puzzles, such as my "Octahedral Cluster," shown in the photos above. But even if you don't plan to ever make the cluster, the little blocks make good Christmas-stocking stuffers, and are pretty to have around. I used to sell them for 35¢ each, and there's a man up in Toronto who's bought about a thousand of them. I'm not sure why.

Some of the corner-waste pieces from those blocks led to another puzzle: When my children were quite small, they used to spend hours in my shop, gluing together scraps to make "puzzles" for their friends. One time, daughter Abbie, merrily gluing corner scraps in different ways, chanced on a fascinating arrangement. As shown in the photo at the top of the facing page, the puzzle has mirror-image halves of six sides each, which fit together to make an R-D, obviously with no difficulty whatsoever. Taking it apart, however, is another matter. Most people will grasp randomly with the thumb and forefinger of each hand and pull. But the puzzle will never come apart that way, because you're always grasping both pieces in each hand. Only by an unnatural three-finger grip with each hand can the puzzle be disassembled. If made carefully, the planes of dissection are practically invisible. My kids made and sold these for a few years at $3 apiece for large ones and $1 for little ones. They used to

From *Fine Woodworking* magazine (November 1984) 49:38-41

The mirror-image halves of 'Pennyhedron' easily slide together to form a hollow rhombic dodecahedron, but getting them apart again requires a three-finger grip that takes most people a while to figure out. Figure 2 shows how to make the puzzle.

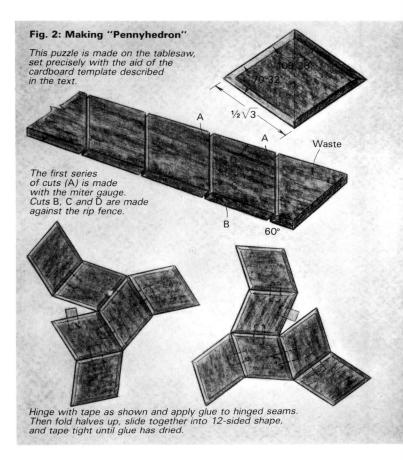

Fig. 2: Making "Pennyhedron"

This puzzle is made on the tablesaw, set precisely with the aid of the cardboard template described in the text.

109°28′
70°32′

½√3

A

A

Waste

The first series of cuts (A) is made with the miter gauge. Cuts B, C and D are made against the rip fence.

D

C

B

60°

Hinge with tape as shown and apply glue to hinged seams. Then fold halves up, slide together into 12-sided shape, and tape tight until glue has dried.

put a penny inside, and therefore named it "Pennyhedron." I think we ran out of scraps and they got interested in other things at about the same time, so production ceased.

"Pennyhedron," which consists of 12 identical rhombic panels, is not difficult to make. Prepare a strip of ¼-in. lauan plywood (or other wood of uniform thickness) about 2½ in. wide and 3 ft. long. You will crosscut this strip at a slight angle—as shown in figure 2—into 12 pieces with the sawblade tilted to 30° and the miter gauge adjusted to the correct angle. This yields one good diagonal cut (A) on each piece. The drawing shows the work as done on a saw whose blade tilts to the right; if your saw tilts to the left, your workpiece will be the mirror image of mine. The other three cuts are simply made against the rip fence as described below. The exact profile of each finished side is shown in figure 2.

It's impossible to set the miter gauge by measuring the angles, but a large-scale cardboard template will do the job. Make a triangle with a baseline of 24 in., and two other equal sides of 20$\frac{25}{32}$ in., as near as you can measure. These are the proportions of half the shape, with the baseline equal to the short diagonal of the piece (the ratio is 1 : ½√3). To set the miter gauge, raise the blade to full height, press one of the short sides of the template against it, and adjust the miter gauge so it aligns with the other short side of the template. Then tilt the sawblade to 30°, lower it to a safe height and make the first series of cuts, a little farther apart than the strip is wide. Next set the rip fence to a little less than the width of the strip (with the blade tilting *away* from the fence, of course, so as not to trap the work) and run the good diagonal cut against the fence to cut the second diagonal. Then cut the other two sides with the same setting.

At craft fairs, we found that people frequently asked what age group a particular puzzle was suited for. This opened the door for one of our favorite tricks: My youngest daughter, Margie, then about seven or eight, would be mingling with the crowd. I would take our most complicated-looking puzzle apart and say, "Anyone who can put this together can take it away." Most adults hung back in fear of embarrassment, leaving an opportunity for Margie to emerge from the crowd, quickly assemble the puzzle, tuck it under her arm and smugly walk away. The crowd always realized that the joke was on them. Children of that age learn very quickly, which leads me to one final tale.

I had licensed one of my designs to a manufacturer, who in turn had contracted with a factory to mold 20,000 of them in plastic. Production was no problem, but the factory couldn't find anyone to put the pieces together for packaging, and was about to jam up solid with puzzle parts. So I made a deal with them and told them to ship the pieces to my factory. My "factory" turned out to be some picnic tables set up on the lawn, and the work force consisted of all the kids in the neighborhood. They all learned quickly, and not one dropped out, especially when I paid them 2¢ per puzzle assembled. The youngest worker was six years old. We finished the job in ten days. □

Stewart Coffin is the author of Puzzle Craft, *which is available from him at 79 Old Sudbury Rd., Lincoln., Mass. 01773, for $12 (1986 price). He is now making canoes and puzzling out designs for ultralight paddles. To put the buttonhole puzzle on, pull the fabric through the loop of string until the far end of the stick can slip through the buttonhole. Then pull the stick until the string tightens. Reverse the steps to remove it.*

Making Marionettes
Carved figures bring life to wood

by Bruno Frascone

Wood has been important to us since the beginning of time. Even today when so many objects and gadgets employ man-made materials, wood is a precious gift that can play all sorts of roles—anything from a box to a home, and sometimes it can dance, talk and entertain.

I began to understand this miracle about 12 years ago while working with a marionette theater in France. I had fallen in love with the fascinating little people, jointed dolls that hang from the strings that control their movements, and I began making them, first with papier-mâché and wire, later from wood. My wooden marionettes worked best, but I knew they needed more sophisticated bodies if I was ever going to eliminate the false or "too-loose" movements that destroy their magical human-like behavior. Thus began my search for the perfect marionette.

By the time I moved to the United States in 1976, I had carved two all-wood marionettes that performed well, but I still was not happy with the way they moved. Then six months later, on my first Christmas in America, my quest ended when my wife gave me a book called *The Dwiggins Marionettes: A Complete Experimental Theater in Miniature* (by Dorothy Abbe, Plays, Inc., 120 Boylston St., Boston, Mass. 02116). William A. Dwiggins, who worked his marionette magic from the '30s to the early '50s, was a remarkable artist who never received enough exposure to become well known (because the actors are seldom more than 20-in. tall and the stage is proportionally tiny, 30 to 40 persons is the maximum audience for a live marionette show). He was not only a good woodcarver, but he had learned how to balance each part of a marionette's body (figure 1) so that the control strings

Father Time hobbles along in an endless march. His clothes conceal a variety of lever-like limbs and hinged joints custom-carved to duplicate the movements of the human body.

working against the pull of gravity produced what he called "almost automatic human motions." I had found the system that would give life to my designs, like Father Time (photo at left). Even though Dwiggins showed me the secret of lifelike movement, he did not limit me to copying his work. I still could create my own individual world of marionettes: in terms of human anatomy, an old man doesn't have the same type of body as a ballerina or a juggler, so you could say their designs are not the same, even though the basic systems that give them life and movement are identical.

With the Dwiggins system, though, you don't have to create a perfect replica of the human body to make a good marionette. Since the body will be clothed, its appearance is not too important. Strings hook the body parts together (figure 2) and regulate posture, so you don't have to carve realistic knees or elbows, but these joints must be cut accurately for the marionette to move properly. Since the hands and head are painted, you can create many details with a brush instead of a carving knife.

Sketching and shaping—I first draw the front and side view of the figure I want to do, usually making it 14 in. to 20 in. tall. (Very small or very large marionettes behave erratically on the control strings.) Once you've got your basic sketch, try to visualize how the figure is broken down into its basic components according to the Dwiggins system, as shown in figure 3 on p. 32. Sketch these parts on both views of your figure, if you like. For a start, just use the Dwiggins pattern for a generic male (figure 4) to make cardboard patterns for both views of each piece. If the dimensions shown on the grid are respected, the marionette won't fail. With experience, you'll probably want to modify some of the

From *Fine Woodworking* magazine (May 1985) 52:30-35

The Dwiggins system

A marionette hangs from its head. So much of its natural action depends on accurately locating all points of support from the neck to the feet in a single plane perpendicular to the ground, as represented by the line through figure 1A. In this way, gravity does all the work—the strings simply control the motions that result from the pull of gravity.

The body parts themselves are simple levers that move in circular tracks about fixed points or fulcrums. The shapes of the parts, the mechanical design of the joints and the tension of the strings used to connect them limit the motion of the levers to certain planes and arcs of travel. The limits (what Dwiggins called stops) for these arcs and the slants of the planes are determined by watching a human being move, then carved into wood by a trial-and-fitting process. Dwiggins' goal was to make the action of every single articulation or joint as close as possible to its counterpart on the human body, although he used the same system for both males and females.

The torso is divided into three individually shaped cones representing the shoulders, waist and hips. The pieces are held together by a string that acts like a spinal cord from shoulders to hips. A loop called a side string, extending through the three pieces, in conjunction with the beveled center piece, controls how much the figure can bend from side to side and front to back. —B.F.

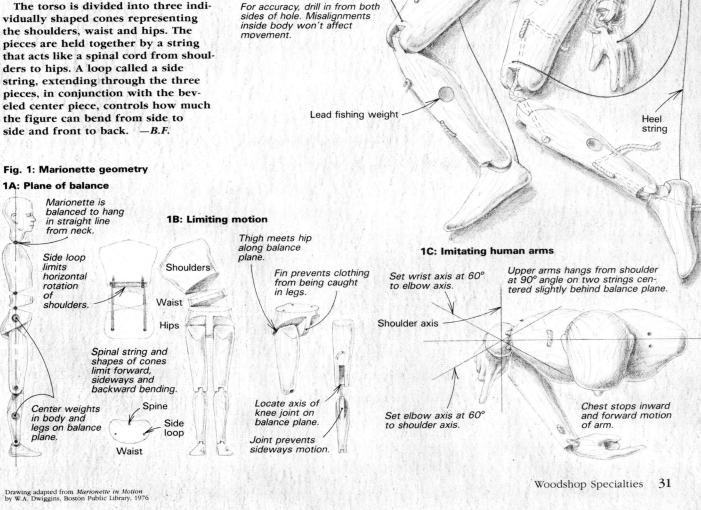

Fig. 2: Stringing a marionette

Forehead string

Head string

Shoulder string

Drill ⅛-in. hole for metal rod to support head.

Drill 1/16-in. hole through center of three torso sections for spinal string.

Depth of groove determines how much screw eye restricts body movement.

Hand string

Elbow string

Add weights to stabilize figure.

Leg string

For accuracy, drill in from both sides of hole. Misalignments inside body won't affect movement.

Lead fishing weight

Heel string

Fig. 1: Marionette geometry

1A: Plane of balance

Marionette is balanced to hang in straight line from neck.

Side loop limits horizontal rotation of shoulders.

Spinal string and shapes of cones limit forward, sideways and backward bending.

Center weights in body and legs on balance plane.

Shoulders

Waist

Hips

Spine

Side loop

Waist

1B: Limiting motion

Thigh meets hip along balance plane.

Fin prevents clothing from being caught in legs.

Locate axis of knee joint on balance plane.

Joint prevents sideways motion.

1C: Imitating human arms

Set wrist axis at 60° to elbow axis.

Upper arms hangs from shoulder at 90° angle on two strings centered slightly behind balance plane.

Shoulder axis

Set elbow axis at 60° to shoulder axis.

Chest stops inward and forward motion of arm.

Drawing adapted from *Marionette in Motion* by W.A. Dwiggins, Boston Public Library, 1976

Fig. 3: Father Time

These are the author's working drawings for the marionette pictured on the previous page. The outline of the body parts used in the Dwiggins system can be seen under the clothes. A thin wire run like a control string from the figure to the control paddle lets the author turn the lantern on and off during performances.

A pensive ballerina relaxes among the spring blossoms, her body parts delicately shaped to give her the flexibility and grace of a prima donna. Makeup paint conceals the joints in her limbs.

parts, perhaps increase the angles of the cones forming the shoulders, waist and hips to create a limber ballerina (photo, above), or make the knee joints smaller and tighter to imitate the restricted gait of an elderly person.

For now, you'd be wise to limit your customizing to the proportions and characteristics of the feet, hands and head—details that are so important in conveying the personality of a marionette. The clown always wears big shoes, and the hands of the maestro are always large and delicate. A marionette head looks best if it equals one-quarter to one-fifth of the full height of the figure. Since marionettes are usually viewed from a distance, it's better to make the head too big than too small.

Once you've prepared all your patterns, trace them onto blocks of wood. Red cedar, white pine or some other soft wood is fine for the body parts, but hardwoods like mahogany, beech and birch are better for the more intricately carved head, hands and feet. So you'll be able to carve sym-

metrically, mark accurate centerlines on each face of every piece. If you have to cut off one of the centerlines in one operation, you can reestablish it using the remaining lines for reference. I carefully bandsaw one view of each piece, then tape the waste on so I'm working with a square block to cut the second view. Work by pairs—upper arm with upper arm, upper leg with upper leg, and so on—so you can remember to maintain the left and right mirror effect of each pair. Beginners should make two sets of pieces, just in case the first set isn't good enough or something breaks. Leave the edges of each piece square for now. You don't want to shape anything until after you've cut the tenons and notches that will form the joints. These joints, what Dwiggins called articulations, must be cut carefully because they determine how well the marionette will move.

Bandsaw the torso pieces to shape, but don't try to carve away any sharp ridges. Be very careful when cutting the hip joint, basically two notches flanking a center

ridge, into the lower torso. For the marionette to walk straight, the two notches must be identical—cuts on one side of the torso must be exactly parallel and in the same plane as cuts on the other side. I use a flexible plastic ruler to lay out the joint lines, then bandsaw the waste, cleaning up with a chisel or knife as needed. With a small gouge, cut a ¼-in. groove under the top part of the torso for the side string.

The mechanism of the leg works in a straight line, and each leg is parallel to the other. I notch the bottom of the knee joint by making two parallel bandsaw cuts, then clearing the waste with a ¼-in. chisel. You can bandsaw freehand, since the gently curved parts have not been shaped yet, but you might want to reattach the waste you previously cut from the back of the leg to help in cutting nice, parallel articulations. To cut the tenons for the knee notch, I angle the piece on end and make two cuts parallel to the length of the piece to establish the ¼-in. wide tongue, then I carve away the sides until the tenon fits into the notch and the upper and lower knee work nicely together. The farther back the tenon shoulders are, the more movement the joint will have, so be sure to leave enough of a shoulder to prevent excessive, unnatural movements. Cut the ankle joint the same way—bandsawing and chiseling a notch in the lower leg and carving the tenon on top of the foot to fit.

The mechanism of the arms is far more complex than that of the legs, and can be best understood by looking at your own body. If you let your arm hang naturally from your shoulder, you'll notice that the axis of the elbow joint points slightly inside of the straight-ahead mechanism of the knee. The wrist also works on another axis, pointing out this time, relative to the axis of the elbow. Dwiggins calculated that the difference between the axes of the shoulder and elbow and between those of the elbow and wrist was 60° in each case. You can use this 60° figure as a general guideline and work from your own body. Cut the elbow notch and tenon straight, just as you did for the knee joint. Establish the elbow angle by carving away the top of the arm where it hangs against the upper torso. Shape the upper arm until the marionette's arm hangs the same way yours does. Again work in pairs so the joints on the left side mirror those on the right side. After doing the elbow, use your body as a guide to approximate the wrist angle and carve out this articulation.

Now you're ready to shape all the body parts with a sharp knife. Use the centerline of each piece as a guideline and work the pieces in pairs to ensure symmetry. Your carving should accentuate the twist you've created in both the upper and lower arm. Proceed slowly, carving away the sharp corners left by the bandsaw. Remember, the pieces need not be perfectly shaped, since the body will most likely be clothed and viewed only from a distance.

Hands are the hardest part of the figure. Think how much you use your hands to express yourself—if you mess up the hands, you may kill the expressive effect of the marionette. One nice thing about creating little people, however, is that you always have a model with you. Use your own hands and other body features (keep a mirror handy) to answer any questions on shapes and gesture that might come up as you carve.

I begin by drawing the hands directly onto a small block of wood, arranging the block so the grain follows the fingers for maximum strength in these delicate areas. The fingers will also be stronger if you

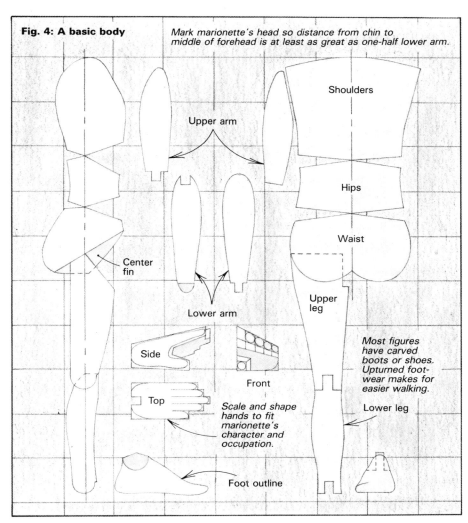

Fig. 4: A basic body

Mark marionette's head so distance from chin to middle of forehead is at least as great as one-half lower arm.

Upper arm

Shoulders

Center fin

Hips

Waist

Lower arm

Upper leg

Side

Top

Front

Most figures have carved boots or shoes. Upturned footwear makes for easier walking.

Scale and shape hands to fit marionette's character and occupation.

Lower leg

Foot outline

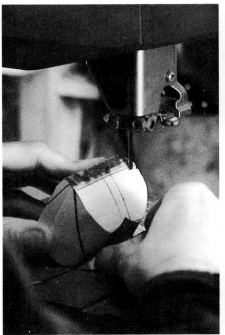

Steady the cone-shaped hip section with a scrap wedge while bandsawing the notches that accept the thighs, above left. Hold the leg piece on end and bandsaw parallel cuts to establish ¼-in. tenons, above right. Carve the shoulders with a knife.

Flexible wrist joints give the ballerina, left, such a repertoire of gestures that her wooden hands seem real. Study your own body to determine how each hand should be formed. Use a small file, below, to shape delicate areas of the palm and fingers where a knife might be too large or where there is danger of breakage.

During carving, Frascone frequently checks the marionette's emerging face from below. The change in perspective makes it easier to spot flaws and to visualize what the finished character really will look like.

carve them joined together, rather than as five individual units. I clamp the block in a small vise and carve the fingers with a ¼-in. chisel, the chisel width setting the width of individual fingers. Small jewelers' files are very useful for fine details on hands, as well as on feet and heads.

Being aware of the centerline is especially important in carving the face and head. Take a block of wood large enough for the head, trace the outline of the head, and mark its centerline on front, back, top and bottom. I cut the main angles of the face with a bandsaw. If you make a cut on one side of the centerline, you must make a similar cut on the other side; if you curve one edge, curve the other. Never try to finish one side or a detail of one side before roughing out the other. I do most of my carving with ¼-in. and ½-in. shallow gouges, a small skew-shaped knife and a spade-foot knife, but the tools really don't matter as long as you never lose sight of the centerlines, or forget that you are working on two profiles—the front and the side. When you carve the eyes, make sure they are on the same level and square. As I carve, I look at the face from underneath, side and top, not just from the front. I also like to use a small mirror to view the emerging face—I always discover a totally different view there.

All pieces of the body are joined with and supported by string—30-lb. test braided nylon fishing line for controls and waxed string used in leathercraft for the joints. A 1/16-in. dia. metal pin supports the ankle, but string permits more supple movements in the other joints. Also, if you should accidentally drop the marionette, the string is likely to break or pull out, whereas metal pins tend to break the wood.

Stringing the body—To assemble the body, drill 1/16-in. holes at the locations shown in the plan. It's normal to have to do some final trimming as you string the pieces together. First, run the spine string through the three sections of the torso, leaving it loose, then add the side string. The side string runs from the lower front of one side, up the side hole of the center part, through the screw eye located in the groove of the upper part, over to the other screw eye, down through the other side hole of the center piece and to a lock hole in the lower section. You'll have to adjust both the side and spine strings to allow the right amount of motion, then secure the ends of each by driving sections of round toothpicks into the lock holes. Drill the holes for the knees and elbow and string these joints together. The shoulder

Marionette motivation

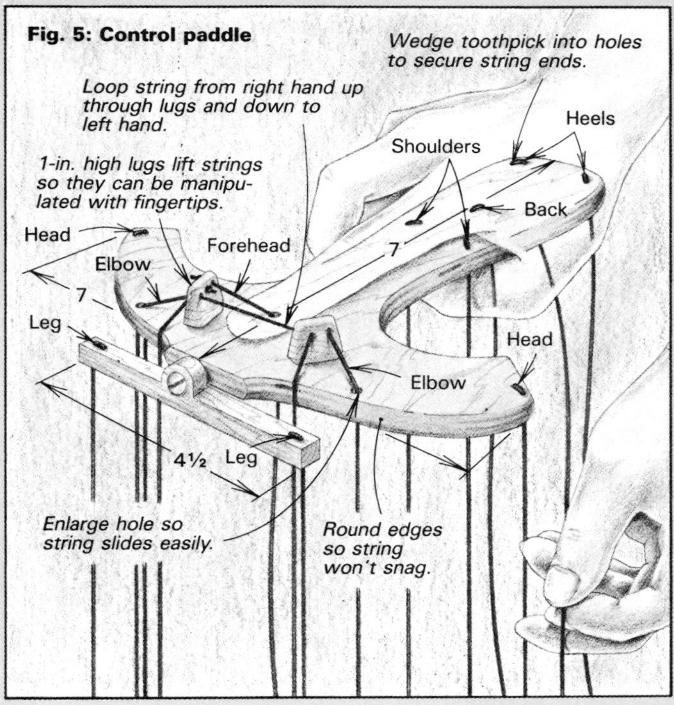

A balanced, well-made marionette comes to life with a series of strings using the control mechanisms Dwiggins developed. His controls are comfortable and fun to use, and comparable to a musical instrument that lets you discover chords, rhythm and melody.

The control is basically a smooth, paddle-shaped piece of ⅜-in. plywood, along with an auxiliary bar, that holds and separates the strings. The two lugs on top of the paddle make it easy to reach the strings most important to the marionette's expressions—they control the arms and hands, and move the head up and down. The strings should slide through the holes without resistance.

I suggest using about 4 ft. to 4½ ft. of string to connect the marionette to its control. Since the entire marionette hangs by strings in the head, these must be inserted first. Attach them just over and slightly forward of the ears. When you set these strings, the control must stand perfectly horizontal. As before, drill ⅟₁₆-in. holes for the strings, then wedge the ends in place with toothpicks.

You'll need at least 11 strings to control the figure. The hand-to-hand string loops from one hand through the holes of the two lugs, then down to the other hand. This string should be slightly taut and

support both hands naturally. The elbow strings are attached to the forearm right below the elbow articulation. They should be taut without carrying any weight. The knee strings, attached right above the knee articulation, are similarly taut and set on the pivoting bar in the very front of the control. The shoulder and back strings should be set so they support and control the body when the head is lowered.

Now you should be ready to experience the true magic of a marionette. With your thumb and middle finger, grasp the narrow part of the paddle handle from above, roughly parallel to an imaginary line connecting the head strings. Use your forefinger to manipulate the head string. Curl your remaining two fingers under the paddle to reach the shoulder and back strings. Use your other hand to manipulate strings to make the figure walk and move its hands and legs. You'll develop your own methods, but here are some guides to get you started.

Head: Tilting the control paddle down and forward will bow the head. Keeping the control in this down position as you alternately roll the paddle from right to left along its axis will produce a shaking-my-head "NO" movement. Holding the control horizontal while

Fig. 5: Control paddle

Wedge toothpick into holes to secure string ends.

Loop string from right hand up through lugs and down to left hand.

1-in. high lugs lift strings so they can be manipulated with fingertips.

Heels

Shoulders

Back

Head

Elbow

Forehead

7

Head

Leg

7

Elbow

4½   Leg

Leg

Enlarge hole so string slides easily.

Round edges so string won't snag.

lifting the forehead string with your index finger will lift the head. Pulling and releasing the forehead string with the control slightly bent down will give a "YES" nod. You can make the marionette bend or twist by using one of the fingers holding the control to manipulate the back and shoulder strings from below the control.

Arms: Use your second hand to manipulate the hands and arms. Pulling the hand string in combination with the elbow strings will give a variety of movements and expressions.

Legs: Make the legs walk by rhythmically moving the control forward and pivoting the bar carrying the

knee strings. When the control is tilted backward, allowing the back, shoulder and head strings to drop, the marionette will sit.

After you learn to control these basic strings, you may want to add others. Just remember—every additional string increases the chance of tangling. Despite that danger, you can create some interesting results by attaching strings to the bottom of the marionette's heels. The strings should hang very loosely so they don't interfere with normal walking, but when pulled they should lift the back of the feet, allowing the marionette to get on its knee, or fly like Superman, or dance on one leg.   —B.F.

and the hip each hang by two strings which are adjusted to allow a natural looseness to the hips and shoulder. Drill the holes of the wrist and ankle and join them together.

Now that your marionette is all together, check its body mechanism. Hold the marionette by its head and lift the knee by the upper leg, watching the body and the lower legs—if they swing too much, add lead fishing weights to the lower legs until the movement seems natural. Check

all articulations to make sure they are not too tight or too loose. This takes practice, but you'll soon see how to work the strings and weights to balance the marionette.

I paint the marionette's hands, legs and face with two coats of gouache water paint (available at any art supply shop). I use fine wool or yarn for hair, drilling into the skull, inserting strands of fiber and pinching them in place with a toothpick. Now the marionette must be dressed. Generally, the clothes are simple designs, made of

lightweight fabrics or leather, and baggy enough to allow free movement. I'm not a tailor, so you're on your own. When the marionette has finally found something to wear, it is complete, although asleep, waiting only for control strings and your skills to give it full life.   □

Bruno Frascone is a professional marionette maker who teaches marionette making and produces miniature theater programs in Charlotte, N.C.

Langton's Wooden People
Character is in the details

by Dick Burrows

Anyone who has ever slept on the ground knows how hard it is to straighten up after a long, cold night. You ache as you slowly stretch each stiff joint. The cowboy pictured below makes you feel that pain, but he can't complain about his backache because he's made of wood.

The cowboy, named Gene, is one of 46 dolls created by Michael Langton of Alton, N.H. Even though the carvings are small, about 20 in. high, the details of their features are overwhelming—veins and wrinkles, fingernails, tendons, warts. To see more on a living body you would have to use a magnifying glass.

Langton says that the details are what grab people, letting them sense the power that enables humans to love and strive and hate, and the cares of the world that abrade and twist their flesh and minds. To him, the best carvings are those that best show life's scars—like David, a spunky paraplegic whose eyes follow you around the room, and Josh, a Bible-reading farmer (photos, facing page).

Langton claims to have no secret methods for his carving—just hard work, concentration and about 200 hours per doll. He uses ordinary carving gouges, attic-sale knives and 5X-7X-12X power magnification goggles. Usually he works directly from life, often taking a series of photographs that illustrate an attitude he wants.

Tung oil is his only finish, except for the eyes, which are colored with pencil crayon. Langton says that the way to get distinctive, natural-looking details is to oil the nearly completed figure two or three times, carve in the finest details, then oil again to soften the delicate lines.

The mobility that Langton's dolls exhibit is as impressive as the detailed carving. Posture and movement can tell as much about a person as facial features, and Langton's realistic figures shrug their shoulders, put on their shoes, sit or walk, cross their legs, even cast a fishing fly. On some figures you can tell whether the person is left-handed or right-handed. The elaborate system of carved body parts and wood-and-metal ball-and-socket joints that makes all this possible is camouflaged by perfectly tailored clothing created by fellow craftsperson Barbara Itchkawich, handmade buttons, even custom-made eyeglasses.

Langton's first doll, a sailor boy named Elmer, was Katherine Hepburn's alter ego in the movie *On Golden Pond.* The producers had rejected about 300 dolls before they found Elmer in New Hampshire where the movie was filmed in 1980. At the time, Langton was carving signs while trying to combine his interest in wood and his art-school background into something more meaningful. "Now, that's not half bad," said Ms. Hepburn when she saw Elmer.   □

Dick Burrows is an associate editor at Fine Woodworking.

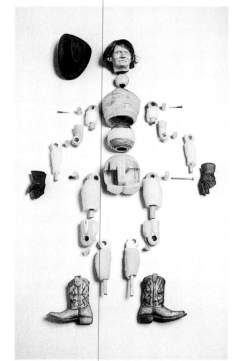

About 60 parts made of plywood, metal, and carved maple and pine let Langton's dolls imitate human movements.

Furrowed face, calloused hands and old boots create a lifelike illusion—until you see that Josh is sitting on two human-size books.

High-Rise Millwork
Working wood inside the glass and steel monolith

by Jeff O'Hearn

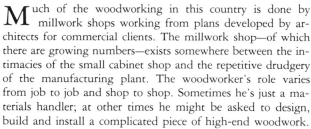

Much of the woodworking in this country is done by millwork shops working from plans developed by architects for commercial clients. The millwork shop—of which there are growing numbers—exists somewhere between the intimacies of the small cabinet shop and the repetitive drudgery of the manufacturing plant. The woodworker's role varies from job to job and shop to shop. Sometimes he's just a materials handler; at other times he might be asked to design, build and install a complicated piece of high-end woodwork.

The range of items custom-built by millwork shops is far more diverse than that of most small manufacturers, who tend to specialize in only a few products. A fully equipped millwork house can simultaneously produce specialty moldings by the linear mile, cabinetry, raised-panel doors, circle-head windows, entire storefronts and matched veneer panels, all in a physical plant that makes no distinctions between departments. These products can be made from any type of wood and brought to any stage of completion, from partially assembled to fully installed.

This ability to meet a customer's unique demands has always been a trademark of the millwork industry, but the industry has undergone a renaissance during the past thirty years. Around the turn of the century, the number of millwork houses began to decline steadily as the products they once made by hand poured off factory assembly lines at low prices. Today, however, the millwork market has bounced back in a new, vigorous form, partly because of the phenom-

enal growth of the contract-furniture design industry and partly because of the growing interest in renovating buildings and offices. Every year, thousands of new offices are built, and designers want distinctive moldings, bookshelves, paneling and furniture. Working directly with architects and designers, the millworker fills the custom demand in ways that a furniture factory cannot.

Huge sums of money go into office woodwork: a millwork contract might specify scores of individual items totaling a quarter of a million dollars or more. As project engineer at Art Woodworking, a large mill house in Cincinnati, I'm the liaison between the designer and the woodworker, corralling all the details and making sure the work gets done right and on time, all the while satisfying the often divergent interests of the architect, the job superintendent, and the client who's paying for the work. Art Woodworking, founded in the 1920s by Henry Dickman, once produced turnings for Cincinnati's thriving furniture factories. Henry's sons, George, Ray and Bill, all went into the business and today Ray heads the company. With some 38 employees, our production setup is typical of the industry, so a recent renovation job we did provides an interesting glimpse into the mechanics of high-rise millwork.

We had been awarded a contract for a three-floor renovation in the DuBois Tower, a 30-story high rise built in 1972 and located in downtown Cincinnati. A law firm, Dinsmore and Shohl, was expanding its offices in the tower, a project

From *Fine Woodworking* magazine (July 1984) 47:30-36

The elegant, seamless wood-work in a modern high-rise building—such as that in this law office in Cincinnati's DuBois Tower—belies the considerable ingenuity that goes into its construction. Working from the architect's plans, millworkers 'fit up' a building's steel and concrete innards with custom-made paneling, molding, furniture and specialty fixtures such as the non-structural column, far left, made by veneering a cardboard form called a Sonotube.

that involved first stripping out sections of the old walls and ceilings right back to the building's concrete skeleton. After that, new partitions were built, using drywall fastened to metal studs. Then new electrical wiring, phone lines, ducting and lights were installed, ceilings were hung, and wallcoverings, paint, carpet and trim were applied.

Our job was part of the "fit-up," an industry term for the process that turns a building's concrete shell into comfortable, attractive offices. The architect, Granzow and Guss of Columbus, proposed a fit-up that would exude a quiet, modern elegance. Most of our work was installed in the central lobby of each floor, poised—as is typical with most fit-ups—to give a strong first impression to people getting off the elevator. We paneled the three elevator lobbies in bookmatched white oak veneer and built identical oak reception desks for each lobby. In each of these areas, the architect called for decorative white oak columns with soffits leading into sets of bookcases. On paper, the columns looked straightforward enough, but actually building them provided some troublesome moments.

One of the most difficult parts of the job was a pair of circular staircases, with all the attendant trim and moldings, which were hung in a shaft paneled in gray fabric. We also provided hundreds of other items, including 150 veneered office doors and some plastic-laminate cabinetry for employee kitchens. Later in the job, we were asked to build some additional furniture, including a 26-ft. conference table veneered in ash burl. By any standards, it was a very healthy job.

Before we actually got the contract, we had to give the architect a detailed cost estimate. Sometimes bidding is "open," which means that the architect has sent his plans to a local branch of a national bid-announcement service such as F.W. Dodge Company. Millwork outfits like Art Woodworking subscribe to this service and submit bids on work that interests them. Often, the architect won't risk unknown problems with a new company, and he'll "close" the bidding by specifying as qualified bidders two or three companies he's already worked with. That's what happened with the Dinsmore job. We were written in as one of two qualified bidders. The other, a New York firm, was unlikely to take on a job in Cincinnati.

Estimating a bid accurately is an acquired skill that succeeds most surely through religious attention to detail. Each bid is prepared by closely examining the architect's drawings, dissecting each item into the time and material needed to make it. Labor rates and overhead costs vary from shop to shop and job to job. Some are as low as $20 per hour, others as high as $50. Typically, a profit margin of 15% is aimed for. The most difficult part of the bid is the time estimate—it haunts the cabinetmaker and determines the profits. Les Childress, our senior estimator, figures time estimates with the help of the Architectural Woodwork Institute's *Cost Book* (2310 S. Walter Reed Dr., Arlington, Va. 22206), a manual with tables describing the time required to jig up and make 175 different millwork products. Childress backs up the cost book by referring to our company's own job rec-

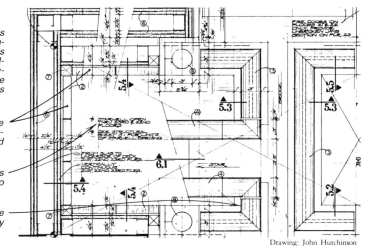

Decoding the architect's shorthand

Though very condensed, this drawing gives enough information about materials, surfaces and dimensions for the millworkers to prepare final drawings and materials lists for the stairwell shown in the photos at right.

Fabric-covered wall panels are shown schematically; the actual dimensions are calculated after drywalling.

Notes say stairwell connects three floors; numbers refer to detail drawings.

Larger-scale details show the mitered and returned stairway railings.

Drawing: John Hutchinson

ords. In our shop, each job is assigned a code number. Cabinetmakers punch their time cards to record how long they work on each job and the cards are tallied daily. At the end of each job, actual and estimated times are compared to reach the moment of truth: Is the job in the red or the black? More often than not, it's in the black.

The work I most enjoy happens after the contract has been awarded: poring over the architect's plans, refining them into working drawings so that the shop can actually build what the contract calls for. There's a clear distinction between the architect's drawings and the shop or working drawings. The architect's plans solve problems of function and appearance, while the shop drawings address construction, assembly and installation. My job is to interpret the architect's intent, adding details where necessary and generally tidying up the tail end of the design process.

I begin by scaling up the architect's drawings, which are often at a quarter-inch to the foot and are thus far too small to show details such as molding profiles and joinery. The details I need to include in shop drawings vary from job to job. The design drawings for the law firm's reception desks, for example, were adequately dimensioned to indicate overall size and shape, and they included notes about veneer grain direction and finish. But decisions about case joinery, the precise size of drawers and the selection of hardware were left up to me. It's a common misconception that the more detail supplied by the architect or designer, the better. Architects don't always know how furniture and millwork are put together, and a drawing that requests a specific type of joinery will frequently be ignored by the millworker, or the price for strict compliance will be very expensive.

Interpreting the architect's intent is akin to detective work, requiring an unfailing eye for detail. The plan view of the open stairways for the Dinsmore job, shown in the drawing above, appears as nothing but a dense crosshatching of lines, cluttered with circles, dimensions and notes. But from this condensed design shorthand, I was able to discern the relationships and sizes of the various millwork components. Fortunately, I had plenty of time to interpret the design drawings. Any questions I had—and there usually are quite a few—were cleared up when the general contractor and the architect reviewed my drawings. I prefer that my drawings return with

red ink here and there. No real review means you're on your own; the architect's approval stamp implies that the shop drawings haven't omitted anything specified in the contract.

Before we can begin making the millwork, we have to fine-tune the shop drawings by adding field dimensions—measurements taken inside the building where the woodwork will actually fit. These are the *real* distances between walls and floors and ceilings, not what the drawings say they ought to be. Even if building construction is behind schedule, we have to wait for field dimensions, in which case the time allotted for our work gets compressed against the tenant's move-in date. To expedite a job, architects sometimes give us "guaranteed" drywall dimensions, but these almost never work out. As the drywallers finish up, I collect field dimensions daily, scheduling work in the shop accordingly. At the same time, I discuss delivery of our portion of the job with the general contractor's superintendent, taking into consideration such factors as the maximum size of shipping entrances and elevators. We prefer to build furniture, cabinets and counters in as few pieces as possible, because the fewer the loose joints, the better the final appearance. On the other hand, particleboard is incredibly heavy stuff. I have been embarrassed to see the agony of seven large men struggling up a small stairway with a plastic-laminate behemoth pinning them into the corners.

While the shop drawings are being reviewed by the architect, there's a bit of a pause, which gives us time to order materials. The Dinsmore job called for 15,000 sq. ft. of white oak veneer, which I was assigned to select from a mid Ohio Valley veneer warehouse. But the most interesting material purchased for this job was the white ash burl veneer for the conference-room tabletop. A Louisville veneer broker had some exceptional burl veneer taken from a truly giant burl flitch—each leaf was 27 in. by 60 in. The flitch we bought had been softened by a chemical treatment, the defects punched and patched, and each leaf glued to a poplar veneer backing for easier handling. The dealer was secretive about the softening process, and I half-expected him to throw in the country of origin and how many elephants it had taken to drag the tree out of the mountains as part of his sales pitch. Such is the effect of a good burl—people seem to enjoy being mystified by the intensity of the wood's twisted growth.

Once the shop drawings have been approved and field dimensions taken, we begin work. Procedures at this point vary

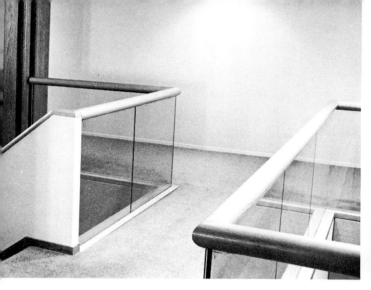

O'Hearn's biggest challenge is understanding the architect's intent and then transforming arcane drawings into woodwork, as shown here. Large-section moldings, which trim the top of the stair's rail, are a main staple of most millwork shops.

widely from shop to shop. At Art Woodworking, we give our cabinetmakers a blueprint of each piece, along with a cutting list describing the size of all the parts. Some of our cabinetmakers prefer only the drawing, accompanied by a careful discussion of critical parts of the design. In other shops I've seen, a senior cabinetmaker does layout and cutting bills, distributes parts lists to machine operators, and supervises assemblers. In our shop, my joinery and construction decisions are often overridden by the foreman or the cabinetmaker, but only after a discussion during which lots of cryptic pencil lines are made on the nearest flat surface.

In the millwork industry, woodwork is done with one constant concern in mind: how to produce the finished product in the least number of steps. As a result, particleboard—veneered or covered with plastic laminates—has become the dominant material for paneling and casework. It's cheaper and stabler than solid wood, and working with it is faster than milling and edge-gluing boards.

The equipment in our shop is geared to particleboard construction. Besides the jointers, tablesaws and planers that any hobbyist woodworker would recognize, we have expensive, specialized machines that greatly speed production. The largest of these are the five machines we use for veneering, which is involved in the majority of the work we do. The steps in production-veneering are the same as in hand-veneering, but we do them a lot faster (see photos, pp. 42-43). First, edgebands are glued to the particleboard substrate by a 20-ft. long machine called an edgebander. The edgebands, which can be either veneer or thin strips of solid wood, are stacked in a feed ramp at the back of the machine. The operator feeds one panel edge into the bander's conveyor, and the machine does the rest. It latches onto the panel and briskly tugs it along, gluing and clamping the edgeband and trimming it flush with the particleboard's length and thickness, all in about 30 seconds.

In hand-veneering, you'd first true the edges of each veneer leaf with a plane, then tape the leaves together to make larger sheets. We do the same, but with a veneer trimmer—a device that trues 15 to 20 leaves at once with a tiny circular saw pulled along a 14-ft. track by a chain. The trimmed (and usually bookmatched) leaves are fastened together by the stitcher, a machine that lays down a very fine thread of hot-melt glue across the seam to hold the leaves together for han-

dling. The stitched leaves are pressed onto the substrate, usually using urea-formaldehyde glue, which sets in about 14 minutes under the 2,000 PSI exerted by the heated press platens. Veneered panels are trimmed, sanded and sent on to the next production step, which might prepare them as wall paneling or as components in casework.

Like virtually all high-rise jobs, the Dinsmore project called for hundreds of feet of custom moldings, some as large as 8 in. in section. We have two molders, an ancient U.S.-made Mattison and a new high-tech Weinig from Germany. Setting up a molder, which is essentially a shaper with many cutterheads, is simple in principle but difficult in practice. Modernist architects often specify that moldings look straight-grained or rift-sawn. It's hard to find thick rift-sawn lumber for big moldings, and we often have to glue up thinner stuff. When we set up the molder, we center the profile cuts so we won't mill too much material off one side, as that could lead to a warp later. Of course, we custom-grind knives when necessary, but most moldings can be constructed from the hundreds of knife shapes that we already have. (These are stored in dusty trays arranged in arcane groups that only Tom Maly, our senior molder operator or "sticker man," really understands.)

In the course of a job, the pace can get frantic, but it's satisfying to see the culmination of two or three weeks at the drafting board pay off. As a building nears completion, meetings have been held and promises made. We'd sure as hell better have some millwork ready by the day circled on the calendar. Two weeks before that day, I'm usually in a frenzy, with three people pushing cutting lists in my face, asking if part 17a isn't really supposed to be $\frac{5}{16}$ in. longer, as I try to handle a phone call telling me that we never did place that order for hinges five weeks ago. All the while I'm thinking about the seven field dimensions I forgot to get, even though I've already visited the job site eight times.

I suppose that the story of any project can be summarized by the problems encountered. The construction business seems particularly chaotic, with deadlines that contractors swear are determined by darts thrown blindly at a calendar, millwork that just won't fit onto the elevator and field dimensions that seem to change mysteriously in the middle of the night. The Dinsmore project had fewer problems than some, but problems nonetheless.

One foul-up involved a machine, which is fairly rare. We

had used our newly acquired edgebander to put 1-in. white oak bandings onto particleboard cores for cabinet doors. While we were milling hinge mortises, we noticed cracks in the face veneer at the banding/substrate joint. In examining the edgebander's glue-capsule data, we discovered that the glue's melting point was 140°F—the same temperature at which we operate our veneer press. The edgeband glue was remelting in the press, then resetting without any pressure against the edge. We couldn't tell how much joint strength had been lost, and we couldn't replace the doors without destroying the veneer sequencing. Our solution was to reheat each panel, then immediately pull the bandings tight with 3-in. screws, plugging the countersunk holes afterward. We've since found an edgebander glue that melts at 400°F, and supposedly won't remelt once set.

The large lobby columns also posed an interesting construction dilemma. We had never made a 30-in. dia., 7-ft. tall veneered cylinder, and we weren't sure how to go about it. We came up with two solutions: The first was a hollow wooden tube made of 2x4s nailed to circular plywood discs, then covered with layers of ⅛-in. Baltic birch plywood. We trimmed, matched and stitched the white oak veneer, and glued it to lauan door skins (thick veneers used for hollow-core door construction), which served as backings. At this point, we were guessing. Would the lauan/oak composite be pliable enough to bend without cracking? All we could do was glue it up and find out. We screwed cleats along both outside edges of each composite skin, brushed the forms with Titebond glue and clamped from cleat to cleat. The procedure worked beautifully. The second time around, we got even better results by gluing the veneer to Yorkite (a paper backing) and gluing it to similarly prepared Sonotubes (giant cardboard cylinders normally used as forms for pouring concrete columns). We used the same method to assemble the pedestal legs for the conference table.

The installation of the law firm's millwork went smoothly. Except for a problem with the finish on some doors, we weren't having the typical deadline crunch. We did have some trouble in the stairwell, however. The 3-in. dia., half-round handrail molding was milled in three sections from a full-size cardboard template that I'd traced from the steel underpinnings on the job site. We bandsawed, shaped and fitted the molding sections to the stairway wall before it was plastered so that the handrail's curve could serve as the plasterers' template. For reasons unknown, or not admitted to, the handrail's joints were broken by the plasterers. Although we reshaped, puttied and refinished the joints in place, they didn't look good.

The blame for such a mediocre result should probably rest with the millworker and the architect. We are at fault because we didn't devise a joint strong enough to resist torquing, but some of the blame must fall on the design itself. The cool geometry of modern design sometimes contradicts its own "be-true-to-the-material" dictum by haphazardly combining dissimilar materials in ways that look good on paper but don't necessarily respect the nature of the materials involved. At the stairway low wall, for example, the three materials—sheetrock, oak and steel—did not combine well. Flush Miesian elegance is not very forgiving of materials that don't stay square or round or flush—or generally geometrically pure.

The accumulation of these sorts of imperfections can detract from satisfaction with the completed job. Most of the

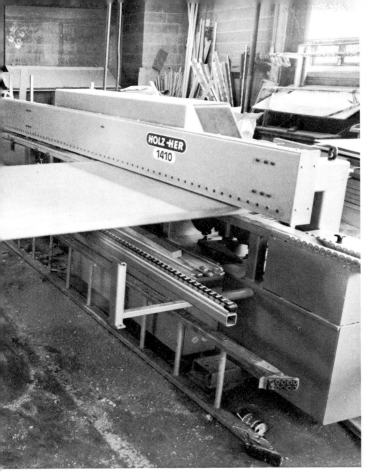

Millworkers get out enormous quantities of work on time by relying on big, expensive machines. In the photo at left, cabinetmaker Herman Unger feeds particleboard through an edgebander, which glues on a solid-wood edge strip before the panel faces are veneered. Below, two veneer leaves are fed through a stitcher, which sews them together with a thread of hot-melt glue.

Though sophisticated machines and jigs ensure consistent results, there's a place for handwork in the mill shop. The radiused corner moldings of the conference table shown at left were hand-turned (above) to match the profile of the machine-cut straight moldings. In the photo below, the disc has been bandsawn into quadrants which will neatly connect the straight moldings.

As the height and rent of a commerical building rise, so too do the scale and cost of the furniture that goes inside. The 26-ft. long conference table shown above is particleboard veneered with white ash burl. Too large and heavy to fit in the building's elevators, the table was made in five sections, then assembled on-site with Lamello plates and knockdown fasteners (photo, left). The pedestal legs are oak-veneered cardboard Sonotubes.

Millwork joinery: engineering, ingenuity

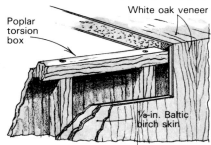

A reception desk—high-rise style

Stringer

Kerfed layer

For the desk's curved front, O'Hearn proposed veneering a sheet of kerfed plywood first bent to the proper radius, then mitered to the veneered fiberboard top.

Poplar torsion box

White oak veneer

⅛-in. Baltic birch skin

The cabinetmaker who built the desk improvised an easier-to-fit alternative: a poplar torsion box skinned with Baltic birch and white oak veneer. The skin was veneered first, mitered on the tablesaw, and then glued to the torsion box.

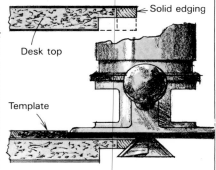

Solid edging

Desk top

Template

To cut the desk top's curved miter, a router fitted with a custom-ground bit was guided against a Masonite template.

Working against delivery deadlines that always seem too near, millwork cabinetmakers don't have the luxury of experimenting with intricate exposed joinery or the fussy hand-detailing that a one-of-a-kind craftsman might lavish on a special piece. Of course, any well-equipped mill shop is capable of executing complex joinery, such as the sticking and coping needed for a multi-pane sash or a fancy frame-and-panel door. By and large, though, the joinery repertoire of a millwork shop consists of the simplest joints strong enough to do the job.

For instance, we usually fasten a carcase together with a dado-and-rabbet, or an offset tongue-and-groove reinforced by screws or staples. Drawer parts are similarly joined. Pieces too large to fit into elevators are built in sections, then assembled on-site with field joints made by the Lamello plate joiner or with a variety of knockdown fasteners. During the past couple of years, I've noticed an accelerating trend toward dowel construction. Using the ingenious combination horizontal/vertical boring machines made in Germany, doweling is faster and more accurate than other

kinds of joinery, and it meshes nicely with the particleboard panel construction so basic to the millwork industry. Our doweling machine can bore up to 25 holes at once, either randomly spaced or set 32mm apart, which matches the standard screw spacing on much European hardware, including drawer slides, hinges and shelf standards.

Our shop drawings try to show ways to make simple joints appear seamless, as in the law firm's reception desks shown on p. 39. Though the visually stark design seems straightforward, the desk top is mated to its front with a tricky curved miter that's 8 ft. long. When I prepared shop drawings from the architect's plans, I proposed constructing the desk's gently curving front by veneering over a core formed by fir plywood kerfed and bent to the proper radius. Solid-wood stringers glued to each edge would maintain the curve. The face veneer could then be glued to a thin plywood backing, its mating edge mitered, and the composite easily bent around the curved core.

Ronnie Bright, the cabinetmaker who actually made the piece, offered another solution. He figured that a narrow miter

would be easier to fit than the relatively wide one my method entailed. After a quick conference in the shop, he decided that we should make the desk front by veneering over a curved poplar framework called a torsion box, the top edge of which fits into a rabbet milled into the bottom edge of the desk top. He milled the desk top's curved miter with a router guided against a Masonite template. Bright's method had another advantage that I hadn't figured on: the back of the hollow torsion box could be left off during assembly, so screws could be driven up into the top for added strength.

Though we rely on sophisticated machinery and jigs, we do a fair amount of handwork, especially on furniture. The radiused corners of the big ash-burl conference table are a case in point (see photos, p. 43). No machine setup I know of could have milled even that relatively simple (though large) molding in a curved piece. We glued up an oak blank and turned the profile by hand, bandsawing the resultant doughnuts into quadrants which were then fitted between the straight moldings that meet at the table's corners.   —J.O'H.

estimated labor hours have already been used up by this time. Any reworking we have to do is painfully time- and profit-consuming. Traditionally, the architect and the owner tour the completed job preparing a "punch list" of glitches that need attention. We try to anticipate the list as much as possible, yet most jobs don't end gloriously with a final day of delivery, but fade away with a piece of trim filled in here, a scratch touched up there.

The millwork business fills an interesting niche in the construction industry, at the crossroads between old-fashioned stick-built practicality and high-rise corporate elegance. Poised between serving the functional needs of the architect and the

contractor, and the aesthetic considerations of the designers who finish the spaces, millwork is becoming more of a service industry. New materials and machinery allow for a greater diversity in product appearance and production than has ever been possible before. At the same time, designers are delegating more of the detailing to the woodworker. All of this points to healthy, invigorating times for progressive millwork houses, and ample opportunities for success for well-informed newcomers.   □

Besides overseeing high-rise millwork, Jeff O'Hearn makes sculpture in his basement workshop. Photos by the author.

Triangular Sensibility
Intuitive geometry makes strong designs

by John Marcoux

Polished stainless steel fasteners glisten like jewels amid the glass and streaks of color in the 'Tritut' table (honoring King Tut and the Egyptians who used triangles in their furniture), left. In workshops, Marcoux is more whimsical, using yardsticks to show how 'weak materials' make strong furniture.

Kathy Carver

I've been designing and building furniture for many years, and I sometimes found myself locked into arbitrary rules that dictate looks. Things like: Dark wood should be used for serious furniture, light wood for informal furniture; forms should be predominantly rectangular. All that was too inhibiting for me as a designer. I struggled for years to sort out a point of view that would free me up to be a more decisive, adventurous furnituremaker, one who was still able to make furniture that people would want.

Eventually I found that I liked what happened when I heeded a fundamental design rule: Form follows function. I start

with common materials—dowels, nuts and bolts, rattan—and put them together so that they rely on structure as an expression of design; purpose-in-use becomes a reason for being. The small table shown above is typical of my personal solution. There's no highly figured wood added for effect, just distinctive linear patterns and geometric shapes. The table base is triangulated to make maximum use of the structural potential of its parts—thus conserving material or enabling me to build with materials I couldn't otherwise use—and to keep costs down. As I'm a natural conserver and a cost-conscious craftsman, this appeals to me.

My fascination with the triangle as a structural unit is an important part of the development of this furniture. For centuries, ancient Egyptian craftsmen used triangles in their furniture. What puzzles me is that sometime between 1500 and 1000 BC the triangle disappeared as a visible aesthetic and structural element in formal furniture (although it was still seen in rustic and wicker pieces), and rectangular forms became dominant. When I began exploring the design possibilities of triangles, I felt like a prospector who had stumbled across a rich vein in an abandoned mine.

Because triangles distribute weight in several directions, effectively neutralizing

Maple dowels are the main structural components in this weavers' bench. The triangular compartments on each side of the 31-in. high seat are for yarn and tools.

much of the force upon them, small-diameter dowels and other relatively weak materials can be used to create interlocking triangles capable of supporting a lot of weight. The triangle has another special quality: when fastened securely at its three corners, it will not change its shape as long as its joints and components remain intact. Without diagonals to brace them, rectangular constructions put under stress tend to distort into parallelograms. Any triangle, regardless of its included angles, will remain strong and rigid, so I've found that I have a lot of design freedom in creating interlocking triangles.

In any triangulated piece, the parts can be assembled in almost infinite combinations, bringing alive an aesthetic idea in which structure is also decoration. In my tables, I try to create linear and angular patterns that fascinate and delight the eye. Tops, especially those that are transparent or have ports revealing the base, must become an integral part of the table design, not just a platform set on a base. Adding mirrors and glass can create an ethereal dimension that changes with the light and with the viewer's position. When the design is right, I hope the viewer senses one of my favorite ideas: "It does what it's supposed to do with joy."

Bolted construction is a powerful asset in these tables. The legs and struts are fastened with machine bolts ⅛ in. in diam-

eter, so I'm not making holes large enough to weaken any component. To make this humdrum hardware appear gem-like and decorative, I polish faceted stainless steel cap nuts (available from Jamestown Distributors, 28 Narragansett Ave., PO Box 348, Jamestown, R.I. 02835).

In the workshops I teach, I like to introduce design ideas and the possibilities that "weak materials" offer by having people build a small table from yardsticks, like the one shown on p. 45. It's a good exercise, and you don't even need any woodworking tools. Tin snips to cut the yardsticks, a drill or a leather punch to make the holes, some wire and a pair of pliers, a screwdriver, some nuts and bolts, and a pocket knife for adding the finishing touches complete the kit. You don't need a tape measure, either—just use the markings on the yardsticks. Start with a couple of dozen yardsticks, and a few hours later you'll have a strong little table and a sense of how triangulated materials work together.

One of my simplest dowel tables, the Tri-table shown in figure 1, can support considerable weight, even though its base weighs only 14 oz. I assembled the table with 1¼-in., #4-40 stainless steel round-head machine bolts with cap nuts. I usually don't worry too much about the initial length of these bolts. After drilling through the two components to be joined,

I insert a long bolt and add a hex nut. Then I cut the bolt close to the nut with electricians' diagonal cutters, unscrew the nut (this helps fix any threads damaged by the cutters) and put on the cap nut. This way, I'm sure that the bolt won't bottom out in the cap nut before the nut can be tightened down. The Tri-table could also be lashed together with cane or rattan. I used rattan only on the top and bottom of the center-column dowels. The top is solid maple, but you could use cane or thin strips of wood in a dowel frame instead.

In constructing the table, I made two simple jigs: one to position three dowels so that I could bore and bolt them together into a triangular unit (figure 2), and one to support the base while I lashed together the center dowels of the triangular units to form a column (figure 3). To make the first jig, I drew a line representing the floor near one edge of a plywood sheet. After deciding the height and size of the tabletop, I drew its side view on the plywood. I angled a dowel between the floor line and the tabletop line until it looked right, then marked the intersections. Next I added blocks and braces to hold the other two dowels needed to build a triangle around the diagonal. I determined the length of the dowels and cut them exactly, although they could be cut after they are drilled.

The dowels should extend about ½ in. beyond the bolt holes. I center-pricked the dowels at the three points where they cross and, using a portable power drill, just eyeballed holes through the center marks. Then I sanded the dowels in a large drum sander (see pp. 48-49) and painted them in three bright colors, which accent the triangles of the base and create a lively pattern as the parts thread through intersections and linear crossings.

To form the base, I lashed the three triangular units together with strips cut from an inner tube. On a plywood base, I made the second jig: I drew a circle large enough to intersect the tops of the legs, divided the circumference into three equal parts, and built traps for the legs at these points. With the three legs set in the traps, I wound the center column with rattan before removing the rubber strips. To secure the rattan, I drilled a hole in one of the dowels, glued in one end of the rattan, wrapped the column, and then worked the other end back into the lashing.

While the base was still in the jig, I added ⅜-in. dowel stabiles, or braces, to keep each leg in the 120° position. Using

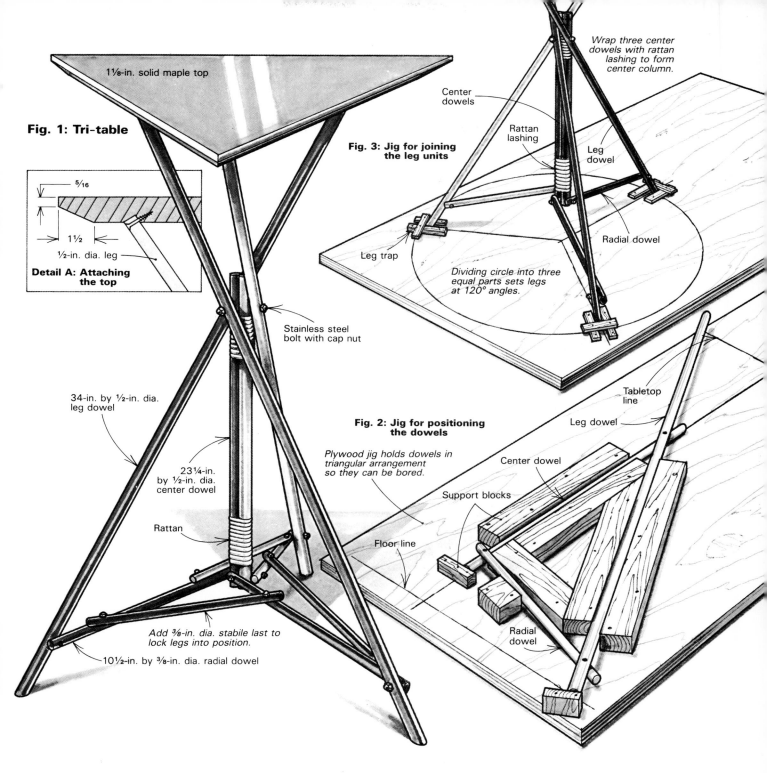

Fig. 1: Tri-table

1⅛-in. solid maple top

Detail A: Attaching the top

5/16

1½

½-in. dia. leg

Stainless steel bolt with cap nut

34-in. by ½-in. dia. leg dowel

23¼-in. by ½-in. dia. center dowel

Rattan

Add ⅜-in. dia. stabile last to lock legs into position.

10½-in. by ⅜-in. dia. radial dowel

Fig. 3: Jig for joining the leg units

Wrap three center dowels with rattan lashing to form center column.

Center dowels

Rattan lashing

Leg dowel

Leg trap

Radial dowel

Dividing circle into three equal parts sets legs at 120° angles.

Fig. 2: Jig for positioning the dowels

Plywood jig holds dowels in triangular arrangement so they can be bored.

Tabletop line

Leg dowel

Center dowel

Support blocks

Floor line

Radial dowel

rubber strips to attach the stabile to the radial dowel temporarily, I positioned it to form an attractive angle. Then I bored and bolted the stabiles and radials together, and removed the rubber strips.

Tightening the bolts and buffing the metal parts completed the base. Holes for the top are bored, as in detail A in figure 1. I left the legs square on their bottoms until after I'd assembled the table. Then I set the table on a level surface,

and cut and sanded the legs until the top was level. Alternatively, you could cut the legs at the floor line while they're still in the jig.

I liked the Tri-table so much that I've expanded the idea to make much more elaborate constructions such as chairs and dining tables. I've also developed a whole series of dual-leg tables with triangular, square or pentagonal tops.

All these tables support my long-held

and stubborn conviction that people will buy furniture that's strong, well designed and reasonably priced. Regardless of the materials used, if you combine a designer's eye with a willingness to experiment and depart from traditional woodworking themes, you can create a variety of distinctive visual effects. *(continued on next page)*

John Marcoux designs furniture in Providence, R.I.

Drawings: David Dann

Working with dowels

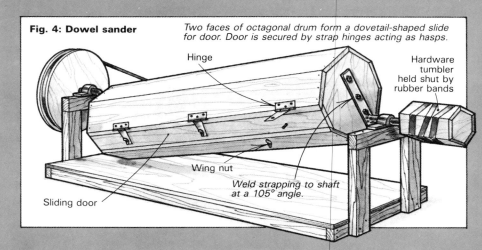

John Marcoux

Fig. 4: Dowel sander

Two faces of octagonal drum form a dovetail-shaped slide for door. Door is secured by strap hinges acting as hasps.

Hinge

Hardware tumbler held shut by rubber bands

Wing nut

Weld strapping to shaft at a 105° angle.

Sliding door

I find dowels to be an efficient and economical building material that gives me a lot of freedom in developing my designs. I prefer maple dowels, if I can find them. Generally, dowels purchased from any reputable lumberyard are maple or birch. Avoid cheap imports—they're spongy and porous and they don't hold up well.

Regardless of where you buy the dowels, they'll probably be pretty rough and covered with mill marks. To avoid tedious sanding, I built an octagonal drum, 47½ in. long and 14½ in. in diameter (figure 4), that tumble-sands 30 to 50 dowels at once. I lined the drum with carpeting to cushion the dowels and to keep

the noise down, but the thing still creaks like an old wooden boat. The brackets that connect the drum to its support and drive shafts are offset, enabling the drum to move up and down along its length as it rotates. For abrasives, I cut sandpaper sheets into thin strips with tin snips. I also attached self-adhering sandpaper to each end of the drum to sand the ends of

the dowels hitting the end walls.

To use the sander, I throw in several handfuls of sandpaper strips with the dowels, turn on the motor, and work on something else for a while. Sanding time depends on how badly the dowels are marked. The drum has to turn slowly, about 25 RPM, otherwise the dowels will be tossed about too roughly and will fall

Marcoux dubbed this 18½-in. high table 'Birdfoot' because of its spindly legs. The top is bronze-colored glass.

Fig. 5: Marking hole centers

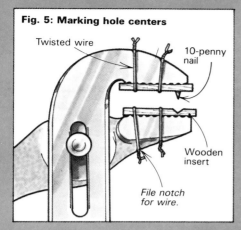

Twisted wire

10-penny nail

Wooden insert

File notch for wire.

Fig. 6: Drilling dowels

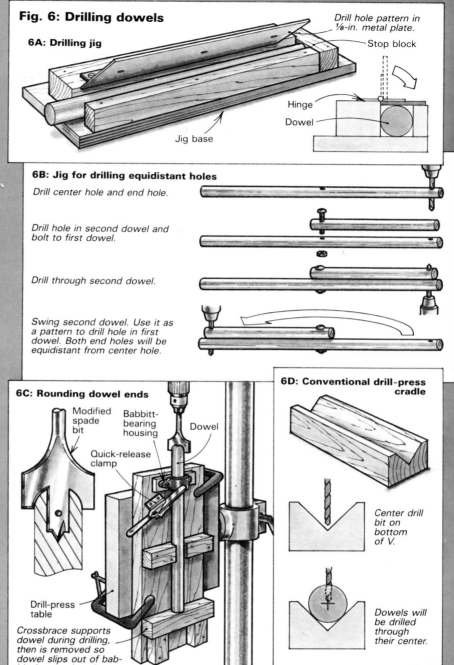

6A: Drilling jig

Drill hole pattern in ⅛-in. metal plate.

Stop block

Hinge

Dowel

Jig base

6B: Jig for drilling equidistant holes

Drill center hole and end hole.

Drill hole in second dowel and bolt to first dowel.

Drill through second dowel.

Swing second dowel. Use it as a pattern to drill hole in first dowel. Both end holes will be equidistant from center hole.

6C: Rounding dowel ends

Modified spade bit

Babbitt-bearing housing

Dowel

Quick-release clamp

Drill-press table

Crossbrace supports dowel during drilling, then is removed so dowel slips out of babbitt-bearing housing.

6D: Conventional drill-press cradle

Center drill bit on bottom of V.

Dowels will be drilled through their center.

from wall to wall. I also added a smaller 5½-in. dia. drum on the support-shaft end for polishing nuts and bolts and other hardware. Tumbling the metal parts with lapidary compound brings them to a bright finish. If I want to clean hardware before it's painted, I tumble the pieces for two hours with medium or fine emery-cloth strips.

When I have to drill dowels, I often use a center punch to make a starting mark and I gauge the angle of the drill by eye. You can make another good tool for marking holes from a pair of Channel Lock pliers (figure 5). In a piece of hard wood, cut a V large enough to hold a dowel and fasten the block to one jaw with wire. Drive a 10-penny common nail though another block, clip off the nail and sharpen the protruding point. Then attach that piece to the other jaw so that the nail will hit the dowel in the V-block. This tool is easy to control, and it makes a hole deep enough for you to accurately start the drill bit.

I also use a variety of blocks and jigs as drill guides. To make an accurate drilling jig for boring identical components, I simply glue two lengths of soft wood, usually about ¾ in. wide, to a base (figure 6A). The first block should be thicker than the dowels to be drilled. The second block should be ⅛ in. thinner to accommodate the thickness of the metal plate used in the jig. Drill guide holes in the metal plate at the locations you want them in the dowels. Next hinge the plate to the first block, so that the plate can be lowered over the dowel. When lowered, the plate should rest on the thinner block and lie flat over the dowel channel between the blocks. Glue the first block to the base, place the correct-size dowel next to it, push the second block lightly against the dowel, and attach the second block to the base. A stop block tacked in the dowel channel positions the dowel.

Another way to guide the bit is to fasten a predrilled dowel to a second dowel with rubber bands and drill through the first hole to make the second. I use a similar technique (figure 6B) to drill holes that are equidistant from a center hole, as for a cross stretcher on a table.

A drill press can also be used for drilling dowels. I bolted the top half of an old babbitt-bearing housing to a wooden base so that it can be clamped down onto a dowel. The size of the housing determines the size of dowels that can be drilled; the one I use fits 1-in. dowels. After turning the drill-press table vertically (figure 6C), I use a modified spade bit to drill and round over the end of a dowel. To shape the tops of the 1-in. legs for the Tritut table (p. 45), I ground down a 1½-in. spade bit so that it rounds over the ends of the dowel as it bores a ½-in. center hole. The center drill bit also stabilizes the outer cutters to prevent chattering which could mar the wood.

Figure 6D shows a conventional V-block cradle for steadying dowels on a drill-press table. The point of the V also helps you line up the drill bit.   —J.M.

Staved Containers
Coopers relied on hand tools and a good eye

by Daniel Levy

Some of the methods historically used by coopers for constructing wooden staved containers can provide alternatives to techniques requiring power machinery. Coopering techniques may be used either to construct entire containers, or to set up staves for turning. They may also be useful to woodworkers using stave construction in other applications, such as curved doors for cabinets.

Daniel Levy teaches courses in woodworking at the University of Maryland, College Park.

A drawknife rounds the outer surface of the stave. If working the stave in both directions chips the grain, hold the stave between a notch in the shaving horse and your stomach.

A hollow knife cuts the concave surface on the inside of the stave.

The staves are checked against a hoop for proper curvature.

Traditionally, the containers made by coopers ranged from casks of all sizes to a variety of straight-sided items. For tight casks, like those used for the maturation of spirits, white oak was generally selected. For less exacting cooperage, various hardwoods and softwoods were used, depending on the type of product to be stored or shipped, the length of time the container would be used and available timber. Both turners and coopers would generally select clear stock that was quartersawn for resistance to warping, reduced shrinkage across the width of the staves and dimensional stability.

Coopers use drawknives to round the outer surface of the staves, which is known as backing. Hollow knives, similar to drawknives but with blades curved for concave cuts, are used to contour the inside of the staves. A shaving horse holds the work. If working the stave in both directions causes the grain to chip, the stave is held between a notch in the shaving horse and the cooper's stomach to complete the cut. These steps are not necessary for turning, but backing makes it easier to check the beveled edges and determine the wall thickness when joining staves of varying widths, and also makes turning safer because the setup is close to a true circle before turning is begun. A hoop can be used to check the curvature—wide steel hoops are best, but a circle made from a wire hanger will do. Check each stave against the same part of the hoop in case it is not a true circle.

A cooper's jointer plane is used to bevel and taper the stave edges. It's 5 ft. to 6 ft. long and is raised at one end on legs. The staves are hand-held at the proper angle, which is judged by eye, and pushed across the blade. To avoid wasting stock, random-width staves are used. Because staves of varying width require different bevels, a fence is not used. For stave turning, a 2-ft. long jointer plane clamped upside-down in a vise serves the same purpose. In either case, be sure to set the plane for a light cut and keep your fingers curled away from the blade. If the container is short, joint the staves two or more times longer than needed and then cut them to length.

Coopers judge the bevels by eye, but the hoop can be used

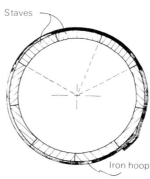

Staves

Iron hoop

Joint the edges of the staves on an imaginary radius line, so the staves will fit tightly in any order.

to check the angles. Joint the first stave so that the bevel angle is on an imaginary radius line to the center of the hoop, or determine the angle mathematically. Both stave edges should be cut at the same angle. Use this stave as a template by clamping it to the hoop and checking both edges of all the other staves against it. If the bevels are cut carefully, the staves can be assembled in any order to form a tight circle. If the

From *Fine Woodworking* magazine (March 1979) 15:74-75

Photos: Mark Sanders

hoop is not a true circle or the template stave is not cut accurately, the diameter may not be what you expected.

Coopers taper their containers either from one end to the other for straight-sided containers, or from the center to both ends for casks. The taper lets the hoops be driven towards the wider part of the container, drawing the staves tightly together. Begin cutting the taper by placing part of the stave past the blade of the jointer plane, like cutting tapers on a power jointer. This procedure can be duplicated for stave turnings. The number of passes determines the extent of the taper, but be consistent on all of the staves for any one container. Full-length passes then clean up the entire edge to the proper bevel.

The staves can easily be assembled in the hoop by leaving the template stave clamped in place. Add the other staves by pressing each one back towards the template. You'll need to hold only the last stave, because the outsides of the staves are wider than the insides, preventing the others from falling in. On a tapered container, you may need to move the hoop up or down to fit the last stave, or perhaps you'll have to replace a stave with a wider or narrower one. When assembling a straight cylinder, a helper can attach a band clamp to draw the staves together, or a wooden wedge can be driven between two staves to hold the assembly temporarily.

A cooper uses scorps and inshaves to smooth the inside of the container, important for a tight leakproof fit of the head (bottom). The outside can be smoothed with spokeshaves or scrapers. The head is set into a groove called a croze, cut with a tool also called a croze, which is composed of a cutter suspended below a board. The board is held against the end of the container and swung around it to cut the groove. The cutter has either saw teeth for small containers, or an iron with two spurs for large ones.

The radius of the head is determined by stepping dividers around the groove. The dividers will be set to the proper radius when six steps around brings you exactly back to the starting point. The head, either one board, or two or more butted or joined with dowel pins, is then scribed and cut. Coopers taper the head from both sides with a heading knife, which is similar to a drawknife, but you may prefer to do this by machine. The tapered edge wedges tightly into the groove. Insert the head by loosening the hoop until the head can be snapped in. Then tighten the hoop.

If you're setting up staves for turning, the cooper's method of setting the head doesn't apply because the staves have to be glued, but you can use the hoops to clamp the staves for gluing. Draw the staves together by driving two or more appropriately sized hoops towards the wider part of the assembly. Coopers hold a driver against the hoop and strike it with a hammer. A hard block of wood will also work. To avoid starved glue joints, do not apply too much pressure. When the adhesive has cured, drive the hoops off the narrow end.

To turn, glue scrap stock to the top end of the staves and attach to a faceplate. Cut a rabbet into the other end of the staves for the base. The head is turned on another faceplate and glued into the rabbet. The scrap stock that was attached to the open end is then cut away, and the container can be turned to a smooth finish inside and out. □

AUTHOR'S NOTE: An interesting gauge for checking the bevels on staves is described in the chapter "Butter Churns," in *Foxfire 3*, edited by Eliot Wigginton (Anchor Press/Doubleday, Garden City, N.Y. 11530).

When jointing stave edges, determine the bevel by eye.

The first stave clipped to the hoop with a scrap of hoop is a template for the other staves.

Each added stave is pushed towards the clip. Because the outsides of the staves are wider than the insides, they won't fall in.

A hoop driver and hand adze are used to tighten the hoops and clamp the staves.

A scorp smooths the inside of the container.

A sawtooth croze swung around the inside of the container cuts a groove for the barrel bottom.

Making Wooden Beehives
Precision homes for the honeycombs

by Kevin Kelly

Within the woods where we gather and saw fine lumber, a few trees conceal, under their bark, hollows stuffed with honeycomb. This is winter food, to sustain a colony of bees while the flowers are gone. But it's a rare tree that has a perfectly shaped cavity to hold all the honey the bees could make. By taking lumber and constructing an ideal beehouse, the craftsman encourages the bees to gather more honey than they'll need for winter, and he pockets the surplus as his rent. The woodworker who ordinarily builds to close tolerances, but is the only one to know it, will find bees to be appreciative guests, for bees care about even a sixteenth of an inch. Mistakes slim to our eyes can cause the bees to construct an unworkable mess inside their hives, to the woe of the keeper.

In the past, bees were kept in all kinds of things, but prin-

Not only must the separate stories of a beehive stack neatly and tightly (left), but such interior spaces as the gap between two frames (right) must be scaled to the bees themselves. Otherwise, the disconcerted insects will glue the parts together, locking up the honey.

cipally, in old Europe, in the dome-like straw "skep" so often pictured on honey jars. In that primitive method both the skep and the bees were destroyed when the honey was harvested. About a century ago an ingenious hive system, made completely of wood, started beekeeping along its modern practice of conserving both hive and bees. Wooden stuff has worked so well with beekeeping that even today, despite the unbalanced tilt toward a world of plastic, most beehives are still made of wood. You can get people to live in plastic houses, but bees, so far, rebel.

The contemporary beehive is a stack of boxes piled up as high as needed and able to be taken down easily. The lowest box is the hive proper, where the bees live and raise their young. The upper boxes, properly called "supers," are where the honey is stored. There are no tops or bottoms inside the stack, but each story is divided within by ten intricate frames, arrayed like slices in a loaf of bread. Hives and supers must stack neatly, and supers should be interchangeable—they will be removed and replaced as they fill. Their outside dimensions are standard throughout the United States, with the inevitable exceptions here and there. Heights, however, can vary, although two sizes, "shallow" and "deep," are most common. Any woodworker making bee equipment should resist the temptation, no matter how compelling, to produce equipment not to standard size.

The side pieces of the box-like super are plain rectangles that fit into rabbets cut on the end pieces. Measurements for the cuts have been planned to form a box with inside dimen-

From *Fine Woodworking* magazine (March 1983) 39:86-89

sions of 18¼ in. by 14⅝ in. (figure 1), which allows a constant space between the edges of the frames and the inside wall. This gap is called the "bee space," and its discovery and application by the Reverend Langstroth in 1851 was the key to modern beekeeping. He measured the natural space maintained between combs built by bees in the wild and found it to be exactly ⁵⁄₁₆ in. ± ¹⁄₃₂ in. Any gap less, even ¹⁄₃₂ in. less, had been caulked by bees with a secretion called "bee glue," and any void wider had been filled with honeycomb. Bees are slightly more tolerant when it comes to the built-in spaces in a wooden hive, but the hive maker, by aiming to construct a consistent ⁵⁄₁₆-in. gap between movable parts of the hive, ensures that the bees will leave the gaps unfilled. Thus, each internal piece will be able to be lifted out, emptied of honey and returned.

Super construction—The sides of the supers are traditionally joined with a finger joint, erroneously called a dovetail joint in bee craft. Finger-jointed hives are strong and durable. By using multiple blades, this is also a quick cut for commercial manufacturers, and this style is childishly simple to assemble—an important feature, since most beehives are sold "flat," to be put together by the buyer. An easier joint to make on

small runs is the half-lap joint, secured with 8d nails, which is adequately strong, and more weather-resistant besides. It has two clear advantages: it creates a windproof corner and it uses shorter sections of boards. If laid out carefully, a 6-ft. board—too short for a finger-jointed super—will conveniently build a half-lap super.

We began building our own hives because we had access to about 1,000 bd. ft. of small but well-proportioned white pine scraps that would otherwise have become winter heat. For half-lap supers, the longest piece need be only 19¼ in., with a width of about 5⅞ in. for the shallow supers and 9⅝ in. for the deep. Small knots, cracks and other minor defects in the wood are for once usable, because the bees will repair them by chinking them with their bee glue, called propolis, a sticky resinous all-round filler, glue and varnish that they apply to interior parts. So ubiquitous is this propolis that one of the very few vital beekeeping tools is a flat prybar, which is used to separate the supers in a stack—the bees automatically glue them together. Don't go overboard with nasty wood, however, because bees have two character traits that will work to your eventual disadvantage. First, they are fussy craftspeople themselves—they will waste much time smoothing rough wood and repairing cracks, instead of going outdoors to

Fig. 1: A modern beehive

Parts must stack neatly—any gaps will be invaded by other bees seeking to rob the honey store. This shopmade hive features windproof, lap-joined corners instead of a commercially made hive's finger joints, but the dimensions are compatible with beekeeping's standard sizes.

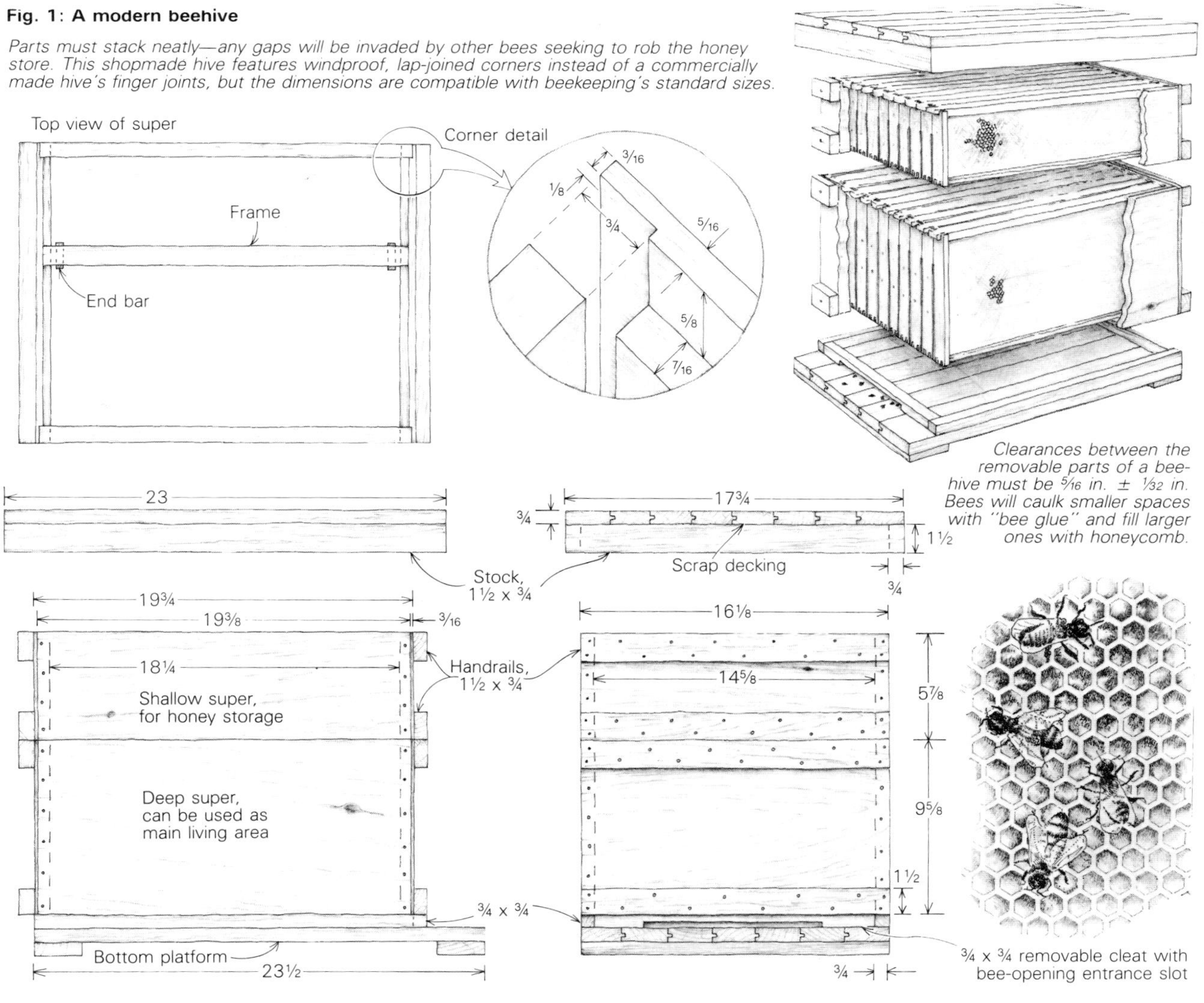

Clearances between the removable parts of a beehive must be ⁵⁄₁₆ in. ± ¹⁄₃₂ in. Bees will caulk smaller spaces with "bee glue" and fill larger ones with honeycomb.

¾ x ¾ removable cleat with bee-opening entrance slot

Woodshop Specialties **53**

Fig. 2: Cutting sequence for top bars

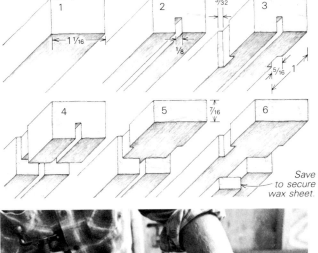

Save to secure wax sheet.

Stacks of parts are dadoed in a 'chute' composed of the tablesaw fence and a length of wood clamped to the table.

Fig. 3: Making the end bars

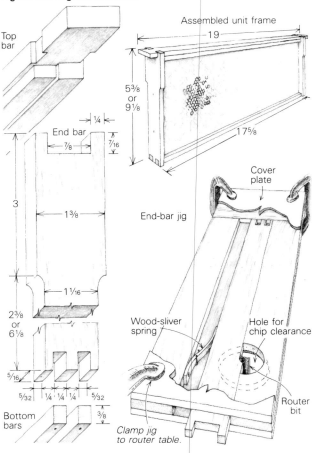

gather nectar. Second, while not exactly what anyone could call lazy, they will take the path of least resistance in their search for sweetness—bees will steal honey from a neighboring hive flawed by an unrepaired bee-sized chink in its armor.

The unit frames, as shown in figures 2 and 3, are a critical construction. Each consists of four parts: two vertical end bars, a horizontal top bar bridging the length of the box, and a bottom bar (which is most easily made from two pieces). The top bar extends beyond the two end pieces to form tabs from which the frame hangs in the super. The bottom bar has a ¼-in. wide slot down its length to hold a sheet of beeswax, the base on which the bees will build honeycomb.

The beeswax sheet is inserted into the slot of the bottom bar, and is supported at the top in a rabbet, secured by the thin wood strip that was cut out when the rabbet was made. Most wax foundation is sold with stiff wire embedded in it so that it does not balloon like a sail and sag into its neighbor. The sides can also be supported with thin wires through holes in the end bars. Once in the hive, all the edges will soon be secured by propolis or by wax comb.

The end bars, by placement and shape, set the proper ⁵⁄₁₆-in. bee space throughout the entire hive. When the frames are placed in the hive, the end bars are recessed from the walls to give the bee space. The end bars are wider than the top bars they hold, so that on adjacent frames the shoulders of the end bars touch, while the top bars have a bee space between them. The length of the end bars is calculated so that they hang exactly ⁵⁄₁₆ in. above the set of frames in the

super below. And the lower half of each end bar is routed on both sides to a narrower width, so that when they are placed side by side there is a passage of ⁵⁄₁₆ in. between frames.

The top bars are easily cut from ¾-in. stock in a sequence of cuts shown in figure 2. The bottom bars are also simple to cut. But because the end bars must measure ⁵⁄₁₆ in. by 1⅜ in., if they are cut from ¾-in. stock, the stock should first be resawn to ⁵⁄₁₆ in. thick and then 1⅜-in. wide blanks cut. The blanks are next arranged face to face in a long train and fed through a chute formed by the tablesaw fence and a board clamped to the table. As the blanks go through the chute, a ⅞-in. dado blade cuts the top notch. With the pieces flipped over and the blade set to take a narrower ¼-in. kerf, two subsequent passes slice the lower notches for the bottom bar.

To rout the contour of the end bars—half a bee space—we devised a simple jig placed on a router table. The jig has a stop and a wood sliver as a spring to keep the piece in place, as shown in figure 3. Routing these pieces is the most tedious task of the run, but when the chips settle, you should harvest a uniform pile of accurately sized end bars.

The assembled parts ought to hug each other snugly. We marry them with Weldwood plastic resin glue. Ordinary carpenters' glue will fail, quickly deteriorating in the tropical conditions inside the hive. Resin glue is waterproof and insectproof, yet seems agreeable to chemically finicky honeybees. The frames will have to undergo a strain of several "g"s while spinning in the centrifuge that whirls the honey from the comb, and they will be battered by tools prying apart propolized pieces, so the units must be rigid. We reinforce each glued joint with 1-in., 18-ga. brads.

The new, cleanly cut frames and inside walls of the hive gradually become stained with a glossy yellow-orange color as the bees use their home, even during the first season. In time the interior collects a lacquer of uneven amber glaze from the thin layer of propolis painted by the bees. I enjoy opening an older hive and inspecting the mellow shellac that's been literally rubbed into the wood by millions of tiny bee feet. This natural finish must have intrigued earlier woodworkers, because Stradivarius and other famous violin makers of old Cremona, Italy, used propolis as a principal component in their varnish.

A beekeeper always finds more propolis than he wants. The stuff is compounded of 30% waxes, 55% resins, and 15% oils and oddments, and it readily dissolves in acetone or ethyl alcohol. Someone with an experimental bent may someday rediscover how to apply this as a radiant wood finish.

To complete the hive, some sort of handhold is needed on each super to enable you to move it around. Full of honey, a deep super weighs 60 lb., and even a healthy farmhand will have to grunt to set it gently on top of a chest-high stack. The shallower, and thus lighter, size is still surprisingly heavy. Customarily, a scalloped handhold is routed into each side of the box. Ormond Aebi, however, who earned the world's production record for extracting 33½ gallons of wildflower honey from one hive, finds that the routed handhold cools the hive at that spot, diminishing yields. Instead, he attaches two wooden rails on each opposite end, which also enables the super to stand on end, taking less ground room when a tall hive full of bees is being dismantled. We now do the same.

Early in this century, hives often sported peaked roofs, shingled like tiny cottages. They were picturesque but uneconomical. Flat roofs can be made of plywood, covered with sheet metal. But both roof cover and the bottom platform are best made of odd pieces of hardwood flooring or softwood decking. For the top, narrow strips should be splined together—it is best not to use wide pieces because they will cup from the rain and sun, even if thoroughly nailed down with 8d galvanized box nails, as we do. For the bottom, join the boards with tongue and groove so that rain water and melting snow can drain out.

Ignoring tradition, we leave our hives completely unpainted. The primary reasons beekeepers paint hives white are to keep them groomed and to prolong the life of the wood. The hives may or may not do better, but the bees inside do not. More often than not, when a colony of bees dies over winter, wet is to blame rather than cold. Cold weather condenses the moisture in the hive onto the comb and walls. This film of pooled water breeds mold and crippling bee diseases. Wood can breathe the wetness out, even as it sheds rain and snow. Paint hinders this respiration. But, even if it made no difference to the bees, and the hives were painted just to keep things tidy, we'd still not lift our brushes. Wood has a grace in weathering, and the natural graying of the pine is genuinely attractive—much like an old barn or a dock. There are other benefits: In remote apiaries, vandals and beehive rustlers may overlook unpainted hives. In towns, neighbors who might protest against bees may never notice them. We once kept an unpainted beehive on a porch roof in the middle of a village—no one realized it was full of bees and honey, because it looked like a collection of old boxes, and as everyone knows, beehives are painted white.

Fitted with sheets of wax foundation and arrayed like slices of bread in a loaf, the precisely fitting frames in each super can be lifted out for inspection or honey extraction.

If one is not careful and lets it, the paraphernalia in any craft will overcome its practitioner. We have deliberately kept our bee supplies to a spartan minimum: a smoker, bee veil and pry tool. The only purchases we must regularly make are wax sheets. These will last for ten years or so, and then can be melted by the sun's heat, sent away as wax lumps to a bee supplier and, for a small fee, "worked" into new foundation sheets. There are a dozen major suppliers and scores of smaller ones, all shipping wax sheets, tools, books, and cages of live bees (sold by the pound!) through the mail. Our favorite for price, variety and service is the Walter T. Kelley Company, Clarkson, Ky. 42726. The bulk of trade for all the suppliers is selling wooden hive parts to be assembled by the buyer. One sample set could be bought to use as a template for building others.

The best time to start a hive and fill it with bees is in the spring, about the time the dandelions bloom. Hopefully you'll need lots of supers—a good colony in peak season can produce 20 lb. of honey a day. Cutting heaps of hand rails, stockpiling rows of end bars, and gluing up frames to be fitted with wax sheets a little later is the kind of relaxing woodwork we fit around the edges of the day's chores. It's best done anytime but summer, when the bees are returning in haste, heavily laden with sweet nectar, unable to wait. What is not stored is lost. What is kept is shared.   □

Besides keeping bees, Kevin Kelly travels and has published Walking Journal. *For more information about bee-keeping, read* First Lessons in Beekeeping, *Dadant and Sons, Hamilton Ill. 62341, 1980, 144 pp.*

Building Doors
Frame-and-panel makes elegant entries

by John Birchard

When the proportions are right, a traditional frame-and-panel door, like Birchard's 80-in. by 32-in. raised-panel door in cherry, is a graceful architectural element.

For a woodworker, a door is like a painter's blank canvas: a well-defined space waiting to be filled with something beautiful. Doors provide me with some of my best opportunities for creative and rewarding woodworking. Making a door for your own home is not only satisfying, it also isn't very difficult.

Doormaking is ideally suited to the small shop. I have only 500 sq. ft. of work space, but that hasn't stopped me from building as many as 12 doors at a time. I don't have room for a stroke sander or other large machines, and I get along fine without them. If time is no object, a door can be built with only hand tools and a tablesaw, but an assortment of basic power tools speeds the task and allows construction methods not possible with hand tools.

A shaper is handy for doormaking, but it isn't essential unless you're planning a production run or making doors with many panes of glass. The shaper is indispensable, however, for cope-and-stick construction (see box, p. 60).

There are two basic types of wooden doors used in residential construction: flush doors and frame-and-panel doors. Built-up flush doors can be as simple as boards joined edge to edge, with nailed-on battens for strength. The most common type of flush door, however, is the hollow-core interior door that hangs in countless tract houses. It consists of a lauan veneer over a cardboard lattice and a light wooden frame. Exterior flush doors are often a veneer skin over a solid core of boards or man-made boards. A thick solid-core door is heavy, and a big one may require strap hinges instead of butt hinges.

I prefer to make solid-wood frame-and-panel doors. Frame-and-panel construction consists of rails, stiles and muntins joined to make a frame. Grooves milled in the framework hold wooden panels in place. This construction results in a strong, du-

From *Fine Woodworking* magazine (November 1984) 49:44-48

Fig. 1: Frame-and-panel door construction

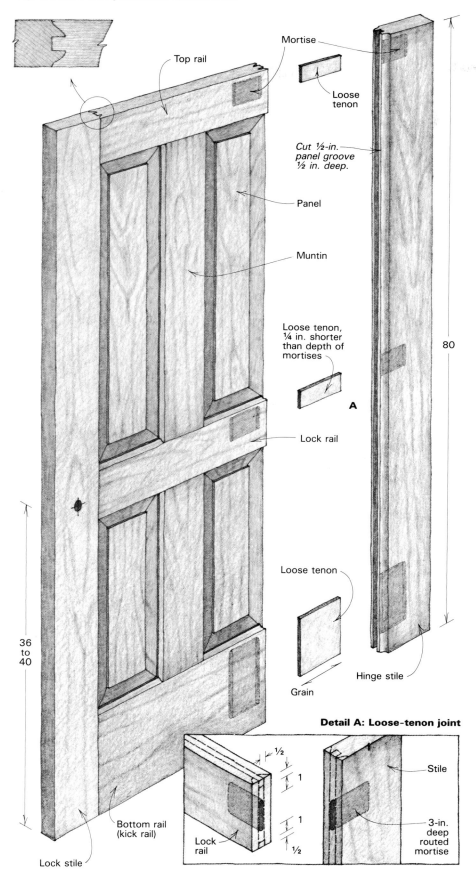

Top rail

Mortise

Loose tenon

Cut ½-in. panel groove ½ in. deep.

Panel

Muntin

Loose tenon, ¼ in. shorter than depth of mortises

A

Lock rail

Loose tenon

Grain

Hinge stile

80

36 to 40

Bottom rail (kick rail)

Lock stile

Detail A: Loose-tenon joint

½
1
1
½

Lock rail

Stile

3-in. deep routed mortise

rable door that's often lighter in weight than a solid-core door, and it minimizes the problems caused by wood movement that plague solid-core exterior doors. The panels in a frame-and-panel door are free to move in their grooves, and can expand and contract without affecting the overall width of the door.

There are countless variations on the basic four-panel door shown in figure 1. Changing panel proportions and varying the shape and arrangement of the framework are just the beginning. Panels can be flat, raised or carved, inlaid with other wood or with brass, or replaced by clear or stained glass. The framework can be carved or beaded—the possibilities are endless.

Design—When I design a door, I consider its size and location, the type and quality of lumber to be used, the joinery, ornamentation, and, of course, the price.

In the United States, the standard height for a residential door is 80 in., but custom doors sometimes exceed this. Exterior doors are commonly 30 in. to 36 in. wide and 1¾ in. thick. Single exterior doors wider than 42 in. present special problems because they're so heavy; for wide openings, therefore, double doors are better. Interior doors are commonly 24 in. to 32 in. wide and 1⅜ in. or 1½ in. thick.

If you're making a door for an old house, existing jambs may vary from the standards and also will probably be out of square. If the latter is the case, make the door slightly oversize and plane it to fit.

In new construction, the doors are most often made after the house has already been completely designed and framed up. If, on a lucky chance, I'm called in before the designs are final, I try to locate the exterior doors in sheltered areas. A door on the south side of a building should have a projecting roof or overhang to protect it from sun and rain. If, as is often the case, a door must be exposed to the elements, I choose a weather-resistant wood such as teak or mahogany, and employ as much glass in the design as possible. I try to design panels for an exterior door as narrow as possible. A large expanse of wood moves more with the weather and is more likely to cause problems.

I design most of my frame-and-panel doors with 5-in. or 5½-in. wide stiles. Most locksets have a 2⅜-in. or 2¾-in. backset (the measurement from the center of the doorknob to the edge of the door). So a lockset with a 2¾-in. backset will be centered in both a 5½-in. stile and the width of the lock rail, I usually make the top and lock rails the same width as the stiles. For visual weight and strength, the bottom or kick rail is usually twice as wide as the other rails.

Doorknobs should be 36 in. to 40 in. from the floor. Since I usually place the center of the lock rail 36 in. from the floor, this means boring through the lock-rail tenon. I've never had a joint fail because of this.

Good door lumber has to be straight and clear. Avoid plainsawn boards or boards with wild grain—they're more likely to cup, warp or twist. This can cause real problems in a door. Quarter-sawn boards are the best choice because they're more stable. I usually buy rough-sawn 8/4 stock so that I can joint any small defects out of the stiles and still end up with stock 1¾ in. thick. My favorite woods are teak because of its beauty and weather-resistance, redwood because it's easy to work and inexpensive where I live, and cherry because it finishes so nicely. Walnut, mahogany and fir are also nice door woods, but harder to work. Oak is popular, but I avoid using it for exterior doors because it blackens with age.

Joinery and layout—Some type of mortise-and-tenon joint (blind, through, wedged, pinned or haunched) is best to join stiles and rails. Traditionally, rails that are wider than 8 in. or so are joined with a twin mortise-and-tenon to minimize the effects of wood movement. In a frame-and-panel door, the greatest load is concentrated on the joint between the top rail and the hinge stile, so it's particularly important to make this joint strong.

I often use cope-and-stick construction. (The molding on the frame edge is called the stick, and the process of cutting it is called sticking. Likewise, its female counterpart on the rail ends is the cope, and the process is called coping.) Since a traditional tenon will interfere with coping the rail ends on the shaper, I've developed the loose-tenon joint shown in figure 1, detail A. I think that it's at least as strong as a blind tenon, and easier to make. I sometimes use dowel joints in combination with cope-and-stick construction, but only on lightweight interior doors. I don't recommend dowel joints for exterior doors.

I'll explain how to make a cope-and-stick frame-and-panel door with the loose-tenon joint. If you don't have a shaper, you can cut the panel grooves and beading with a router. Or you can apply

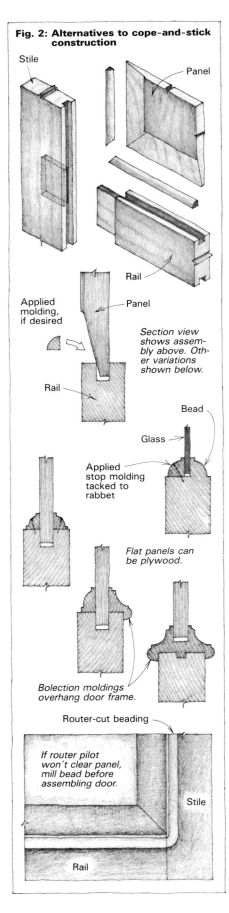

Fig. 2: Alternatives to cope-and-stick construction

Stile

Panel

Rail

Applied molding, if desired

Panel

Rail

Section view shows assembly above. Other variations shown below.

Bead

Glass

Applied stop molding tacked to rabbet

Flat panels can be plywood.

Bolection moldings overhang door frame.

Router-cut beading

If router pilot won't clear panel, mill bead before assembling door.

Stile

Rail

molding as shown in figure 2, or eliminate it altogether.

I begin by ripping the frame pieces about ½ in. wider than their finished size, then jointing one edge and one face. Next I plane all the wood to thickness, then rip to finished width. If I don't have stock wide enough for the kick rail, I glue it up. All parts must be square and straight.

The length of the rails depends on whether you cope and stick the joints or not. For example, let's take a door 36 in. wide with 5½-in. wide stiles. If I don't cope and stick, I'll cut the rails 25¼ in. long—door width minus the combined width of the stiles, plus ¼ in. For cope-and-stick construction, I add to this measurement the amount that the coping overlaps the sticking on the stiles. The extra ¼ in. makes the door 36¼ in. wide to allow for any irregularities in the jamb, and so I can clamp the door without worrying about scarring the edges. When I hang the door, I'll plane it to fit. (For traditional mortise-and-tenon joints, allow for the length of the tenons when figuring rail length.) I cut all the frame members to length with a cutoff jig on the tablesaw, using a 60- or 100-tooth carbide blade. These cuts must be perfectly square in both directions. If they're not, the joints won't be tight or the door will be twisted.

Once I've cut all the frame pieces to length, I lay out the door on my assembly table and mark where the rails join the stiles. Then I line up the stiles next to each other, inside edges up. I mark the locations of the mortises with a square and a marking gauge, centering the mortise on the stiles. I usually start the mortises about 1½ in. from the top and bottom of the door, and 1 in. from the other rail edges so the tenons won't interfere with the ½-in. deep panel grooves.

I cut the mortises with a plunge router before doing any slotting or shaping on the stile or rail edges so that there's a flat surface for the router base to slide on. Drilling a ½-in. dia. hole 3 in. deep at one end of each mortise eases the plunge of the router bit into the wood, and makes the bits last considerably longer. I cut 3-in. deep blind mortises by making several passes with a 4-in. long, ½-in. dia. spiral fluted bit, checking the router-fence adjustment often to make sure that the mortise is exactly centered in the thickness of the stile. Next I rout mortises in the rail ends, holding the pieces in the bench vise while mortising. A length of 2x6 clamped to the benchtop helps stabilize the router, and raises the work high enough off the

Plunge-routed mortises begin with a ½-in. hole drilled at one end to ease the bit's entry (above). Several passes with a ½-in. fluted router bit cut a mortise in the stile (right) and the rail end (below) for a loose tenon. A 2x6 clamped to the bench provides support for the router base.

bench so that the router fence clears the vise.

To make the loose tenons, I plane a board to ½-in. thickness, rip it to the correct width, and cut the tenons ¼ in. shorter than the total depth of both mortises. The tenons should be a friction fit in their mortises. The router-cut mortises have radiused corners, but I don't feel that it's necessary to round off the edges of the loose tenons. The gaps at the mortise ends won't affect the strength of the joint. It's also very helpful to be able to slide the rail up and down a little during assembly.

With the joints cut, I'm ready to cut the panel grooves and the decorative beading along the inner edges of the stiles, rails and muntins. For a raised panel, I usually make the grooves ½ in. wide and ½ in. deep, but for a 1¾-in. thick door, I sometimes make them ⅝ in. wide.

On the shaper, I cut the cope first on the ends of the rails and muntins. Then I cut the stick the full length of each frame member. Alternatives to coping and sticking are shown in figure 2. One of the easiest is to dry-assemble the frame, then rout

the beading around the panel openings with a pilot-bearing bit and rout the panel groove with a slotting cutter. Make sure that the bit's bearing rides on a true surface, not on the beading. The corners of a routed panel groove will have to be cleaned out with a chisel.

One nice feature of cope-and-stick joints is that the beading appears to be mitered where the stiles and rails intersect. This gives a nice sharp look to the corners, which in many designs is more appealing than the rounded corners produced by beading an assembled door with a router.

When the framework is finished, I cut the panels to size. To determine raised-panel thickness, I usually add ½ in. or more to the width of the panel groove (i.e., a ½-in. wide groove gets a panel 1 in. thick at its thickest section). To determine panel size, I dry-assemble the framework and measure from the bottoms of the panel grooves. I make the panels about ³⁄₁₆ in. smaller than this measurement to allow for cross-grain wood movement. The panels are never glued in place—

they must be able to float in the grooves so they can expand and contract.

I raise panels on the shaper, but this can also be done on the tablesaw or with a router. I sand and finish the panels completely *before* gluing the door so that I can apply finish to the edges that will be fit into the grooves. It's a good idea to apply finish to the insides of the panel grooves, but be careful not to get any on the glue joints.

Assembly—I use plastic resin glue (urea-formaldehyde resin) on all my doors. It's water-resistant and slow to set up, which gives me more assembly time. I assemble most of my doors flat on a Formica-topped table that has access on three sides, but sometimes I clamp one stile in the bench vise and work up from there. The most important thing about assembly is to check for square and make sure that everything—especially the panels—fits perfectly before applying any glue. Be sure to put clamps on both sides of the door to keep it flat. After the glue has cured, I hand-plane the frame to flush the joints and to remove surface blemishes. Between planing and the final sanding, I trim the edges and the top of the door with either an electric hand-planer or a straight-fluted router bit like the one I use for mortising. A straightedge clamped to the door guides the router. Before trimming the top or bottom, I bevel the stile corners with a block plane so that the router or planer doesn't tear out grain at the end of the cut.

I install the top hinge 7 in. from the top of the door and the bottom hinge 11 in. from the bottom, with a middle hinge, if used, centered between the two. I cut the hinge mortises by defining each end of the mortise with a chisel cut, setting the router fence for the width of the hinge, and hogging between the chisel cuts. Then I carefully square up all the corners with a chisel.

If possible, I hang the door and do any final fitting before applying the finish. A door hung during the dry season can be expected to swell. I compensate for this by allowing a little extra clearance between the door and the jamb. Except for the hinges, I wait to install the hardware until after finishing.

Finishing—Paint is the best protection for an exterior door, but it obscures the natural wood. I don't recommend straight, unthinned varnish on the surface of exterior doors because varnish degrades quickly and is difficult to renew. Straight oils aren't protective enough either. If a door is well sheltered from the sun, a finish of equal proportions of spar varnish, boiled linseed oil and mineral spirits will protect the wood if periodically renewed. Be especially sure to finish the door's top and bottom edges and any exposed end grain. For a hand-rubbed look, I flow on one coat, wait a few minutes and then wipe off the excess. Before the first coat has dried, I scrub on a second coat with 00 steel wool. After I've wiped off the excess, I let the finish dry overnight. I repeat this process several times. This finish is easy to renew. Just flow on a new coat and wipe off the excess—the mixture will soak in just where it's needed.

A properly made and properly hung door should give its maker a satisfying feeling of accomplishment, and its owners a lifetime of service. □

John Birchard is a professional woodworker in Mendocino, Calif. Black-and-white photos by the author.

A shaper makes it simple

If you're making more than a few doors, a spindle shaper is a good investment. It can cut interlocking cope-and-stick joints which speed the making of frame-and-panel doors, give the appearance of mitered beading, and produce a stronger glue joint. And for doors with lots of sash work, a shaper is essential.

The shaper has a high-speed vertical spindle that protrudes through a hole in the middle of a table. A fence guides the stock. Cutters fit on the spindle singly, or they can be stacked in combination with spacers and bearings to make all sorts of different moldings, grooves or raised panels.

One way to tool up for a cope-and-stick joint is to buy a cope-and-stick cutter set. This is sometimes called a door-lip set, and it consists of two matching sets of cutters: one to cope the rail ends, and one to mold, or stick, the entire length of the stiles and rails. One pass mills the panel groove and beads both edges. These carbide cutter sets are convenient, but at more than $300 they're expensive.

It's cheaper to stack several high-speed steel cutters to get the profile you want. I prefer high-speed steel cutters to carbide ones because in addition to their being less expensive, I can regrind and resharpen them myself on a carborundum wheel. One of my favorite shaper cutters is the Powermatic #6178048 (available from Woodshop Specialties, Cold River Industrial Park, Quality La., Rutland, Vt. 05701). It's a reversible S-curve that can be used to stick the edges of the stiles and rails, and then flipped over to cope the rail ends. Using the Powermatic in combination with straight cutters, as shown in the drawing, I can get a panel groove on the stick or a matching stub tenon on the cope. If you use a reversible cutter, you'll need a reversing switch on your shaper so that you can flip the cutter from stick to cope cut.

As with most machines, shaper set-up is extremely important. You shouldn't alter the spindle height between cuts, or the door parts won't line up. Remember also that the stock needs to bear against the shaper fence after it's passed over the cutter as well as before. Position the fence so that some part of the original stock surface remains to bear on the fence during the last cut. If this isn't possible, you can build up the outfeed fence

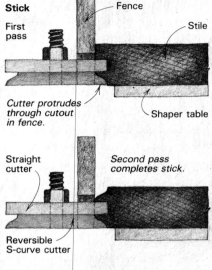

Cope and stick with reversible shaper cutter

Stick
First pass
Fence
Stile
Cutter protrudes through cutout in fence.
Shaper table

Straight cutter
Second pass completes stick.
Reversible S-curve cutter

Flip cutter and reverse shaper rotation to cut cope.

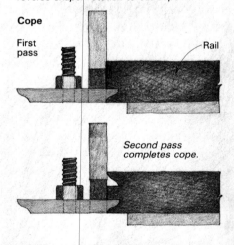

Cope
First pass
Rail

Second pass completes cope.

to contact a cut surface. The gap in the fence for the cutter can be a problem, particularly for end-grain coping on narrow pieces. To guide narrow stock past the gap, I let a piece of wood into the fence to span the gap at the height of the stub tenon.

It's easy to spend thousands of dollars on a shaper and thousands more on carbide cutters, but I didn't. For much less than the cost of one heavy-duty machine, I bought two ½-in. Sears Craftsman shapers and outfitted them with 1-HP motors and heavy-duty pulleys. These small shapers can't do everything a big machine can, but they're fine for cope-and-stick work. Having two machines cuts down on set-up time. —J.B.

Q & A

Dashboard restoration—*I'm doing restoration work on 1940s Jaguars and Bentleys. What did manufacturers use to glue and finish the veneered dashboards? This finish has to be glass-smooth, withstand extreme fluctuations in temperature and humidity, and protect against ultraviolet light.* —Richard W. Morton, Redwood City, Calif.

DONALD STEINERT REPLIES: In the 1940s, hot hide glue was used to attach the veneers. A modern alternative is hot-melt glue sheets (available from Bob Morgan Woodworking Supplies, 1123 Bardstown Rd., Louisville, Ky. 40204), which are heated with a household iron. Don't use contact cements.

The dashboard veneer was finished with either varnish or lacquer, neither of which is immune to the effects of temperature, humidity and ultraviolet rays. Even today, there is no clear finish that will stand up to the extremes a dashboard can experience. I refinish the woodwork in many $120,000 Rolls Royces that are less than three years old!

In my restoration work, I spray on a catalyzed polyester resin; this is toxic stuff, and tricky to work with because of its 20- to 40-min. pot life. You can use a varnish such as McCloskey's Bar Top Varnish, or a bar top lacquer. Both require many light coats, followed by wet-sanding with very fine-grit wet-or-dry paper. Finish with rubbing compound.

Bending around a short radius—*I'm an orthodontist and want to make an oversized toothbrush for health demonstrations. I am using ¼-in. hardwood dowels for the bristles but am having trouble steam-bending them on a short radius (to represent worn bristles on the outer row) without breaking them. Do you have a better way?* —Kent Shacklett, Tulsa, Okla.

SETH STEM REPLIES: You can reduce the chance of breakage by using a backing strip to compress the wood fibers while you are bending the steamed wood. For small stock or rounded shapes like your ¼-in. dowels, rig up a backing strip from ½-in.-wide twill tape (a non-stretching fabric strip available in yard goods stores), which will conform to the dowel's contour. Cut the dowels to length, then staple or glue the twill tape to 2¾-in. by ¾-in. by 8-in. pine scraps, as shown in the sketch, so the dowel just fits between the pine pieces. Make a

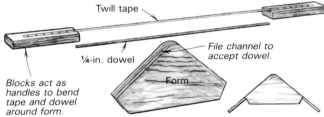

Twill tape
¼-in. dowel
File channel to accept dowel.
Form
Blocks act as handles to bend tape and dowel around form.

wooden form of the radius you want and use a round rasp to cut a channel for the dowel. After steaming or boiling the dowels in hot water for 10 minutes, bend the dowels over the form with the twill tape strap on the outside. The pine acts as handles, and the strap will keep the dowel in compression. Clamp the dowel in place until it dries. You should be able to bend ¼-in. dowels to at least a 1-in. radius with this system. With production chair making, each of the curved parts is bent individually using similar methods. Since you need many identical bent pieces, you might try making a larger form, using six backing strips between two strips of plywood to bend six dowels at once. If possible, use oak dowels (available from Cryder Creek Wood Shop, Box 19, Whitesville, N.Y. 14897, or Woodworker's Supply of New Mexico, 5604 Alameda N.E., Albuquerque, N.M. 87113), which have long fibers and bend well.

Production Problem
Making hundreds of square frames

by Henry Jones

In a review of two David Pye books in its November 1978 issue, *Fine Woodworking* discussed the distinction between operations of risk and operations of certainty. Those of us who produce wood objects in some quantity must, of necessity, be concerned with the latter. More than that we must be inventors, even Rube Goldbergs, in a continuous quest for easier, faster, surer methods. A set of operations that turns out a product in the fewest minutes without compromising design or quality is the key to profits, even small ones.

Recently we went to work on the problem of making frames by the hundred: plain, ordinary frames such as you might require for a mirror or picture, a small glass showcase, or—our particular application—a stool/table with a panel top. We have developed a method that allows us to get the job done fairly rapidly, but it leaves something to be desired. We suspect that other readers have devised better ways and will think our method slow, even naive. Perhaps they will deluge the editors with mail. What we would like to see is more articles on methods and tooling for small production shops.

Here are the details of the frame problem and our solution: We produce square frames using hardwood 2x2s 16 in. long in batches of 100. That means cutting 800 ends, setting up four pieces at a time, gluing and clamping them, allowing time for the glue to set and removing the clamps. The assembled frame must fit over other jigs for routing and shaping. Thus, each frame must vary less than 1/32 in. in dimension, squareness, twist of stock, flatness or any combination, or the frame won't fit over the subsequent jigs or will rattle loosely on them. We held the dimensions within about 1/64 in. on all but five frames of the first hundred.

After experimenting we chose a plain miter joint with a corner block added later because, first, we could control length to within a few thousandths of an inch; second, we could apply glue quickly to the flat miters; and third, the joint would look good after we put a 1-in. radius on the corners. The glue block strengthens the frame (yet is hidden by the panel that fits into the frame) and enlarges the area against which a hanger-bolt and nut draw the leg top.

What seemed simple next

Photo (top) shows spot face on which leg top is seated. Hanger-bolt and nut (bottom) draw leg onto frame and glue block.

was to build a jig to clamp the four pieces in position so the glue could set. The jig had to be quick to load, each piece being automatically positioned, and the clamps had to bring the pieces into intimate contact for a strong, tight joint. It had to be accurate yet able to cope with a frame of four pieces, each of which might vary as much as .004 in. in length. We decided on an epoxy glue, WEST (for "wood epoxy saturation technique"), which penetrates the wood, remains slightly flexible and sets hard enough in two hours to permit the clamps to be removed. Whoops! That's 200 hours just waiting for the glue to set, five weeks of eight-hour days. Economics demanded that gluing take no more than three or four minutes. Okay, build 25 jigs. But what would *that* cost? If there were a glue that set in one or two minutes, assembly would require only two jigs, but the timing would be tricky.

Finally we hit upon a Novaply (high-density particle board) base with three pins in its center to locate a removable Novaply square. A lever-action cam clamp is mounted on the base opposite the midpoint of each side of the square. We quickly made 16 of the removable central squares all exactly the same with an accurately set radial arm saw, and waxed the corners where there would be contact with glue squeezed out from the frame joints. Thus we can glue up one-sixth of the entire batch of 100 frames at once. Line up 64 of the mitered sticks, their ends overhanging the bench edge. One or two strokes with a small roller carrying epoxy glue butters one end of the whole batch. Turn the sticks and butter the other ends. To set up the jig, install a square over the three locating pins, place four sticks around the square and close the clamps. Because the clamp pads are only 6 in. long and 1 in. high, most of the edges of the frames remain exposed. A large, powerful rubber band stretched around the frame holds it snugly against the central square, so the clamps can be released and the frame with the square moved to a flat drying bench. With another

square installed on the base, the cycle can be repeated. When all 16 frames are glued up, they are left to dry while other operations are performed. After two hours, remove the rubber band and the central square, rewax the squares and clean the frames for the next operations—routing, shaping and sanding—before applying the corner blocks.

In summary, with enough central squares, one worker could assemble 100 frames in less than a day, mixing glue, buttering ends, loading and unloading the jig, removing excess glue, stripping the frames of rubber band and central square, stacking dry frames and taking coffee breaks. But the time to cut and install the corner blocks must be added before the joint is complete. Since we run only 100 frames at a time, production time works out to more than two days—adding time for the operator to set up the jig, get his rhythm going and up to speed, then to clean up and put it all away. Our actual time for making 100 frames is about 14 hours, or about 8½ minutes per frame, not counting the 12 hours for drying (when done in 6 batches of 16, the optimum number for our jig considering WEST epoxy's open-assembly time). While the glue is drying, many of these and other operations can be performed on units that are not drying. We find that the total time breaks down as follows: About one-quarter of the time is spent cutting and deburring the miters, one-quarter gluing up at the jig, one-eighth stripping the dry frames of the rubber band and central square, and three-eighths cutting and applying the corner blocks. This means that the clamping-jig operation time averages out to two minutes per frame.

The weak points of the method are that the tolerances sometimes add up unfavorably and we get an out-of-square frame or one that is not quite flat. Our clamps are not quite powerful enough to make the glueline as inconspicuous as we would like it to be. In spite of this, tests have shown the joint to be very strong.

Frame-clamping jig

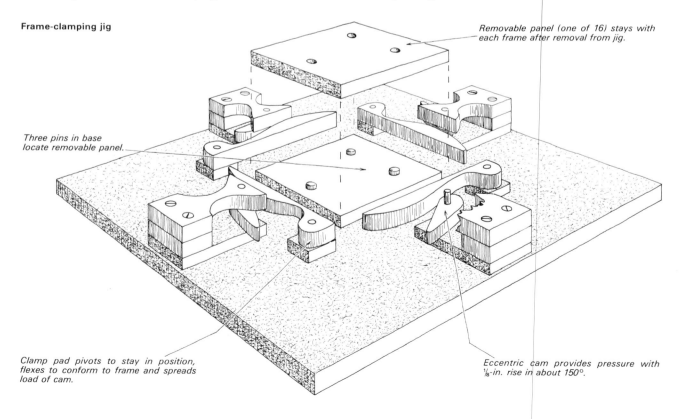

Removable panel (one of 16) stays with each frame after removal from jig.

Three pins in base locate removable panel.

Clamp pad pivots to stay in position, flexes to conform to frame and spreads load of cam.

Eccentric cam provides pressure with ⅛-in. rise in about 150°.

Photos: Staff; Illustration: Christopher Clapp

1. *Buttering mitered ends with epoxy glue.*

2. *Placing central square over locating pins.*

3. *Loading jig with frame parts.*

4. *Tightening cam clamps.*

5. *Stretching rubber band over frame edge.*

6. *Removing frame, central-square, rubber-band assembly to drying bench. Jones uses removable handle for grip on assembly.*

7. *After frames are routed and shaped, Jones applies corner blocks, using go-bars.*

8. *The finished parts and the assembled stool/table. Central section, not a structural member, is easily pushed up and flipped over to change inlaid table into upholstered stool.*

We have had no trouble with our miters and expect none for several reasons. We are joining 2x2s only 16 in. long. Thus we have a large gluing area, a relatively short glueline (after shaping) and no long levers. Since each joint is supported directly underneath with a leg, racking is minimized. Our corner blocks are small and have less than ⅛ in. nipped off their apexes so they run right to the joint corner, adding glue area but not acting as large fulcrums to open the joint. The penetrating, flexible epoxy we use is superior, we believe, to animal glues in present-day heated houses, to yellow glues on end grain and to plastic resin glues, which are brittle. We allow time for the epoxy to penetrate by buttering many joint faces at a time, and we apply enough so that some oozes out all around. Visual inspection of dismembered joints have revealed they have not been sucked dry. As to the wood we use, it is very dry mahogany (about 8% moisture content) so that we can expect no significant permanent shrinkage. Expansion will be the first result of climatic change, and relaxation of this pressure instead of tension will be the result of the next climatic season. Actually this last does not affect miters as much as right-angle grain joints, but it brings up a small (and

we think important) point of furniture design that is rarely mentioned directly: One reason to start with very dry wood is that one can design more successfully to withstand compression than tension at the glue joint. If the wood shrinks, it's hard to keep it from splitting, but wood can withstand a lot of compression before the fibers are detrimentally crushed. Our joints remain tight and strong for these reasons.

Our jig can easily be modified to handle frames of various sizes. All that is required are central squares (or rectangles) equal to the inside dimensions of the frames to be made, and cam clamps, which instead of being fixed to the jig base, are mounted on individual, movable sub-bases. Locating pins in the bottom of these sub-bases could fit into rows of holes drilled in the jig base from near the center to the base sides.

Still the method seems more complicated than need be. And a very good jig should produce cleaner joints. There must be a faster and easier way to glue up large numbers of simple frames with fine, strong joints. □

Henry Jones is an industrial designer who operates his own small production shop in Vineyard Haven, Mass.

The Mosaic Door
Possibilities of the plywood sandwich

by James Rannefeld

Many woodworkers have become dissatisfied with the design limitations imposed by the typical frame-and-panel door, while others are frustrated by the structural problems of the batten door, which weathers rather poorly. There's another way to make a door, one that presents new design possibilities and offers structural improvements over traditional methods. For the past six years I have been refining a technique for building the mosaic door. Essentially a three-layered composite structure with a dimensionally stable

Mosaic technique offers strength, dimensional stability and design versatility. Playing on Art Deco motifs, this design required joining the central components with splined miters.

plywood panel as its core, this particular type of door can be treated in an endless variety of ways—even made to look like the traditional frame-and-panel door it supplants.

The core panel itself is best made from a single sheet of ½-in. exterior-grade plywood, which is overlaid front and back with solid wood. Though similar in several respects, my doors differ considerably from the two-layered doors that have been made traditionally in New Mexico by Spanish craftsmen, who typically nailed a rail-and-stile facade over a tongue-and-groove panel, or covered the panel with applied trim. These doors often become leaky from wood shrinkage, not only around the jambs, but also between boards in the door. It was this problem that led me to sandwich a stable plywood core between two outer layers of solid material of virtually any thickness.

An exterior door must withstand great stresses. On the inside, the home environment is typically warm in winter and cool in the summer—the exact opposite of climatic conditions on the outside of the door. Normally the home is uniformly dry, while winter snows and summer rains lash the door's exterior. Yet the greatest problem is direct sunlight on the door, which raises the temperature of the outer surface considerably higher than the ambient temperature, especially when dark woods are used.

Because of these conflicting stresses, I spline together adjoining mosaic pieces on the outer surfaces in addition to laminating them onto the stable core. Even under optimal laminating conditions using a press, there is often enough cupping in larger mosaic pieces, or enough variation in the plywood core, to create a less than perfect bond. But with a matrix of splines covering the whole surface, it is virtually impossible for any single piece to become dislodged from the panel. The splining technique also accommodates the expansion and contraction of individual pieces that may be of different species with differing expansion coefficients.

Overlaying the surface with individually splined pieces allows not only mixing wood species, but also using various thicknesses in the composition, sculpting, carving and shaping them at will or whimsy—as long as the spline grooves are in alignment. Additional possibilities include piercing the door and incorporating glass mosaics in the design.

My technique for making mosaic doors is not unlike that used to make stained glass windows. First I design the patterns for the panel surface (inner surface too if it's different) and lay out the design full-size on paper. Then I cut to rough size the larger mosaic pieces, where the same species and lumber thickness will permit. Next the mosaic pieces are bandsawn out and touched up where necessary with a belt or drum sander to achieve an optimal fit along their contoured edges. This part is like making a giant jigsaw puzzle, fitting the pieces together on top of the paper cartoon.

Then I relieve the adjoining perimeters of the pieces on my

Photos: James Rannefeld

shaper, though the same thing can be done with a router, using a chamfering or rounding-over bit. You may, of course, want to sculpt each individual piece with hand and power tools in whatever combination suits you. When all the pieces are shaped, I use my shaper to cut a groove ½ in. deep by ¼ in. wide all the way around their edges. Rather than using a standard depth collar for this, I recommend a ball-bearing collar. Again, a router equipped with a proper slotting cutter can do the same job. Remember, all the grooves must be cut a uniform distance from the bottom of each piece. Next I cut the contoured splines from tempered hardboard or plywood (dark-colored splines look best), but you could use other suitable materials for this.

I cut the plywood panel for the core oversize, and after trial-fitting all the pieces, I start gluing them to the panel, beginning flush at one edge of the design and proceeding outward from there. Then I put the whole thing in my glue press, which has enough screws to handle mosaic tiles of varying thicknesses, apply even pressure and let it sit overnight. The next day I repeat the process on the door's other face, which might have a totally different pattern.

With gluing complete, I cut the mosaic panel to finished size, allowing the core to protrude ½ in. on all four edges. I used to allow a ¼-in. thickness of the mosaic tiles to remain flush with the edges of the plywood, in effect rabbeting them, but the size of the groove this requires in the frame leaves too little stock overhanging the panel sandwich. So now I cut back the tiles to allow only the plywood to protrude. Then I groove the rails and stiles to fit snugly on the "tongue" that's been formed by the protruding core. The joinery of the frame members themselves can vary according to your preferences—½-in. by ½-in. tongue-and-groove plus ¾-in. through-dowels do nicely, though sometimes I spline them together. Next I finish both sides with two coats of a 50/50 mixture of exterior polyurethane and Watco Danish oil and follow these with additional applications of exterior Watco.

I recommend keeping the mosaic pieces reasonably small so that expansion and contraction are minimal. The only problem I have experienced to date has been with a mixed-wood mosaic—a couple of walnut pieces loosened up. At the time I was using a dry marine resin glue. Now I use a resin-emulsion type glue called WP-2200 made by National Casein, 3435 W. MacArthur Blvd., Santa Ana, Calif. 92704. It's a fast-cure (closed assembly time of 20 min.), exterior Type 1 bond that's ideal for doors.

No matter how tight the joints or how good the gluelines between the laminations, the spaces between mosaic pieces on the exterior side of the door will grow and dwindle with seasonal changes—just as a loose panel will move around in its enclosing frame. However, by chamfering or otherwise relieving the edges of individual mosaic elements, these changes appear minimal and often enhance the overall textural quality of the surface.

Recently I have begun to treat the individual mosaic pieces sculpturally, and this has widened the horizons for my designs. Now I'm using the technique on headboards, murals and tabletops. And I'm contemplating the use of stone, ceramics, plastics and glass as potential materials for overlaying wood. □

James Rannefeld (JAWAR) designs and builds furniture and architectural components in Taos, N. Mex.

Section through door

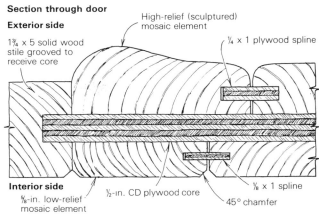

Gap between mosaic pieces is determined by season and location of manufacture, and by the relative size of the individual elements.

The mosaic pieces on this door, called Curvilaminar II, are of different thicknesses; individual press screws with padded feet apply uniform pressure to each piece.

Building Stairs

Harry Waldemar shows the old-time way to a custom job

by Deborah Fillion

When Harry Waldemar, of Ardsley, N.Y., began his four-year apprenticeship in 1925, the stairbuilding trade had already begun to decline. During the 19th century, New York stairbuilders were known all over the country, and were called in for the toughest jobs everywhere. This was chiefly because the typical New York brownstone house contained a difficult stair whose handrail required a hairpin twist. The stairs were built and assembled in the shop, then shipped to the site for installation.

In 1903, a new law required all stairs over three stories to be fireproof, so much new construction turned to metal stairs. Then in 1925, the year Waldemar started in the shop of Oscar Neilsen, stock parts for making treads, balusters and handrails came on the market. Still, the builder of custom stairs was able to compete against the production shop until after World War II, when the postwar demand for housing encouraged quicker techniques and cheaper construction. Production shops took the lead for all but the most complicated stairways. Fewer and fewer men entered the old trade; those who did were older than an apprentice ought to be, and new labor laws made training a man unprofitable. By the time Waldemar retired in 1976, the art of building stairs from scratch had just about died. The situation has improved a little in the last few years, with surging interest in restoring old houses and reviving traditional craft techniques. Waldemar, whose long career includes building and installing a three-story tapering spiral stairway in the Rockefeller house at Seal Harbor, Me., increasingly found himself invited to conduct workshops for young carpenters who wanted to learn his secrets.

An uneasy lecturer, Waldemar finally decided it would be better to record what he knew in the form of precisely detailed knock-down models, at one-half and one-quarter scale, of the various forms that a good stair can take. But no matter how tricky the stair, the basic methods and the standards of the craft remain the same. Waldemar demonstrates these step by step on the following pages, using his model of an open stair (that is, one in which one stringer is fastened to the wall and the other is open to view in the downstairs room). This and his other models have been on display at the New York State Museum in Albany.

An open staircase. The closed stringer fits against a wall, while the open stringer on the handrail side shows in the downstairs room.

Brownstone stairs, at one-quarter scale.

Waldemar disassembles the half-scale model.

From *Fine Woodworking* magazine (September 1981) 30:48-55

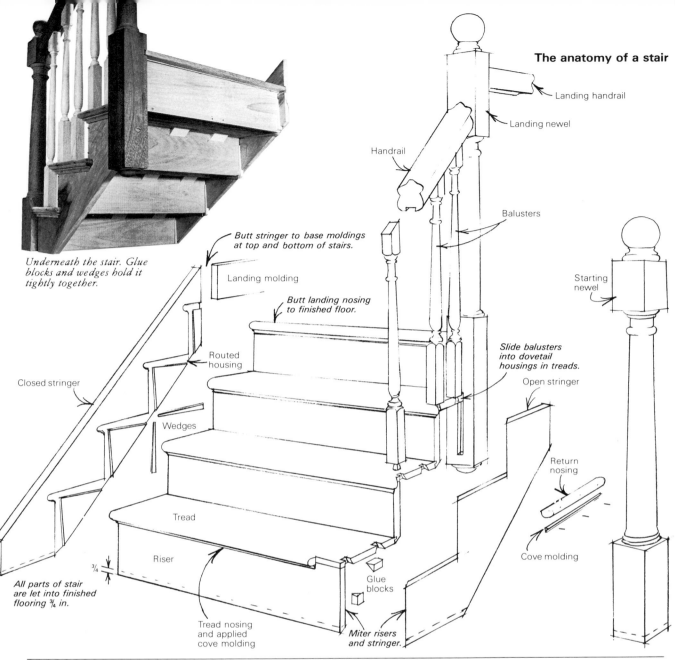

Underneath the stair. Glue blocks and wedges hold it tightly together.

The anatomy of a stair

Landing handrail

Landing newel

Handrail

Balusters

Butt stringer to base moldings at top and bottom of stairs.

Landing molding

Butt landing nosing to finished floor.

Routed housing

Starting newel

Slide balusters into dovetail housings in treads.

Closed stringer

Open stringer

Wedges

Return nosing

Tread

¾

Riser

Glue blocks

All parts of stair are let into finished flooring ¾ in.

Tread nosing and applied cove molding

Miter risers and stringer.

Cove molding

At the job site—A staircase consists of a stack of steps, and a step consists of one riser (the vertical board) and one tread (where you walk). The work begins by accurately measuring at the site; the drawing at right shows a typical flight, although the models that follow contain only four steps. The first measurement is the total rise from finished floor to finished floor. Always verify that the lower floor is level. If it's not, measure the variation at A' and allow for it. Since an average flight contains 14 risers, divide the rise by 14 to obtain the height of one riser. This dimension can vary from one stairway to another, but must be uniform within a flight, or else people will stumble. Risers are usually about 7¾ in. high.

There's always one fewer tread than riser, and an average run is 9 in. Thus 13 treads times 9 in. gives the total run of the flight, providing this run will permit headroom of 6½ ft., as drawn. Tread and riser dimensions can be adjusted, but this rule of thumb should always be observed: Two times the rise plus once the run should total between 24 in. and 25 in.

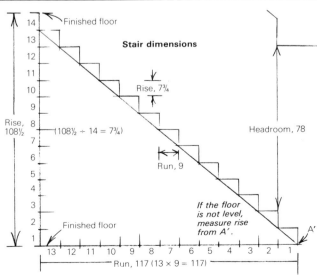

Finished floor

Stair dimensions

Rise, 7¾

Rise, 108½

(108½ ÷ 14 = 7¾)

Headroom, 78

Run, 9

If the floor is not level, measure rise from A'.

Finished floor

A'

Run, 117 (13 × 9 = 117)

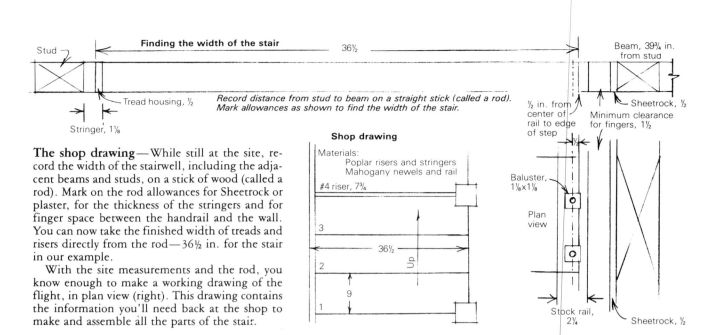

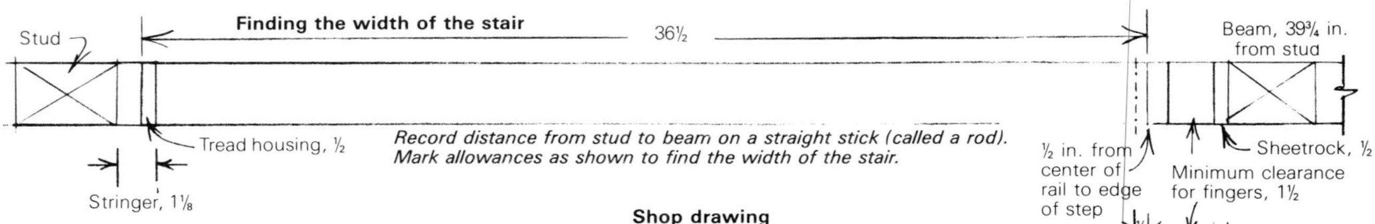
Finding the width of the stair
Stud
36½
Beam, 39¾ in. from stud
Tread housing, ½
Stringer, 1⅛
Record distance from stud to beam on a straight stick (called a rod). Mark allowances as shown to find the width of the stair.
Sheetrock, ½
Minimum clearance for fingers, 1½

The shop drawing—While still at the site, record the width of the stairwell, including the adjacent beams and studs, on a stick of wood (called a rod). Mark on the rod allowances for Sheetrock or plaster, for the thickness of the stringers and for finger space between the handrail and the wall. You can now take the finished width of treads and risers directly from the rod—36½ in. for the stair in our example.

With the site measurements and the rod, you know enough to make a working drawing of the flight, in plan view (right). This drawing contains the information you'll need back at the shop to make and assemble all the parts of the stair.

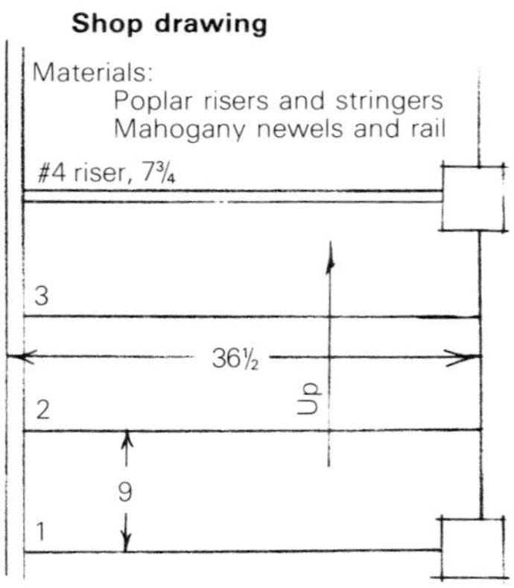
Shop drawing
Materials:
Poplar risers and stringers
Mahogany newels and rail
#4 riser, 7¾
3
36½
Up
2
9
1

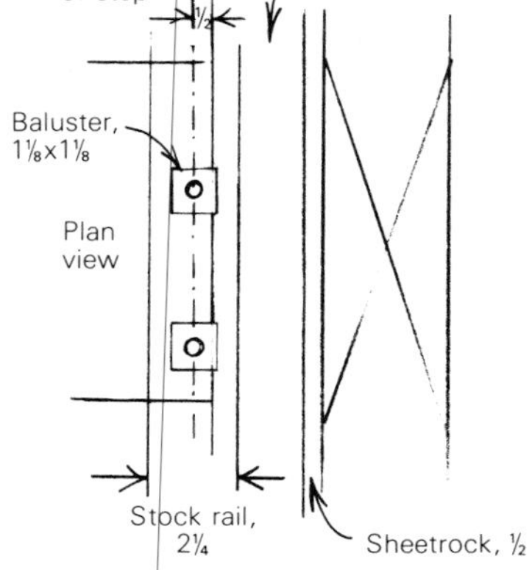
½ in. from center of rail to edge of step
Baluster, 1⅛x1⅛
Plan view
Stock rail, 2¼
Sheetrock, ½

The pitch board—Back at the shop, the first things to make are a pitch board and two stair gauges. The pitch board is a right-angled triangle sawn from plywood, whose sides are the rise of one riser and the run of one tread. The stair gauges, one for the closed stringer and one for the open stringer, are used to position the pitch board when laying out the stringers, as shown below. You'll refer to the pitch board throughout the job, so make sure it's accurate.

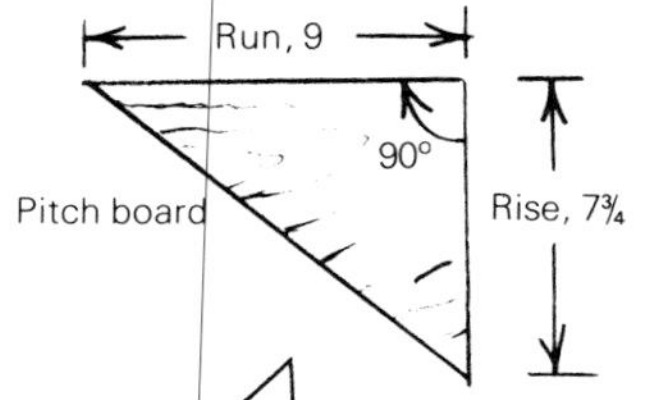
Run, 9
90°
Pitch board
Rise, 7¾

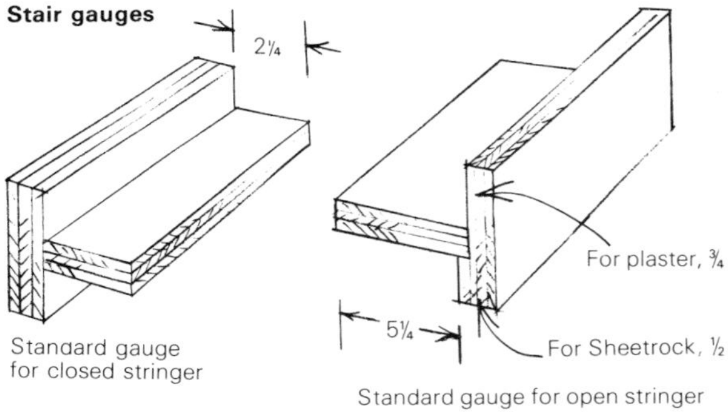
Stair gauges
2¼
For plaster, ¾
5¼
For Sheetrock, ½

Standard gauge for closed stringer

Standard gauge for open stringer

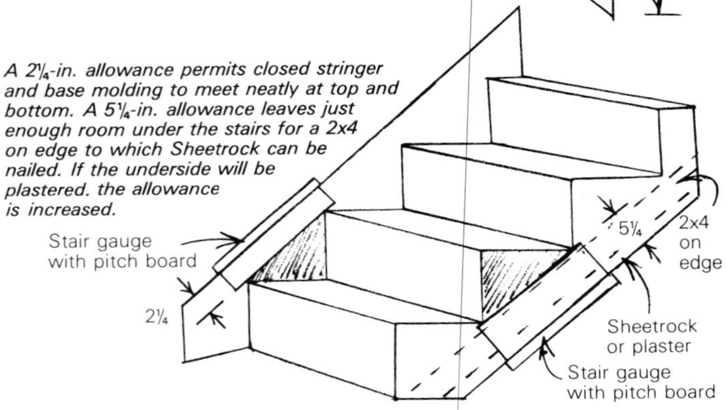
A 2¼-in. allowance permits closed stringer and base molding to meet neatly at top and bottom. A 5¼-in. allowance leaves just enough room under the stairs for a 2x4 on edge to which Sheetrock can be nailed. If the underside will be plastered, the allowance is increased.
Stair gauge with pitch board
2¼
5¼
2x4 on edge
Sheetrock or plaster
Stair gauge with pitch board

The closed stringer—The closed stringer, also called the housed stringer, anchors one side of the stair to the stairwell wall. It starts out as a 5/4x10 board (1⅛x9¼) of pine or poplar. To find its rough length, measure the long side of the pitch board (12 in. in our example) and multiply by the number of steps, then add a foot or two for waste. Normally, for 14 risers, you'll need a 16-ft. board.

Layout begins at the top, using the pitch board and the closed-stringer gauge to establish a line that will be the vertical end of the stringer in the finished stair. Next, shift the pitch board 3 in. to allow for the landing nosing, then trace around the pitch board to locate the outside faces of the first riser and tread. Proceed down the board. At the bottom, add the thickness of the finished floor (usually ¾ in.) to the height of the last riser. Good stairs rest on the subfloor, with the finished floor fit around the bottom step and newel post. Thus the floor holds the stairs in place. If the floor's already installed, you must chop it out to fit.

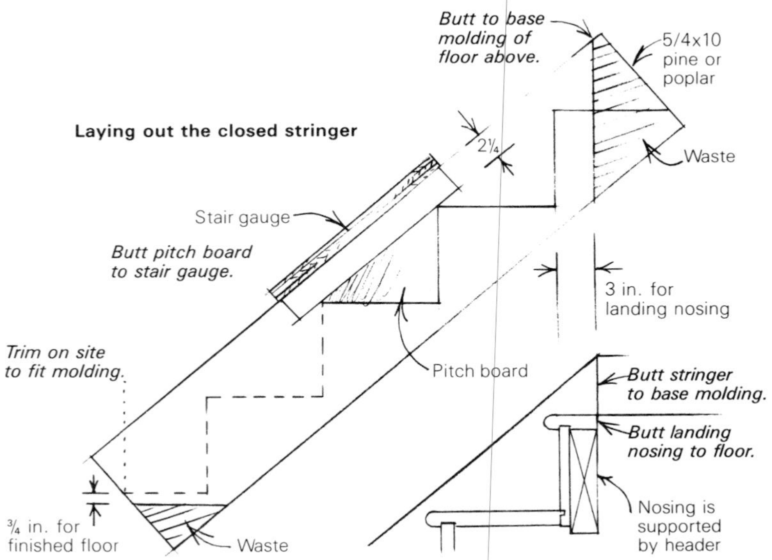
Laying out the closed stringer
Butt to base molding of floor above.
5/4x10 pine or poplar
Waste
2¼
Stair gauge
Butt pitch board to stair gauge.
3 in. for landing nosing
Trim on site to fit molding.
Pitch board
Butt stringer to base molding.
Butt landing nosing to floor.
Nosing is supported by header
¾ in. for finished floor
Waste

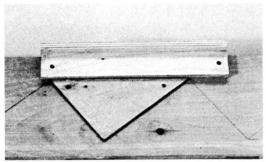

After laying out the closed stringer with pitch board and stair gauge, above, the router template, right (oversize for various size stairs), is used to rout the step housings.

Routing the closed stringer—The zig-zag housing is routed ½ in. deep into the closed stringer, to accept the ends of the treads and risers, plus the wedges that lock them in place. You can make a router template for use with a guide bushing (photo, top right), or you can develop the housing layout from the pitch-block lines and excavate the waste with saw, chisel and router plane. Routing done, finish up by chopping small recesses to receive the end of the cove molding that covers the joint between the tread nosing and the riser below. Production shops merely butt this molding against the stringer.

Typical wedge

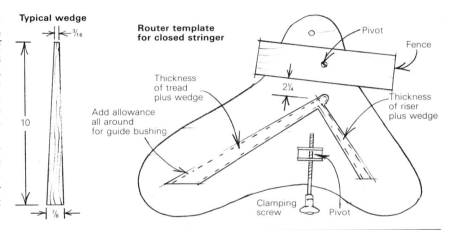

Router template for closed stringer

The open stringer—The open stringer supports the other side of the stair; treads rest on it and risers meet it in a neat miter. At the bottom it rests on the subfloor, at the top it is housed in the landing newel. Thus it is shorter than the housed stringer by the amount of the top riser and the 3-in. nosing allowance. It's also wider, being cut from a 5/4x12 board of pine or poplar. Use the pitch board and the 5¼-in. gauge to lay it out as shown, starting with a full tread at the top and allowing for the finished floor at the bottom. It can be cut out on the table saw and bandsaw, but not easily. Stairbuilders saw it by hand at the bench, using a leg vise that rises several inches above the bench surface. First make a relief cut above the line of each tread, then saw all the treads, then saw the miters for the risers. The miters should be accurate, although they can be undercut by about the thickness of a pencil line to make a neat fit certain.

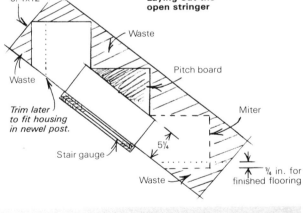

Laying out the open stringer

The completed stringers, below.

Treads—It's usual to buy pre-milled tread stock of white or red oak, 12 in. wide and 36 in. or 42 in. long, planed to 1 in. thick, with the nosing molded on one edge. The tread depth in our example is the 9-in. run, plus 1¼ in. for the nosing, plus ¼ in. for the tongue, a total of 10½ in. Rip the stock to this width.

The measuring stick gives us the length of each tread, 36½ in. This includes the half-inch that's housed inside the closed stringer, but you must still add 1¼ in. for the miter that meets the return nosing on the open side, plus ⅛ in. in order to have a place to start sawing this miter. Thus the treads must be crosscut to 37⅞ in. long; this requires purchasing 42-in. stock. Using the table saw, router or shaper, make the ¼-in. tongue on the back edge of each tread, and the ¾-in. groove on the underside where the riser fits. The spindle shaper is the right machine for these operations, and is essential in the small stair shop because it will also produce moldings, nosings and handrails.

Lay out the nosing miter. On the table saw, crosscut to within 2 in. of the miter, cut the miter itself, then remove the waste.

Section through step

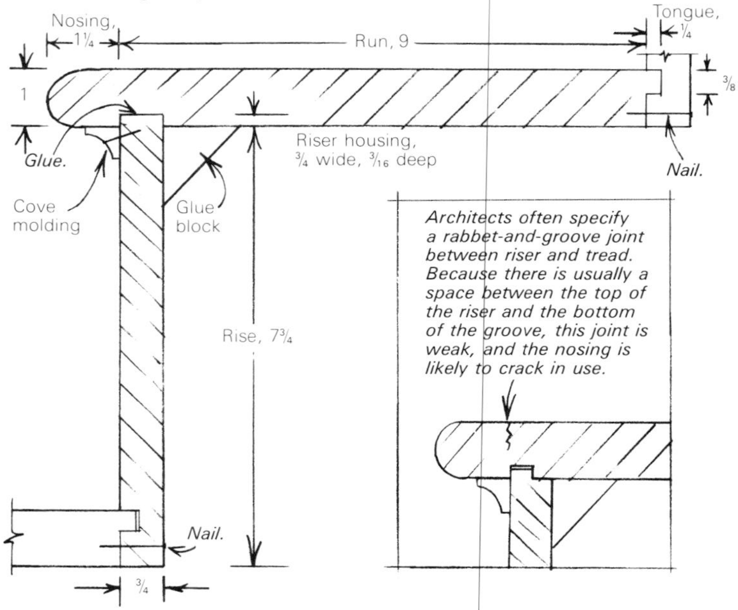

Nosing, 1¼
Run, 9
Tongue, ¼
1
⅜
Glue.
Riser housing, ¾ wide, 3/16 deep
Nail.
Cove molding
Glue block
Rise, 7¾
Nail.
¾
Architects often specify a rabbet-and-groove joint between riser and tread. Because there is usually a space between the top of the riser and the bottom of the groove, this joint is weak, and the nosing is likely to crack in use.

Plan of tread

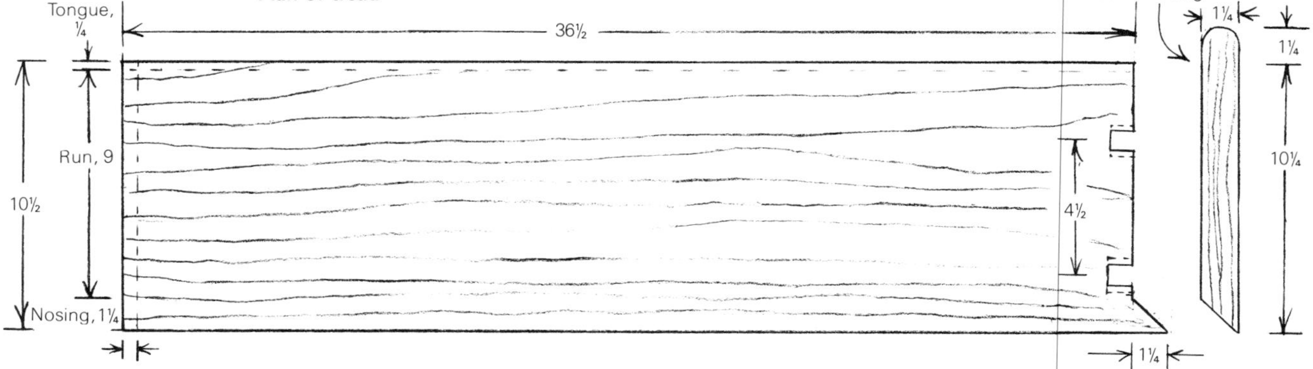

Tongue, ¼
36½
Return nosing
1¼
1¼
Run, 9
10½
4½
10¼
Nosing, 1¼
1¼

Tread is housed ½ in. into closed stringer

Add allowance to tread width for return-nosing miter.

Baluster housings—If you turn your own balusters, you'll be able to make the traditional dovetail on their bottoms, which allows you to mount the balusters from the stair's open side after the handrail is in place. Besides finishing the end of the tread, the return nosing then traps the balusters. You'll need to cut a pair of dovetail housings in the open end of each tread. Position the front housing so the front edge of the baluster is directly over the face of the riser below. The housing is normally ¾ in. wide on the top surface of the tread, spreading to 1¼ in. at the bottom, and a uniform ¾ in. deep.

If you are buying stock balusters, they'll come with a round pin instead of a dovetail. Drill for the pin so that the shoulder of the baluster covers the joint between the tread and the return nosing by 1/16 in. Then saw a slot so the baluster can still be slipped in from the open side. Whether the pin is round or dovetailed, a single nail locks it in place.

Return nosing—The return nosing completes the tread. You can buy it by the running foot, leaving you to shape the back end like the nosing profile and miter the front end to length. Or, you can shape and saw it from tread scrap, starting with pieces 12 in. wide and 14 in. or so long. The strategy is to shape all four edges of the scrap, rip a nosing 1¼ in. wide from each long edge, reshape the cut edges and rip again. Then miter each nosing to an overall length of 11½ in.—the 9-in. run plus 1¼ in. at both ends, as shown below, at right.

Two types of baluster housings

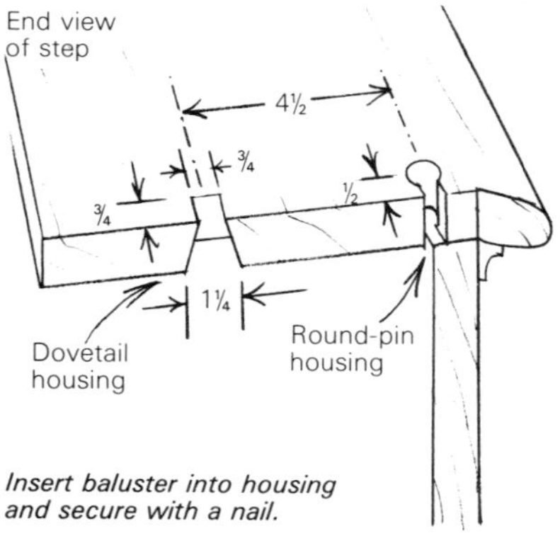

End view of step
4½
¾
¾
½
1¼
Dovetail housing
Round-pin housing

Insert baluster into housing and secure with a nail.

Shaping return nosing

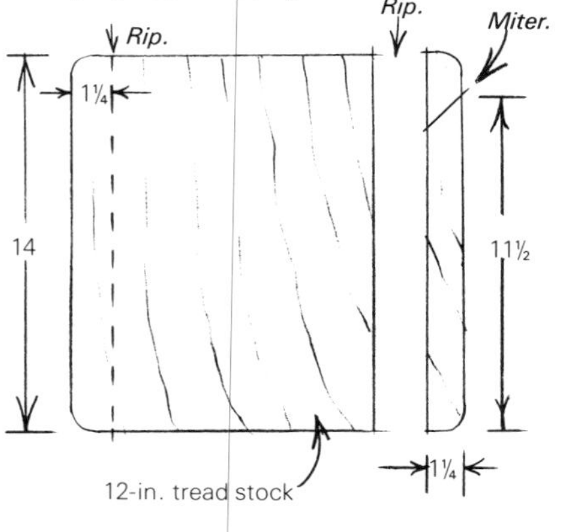

Rip.
Rip.
Miter.
1¼
14
11½
1¼
12-in. tread stock

Here's how all the pieces of a finished step come together at the housed side (left) and the open-stringer side (right). You can see the fine points that make the difference between custom and production stairs. In custom stairs the riser is fully housed in the bottom of the tread, rather than being nailed or rabbeted, as in production stairs. The coved molding at this joint is let into the closed stringer in custom stairs, cut short to abutt it in production stairs. Production builders also often skip the tongue and groove at the back of the treads and lower face of the risers, relying on a few nails here instead. They usually do without glue blocks underneath too. Not much holds such stairs together, and that's why they squeak. Once the stair is installed, there's no way to get in and reinforce it, so it's best to do the job right in the first place.

Risers—Risers can be pine, but if they are to be painted, poplar is better. Buy 10-in. stock planed to ¾ in. thick, then rip it to 7¹⁵⁄₁₆ in. wide—that is, the rise of 7¾ in. plus ³⁄₁₆ in. which will be housed in the groove of the tread above. The waste ripped off can be shaped or routed into cove molding. Miter one end of the riser where it will meet the open stringer, then cut to finished length, 36½ in. in our example, taken from the measuring rod. It's best to cut the groove near the bottom edge of each riser after gluing, or else the steps could come out crooked.

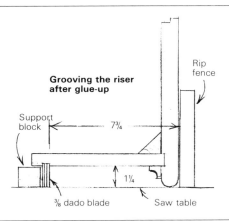

Grooving the riser after glue-up

Support block

Rip fence

7¾

1¼

³⁄₈ dado blade

Saw table

Gluing up—One step consists of a tread and the riser below it. Glue each riser into the groove milled on the bottom side of its tread, add glue blocks to the back, then glue and nail the cove molding to conceal the joint. When the glue has set, arrange the table saw as shown and cut the groove into the face of the riser ³⁄₈ in. wide and ¼ in. deep. The top of the groove will be parallel with and exactly 7¾ in. from the face of the tread. Tack the return nosing in place, using 6d finishing nails—you'll remove them later to insert the balusters. Sand the steps before assembly.

Assembling the flight—Stairs are usually assembled and glued up at the shop, then shipped to the job site in complete flights, although without handrail and balusters. Start at the top, with the first complete step (not the top riser and landing nosing). Lay the closed stringer flat on the floor, insert the step and tap in the wedges that lock it in place. Wedging the top step tight will be enough to square off the flight, so now drop the remaining steps into their housings, wedging loosely as needed. Add the open stringer, nailing through the miter into the end grain of the risers. Three nails per riser will hold it. Next, wedge the closed side, gluing in the riser wedges first and trimming them flush to allow clearance for the tread wedges to be glued in tightly. Then back-nail the bottom of the risers to the treads, spacing the nails 8 in. to 10 in. apart under the tongue. Add glue blocks to the open stringer, one block under each tread and one behind each riser. Like the wedges on the closed side of the staircase, these glue blocks will keep the stairs tight and free of squeaks. Tack the cove molding under the return nosings. Notice that nails are never driven into the face of the treads. Now you're ready to fit the newel posts, top riser and landing nosing, all of which must be done before installation because the finished floor will have to be fit and laid around them.

Open stringer will be glued and nailed to the partially assembled flight.

Starting newel—The starting newel, at the foot of the stair, has a large housing chopped in it to fit around the outside corner of the bottom step. The newel should be laid out before it is turned, usually from a blank 4 in. square by 4 ft. long. Start the layout by scribing a centerline on two adjacent faces of the blank, then locate the shoulders that separate the turned shaft and cap from the sections left square (right). Begin at the top of the post; the important dimension is from the crest of the handrail to the top of the first tread, 30 in. Since the handrail enters at the pitch angle, use the pitch board to establish its vertical thickness. At the foot of the post, the stringer is let in ½ in. past the centerline, whereas the face of the bottom riser goes in right on the centerline. There's also a shallow housing for the tread nosing and its cove molding (trimmed to fit). The return nosing is cut off flush with the newel. Allow an extra ¾-in. to be let into the finished floor. After laying out the newel, turn it and cross-cut it to length, then saw and chisel the housings.

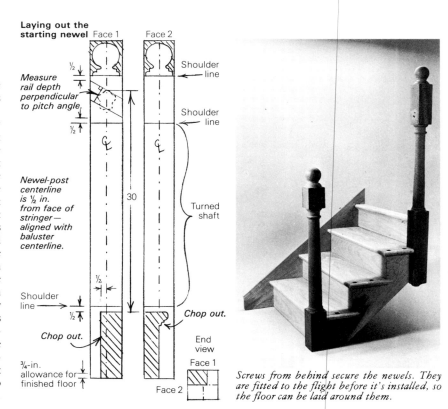

Laying out the starting newel

Face 1   Face 2

Shoulder line
Measure rail depth perpendicular to pitch angle.

Shoulder line

Newel-post centerline is ½ in. from face of stringer—aligned with baluster centerline.

Turned shaft

30

Shoulder line

Chop out.

Chop out.

End view

¾-in. allowance for finished floor

Face 1

Face 2

Screws from behind secure the newels. They are fitted to the flight before it's installed, so the floor can be laid around them.

The landing newel (top) and starting newel, with their housings. Note the difference in the lengths of the turned shaft and of the square sections.

The assembled flight, with newels removed. Portions of the top and bottom treads and their moldings must be sawn away to fit the newel housings.

The starting newel houses the tread nosing and its cove molding.

Landing newel—Because it accommodates a handrail on the landing, and also houses the top riser and the top of the open stringer, the landing newel is taller than the starting newel. A 5-ft. blank is usually long enough. The landing handrail runs straight out the back of the newel (face 1, right), so this newel must be laid out on three adjacent faces, beginning from centerlines and working down from the top. As before, the critical elevations to establish are the level of the landing itself, and of the shoulders that define the newel's turned portions. The crest of the landing rail is 34 in. above the landing nosing, and the crest of the pitched handrail is 30 in. above the landing, as it was on the starting newel. With these points established, you then scribe onto face 2 of the newel the profile of the nosing itself, of the top riser, and of the back end of the top tread, all of which should be cut back so they fit in what will be a ½-in. deep housing. The step profile and the end of the open stringer may then be scribed onto face 3. Leave 1¼ in. below the stringer before laying out the drop that completes the newel. Finally, scribe the housings for the landing rail. The pitched rail need not be housed. This layout is more difficult to describe and draw than to do; its logic is apparent when you have an assembled stair or a model that you can refer to.

Screws through stringer and riser, from beneath the stair, secure this type of newel in place. Newels are usually fitted to the flight before it leaves the shop, then removed for shipping. Make sure they're plumb, then measure between the newels to find the length of rail stock you need.

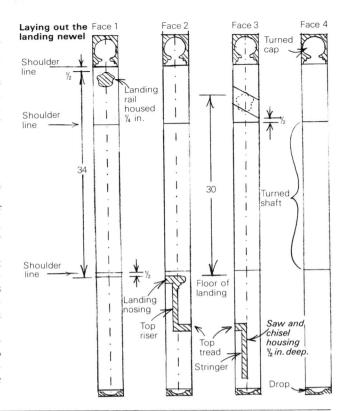

Handrailing—You can buy handrailing, or you can shape your own on the shaper. Either way, start by plowing a groove ¼ in. deep down the center of the underside of the rail, wide enough to fit the square section atop the balusters. Use the pitch board to miter the ends of the handrail, to the length you took by measuring between the newels. Butt the handrails to the newels and secure them with nails or screws.

Balusters—Each tread carries two balusters, one shorter than the other because of the handrail's pitch. They look best when the turned portion begins at the level of the top of the next tread, and ends at a uniform distance below the handrail. Thus the difference in length is accommodated in the central turning, not in the square sections at top and bottom. To lay them out, draw a full-size side elevation of one step. The turning must include stock for the dovetail pins that fit the housings in the ends of the treads. These dovetails can be sawn in the square baluster, but it's quicker to turn a cone-shape and trim it to fit. Leave the tops of the turnings overlong, and use the pitch board to trim them to length, not forgetting the extra ¼ in. that fits into the handrail. Two finishing nails into the handrail, and one through the dovetail, hold them in place. Replace the return nosing and its cove molding, gluing the mitered ends. Set the nails, drive a nail through the miter, and you're done. □

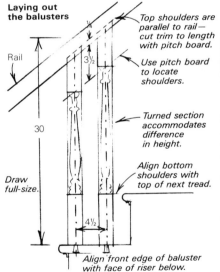

Two nails secure each baluster to the bottom of the handrail. The top of the baluster is sawn at the pitch angle.

A single nail locks the bottom of the baluster to its tread.

Antebellum Shutters
Movable louvers from simple jigs

by Ben Erickson

Antebellum frame houses are still common in my part of western Alabama. Some of these Greek-revival gems have decayed beyond repair, but many are being restored. Back then, all fine Southern houses sported exterior louvered shutters, many of which had movable louvers to control ventilation and light. After a century-and-a-half of sun and rain, it's a rare restoration indeed that doesn't need at least a couple of new ones. Reproducing these shutters is an important sideline of my woodworking business and I've developed some ways to speed the process.

Old shutters in my area are usually heart pine or cypress. These woods are scarce now so I use clear redwood. It's stable, holds paint well and is naturally resistant to decay. Windows in these old houses average 3 ft. by 6½ ft. and it takes about 50 b.f. of 2-in. lumber to make a pair of shutters for a window this size.

The frame is through mortised and tenoned, just like a frame-and-panel door frame. Pegs alone held the old ones together. I usually use a haunched tenon for the top and bottom rails. Figure 1 shows how a typical antebellum shutter goes together. If I'm making several shutters for the same house, I try to find an average one to copy because the dimensions can vary considerably from shutter to shutter. Old windows vary too, so it's best to measure each window. When laying out, add ¼ in. to the width of each shutter to allow for the rabbets where the shutters overlap in the center of the window.

After dimensioning the frame stock, lay out and chop the rail mortises in the stiles. I use a ⅜-in. hollow-chisel mortiser in the drill press. Next, I cut the rail tenons on the tablesaw. I mount two combination blades on the arbor, with washers and sheet-metal shims between them to get the right spacing. This setup cuts both tenon cheeks in one pass. Check the tablesaw setup with scrap stock exactly the same thickness as the frame stock and trial fit the test tenon in the stile mortise. The tenon should slide snugly into the mortise. Mark the face side of the rail stock and always keep this side against the fence of the tenoning jig as you cut the tenons to avoid alignment problems later. I cut the shoulders on the radial-arm saw and saw the haunch, if any, on the bandsaw. A stop block against the radial-arm-saw fence ensures that all the tenons are the same length.

Dry assemble the frame and check the outside dimensions against the window measurements. If you've made an error, it's best to find out now, before proceeding.

If you're copying an old shutter, measure the distance between the centers of the holes the louvers pivot in. These will probably vary, so measure several and average them. If you're working from scratch, here's one way to space the holes: On the

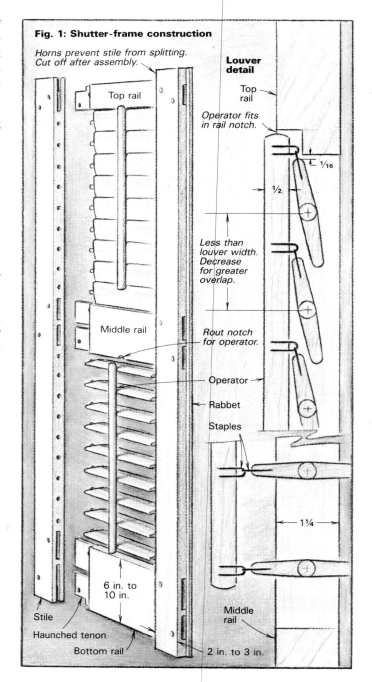

Fig. 1: Shutter-frame construction

Horns prevent stile from splitting. Cut off after assembly.

Top rail

Middle rail

Stile

Haunched tenon

Bottom rail

6 in. to 10 in.

2 in. to 3 in.

Louver detail

Top rail

Operator fits in rail notch.

1/16

1/2

Less than louver width. Decrease for greater overlap.

Rout notch for operator.

Operator

Rabbet

Staples

1¼

Middle rail

Drawings: Lee Hov

With two blades on the tablesaw arbor Erickson cuts both rail tenon cheeks in one pass, above. Rather than risk fingers cutting free-hand, he's designed a tenoning push stick that rides the rip fence and holds the stock upright. A 1x2 table and fence support the stile while drilling the louver holes, right. The block system shown below ensures accurate hole spacing.

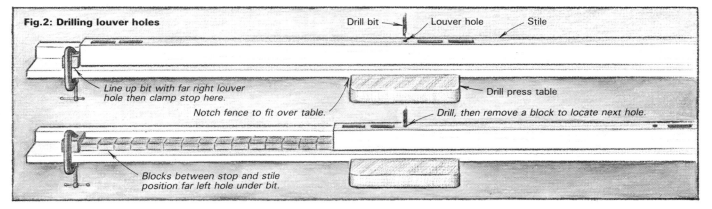

Fig.2: Drilling louver holes

Drill bit — Louver hole — Stile

Line up bit with far right louver hole then clamp stop here.

Notch fence to fit over table.

Drill press table

Drill, then remove a block to locate next hole.

Blocks between stop and stile position far left hole under bit.

stiles, mark the holes for the top and bottom louvers in each opening. These louvers should clear the rails by about $\frac{1}{16}$ in. to allow the louvers to close completely. So, for a $2\frac{1}{4}$-in. wide louver, you'd mark the centers $1\frac{3}{16}$ in. from the rails. The louvers should overlap each other about $\frac{1}{4}$ in. Divide the distance between the two centers you just marked by the number of louvers you want. The result should be about $\frac{1}{4}$ in. less than louver width, or roughly 2 in. for $2\frac{1}{4}$-in. wide louvers. If larger, the louvers won't have enough overlap, so add another louver and divide again. If a lot smaller than $\frac{1}{4}$ in., try removing a louver. For example, to fit seventeen $2\frac{1}{4}$-in. wide louvers into a 35-in. space, divide 35 by 17 = $2\frac{1}{17}$ in. Rules aren't graded in 17ths so set your dividers as close as you can and step off the distance (or measure in metrics and eliminate the fractions).

The method I use to drill the holes, shown in figure 2, ensures accurate spacing. I set a stop block on the radial-arm-saw fence and cut scrap blocks as long as the center-to-center distance between holes. A long combination fence/table extension on the drill press supports the stile. With the bit over the first hole on the right, I clamp a stop on the fence at the left end of the stile.

When I line up the blocks between that stop and the left end of the stile, the bit should be directly over the first hole on the left. You may have to make several sets of blocks with just slight variations in length before you get it right. Line up the blocks, drill a hole and remove a block to position the next hole. Both stiles may be drilled on the same setup.

Antebellum louvers are usually about $\frac{3}{8}$ in. thick and $1\frac{3}{4}$ in. to $2\frac{3}{4}$ in. wide. Viewed from the end, the louver has an elongated diamond shape. I find it convenient to plane this shape on 4 ft. to 8 ft. lengths, then cut them to exact louver length.

After the stock is dimensioned rectangular (usually $\frac{3}{8}$ in. x $2\frac{1}{4}$ in. or so), I taper the louvers on the thickness planer. As shown in figure 3, page 76, my taper setup is simply a strip of wood as wide as the louvers and as long as my planer bed, ripped to a 3° angle. It's sandwiched tightly between two wooden guide strips which are clamped to the bed. I just feed the louver strip through on top of the angled wooden strip for the first two passes and double the angle for the third and fourth passes. Start with some sample pieces and run a marking gauge down the center. Scribble on the

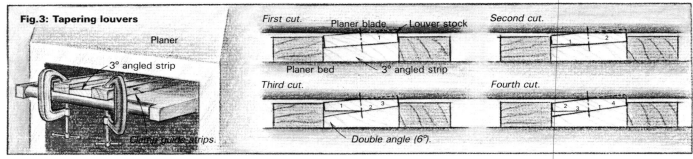

Fig.3: Tapering louvers

Planer

3° angled strip

Clamp guide strips.

First cut.

Planer blade — Louver stock

Planer bed — 3° angled strip

Second cut.

Third cut.

Double angle (6°).

Fourth cut.

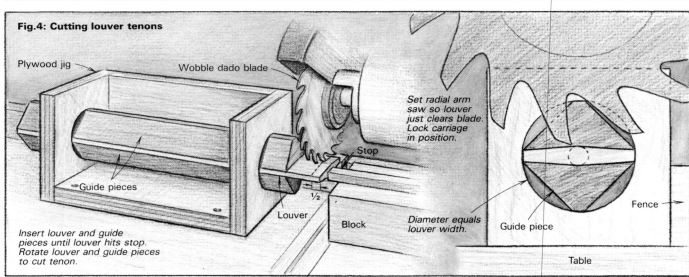

Fig.4: Cutting louver tenons

Plywood jig

Wobble dado blade

Set radial arm saw so louver just clears blade. Lock carriage in position.

Guide pieces

Stop

½

Louver

Block

Diameter equals louver width.

Guide piece

Fence

Table

Insert louver and guide pieces until louver hits stop. Rotate louver and guide pieces to cut tenon.

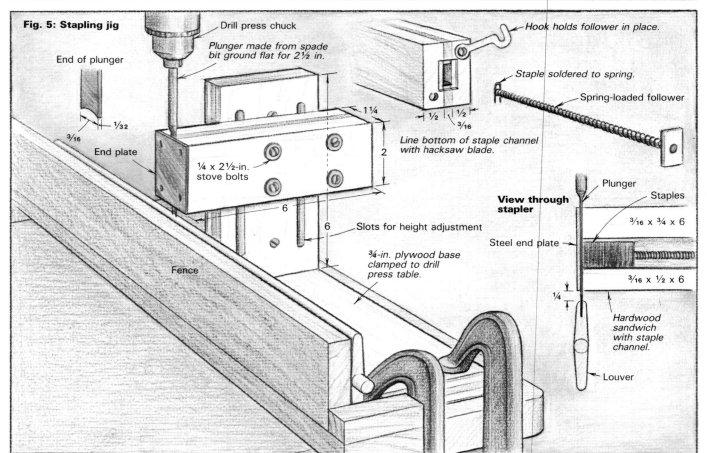

Fig. 5: Stapling jig

Drill press chuck

Plunger made from spade bit ground flat for 2½ in.

End of plunger

Hook holds follower in place.

Staple soldered to spring.

Spring-loaded follower

½   ½

3/16

Line bottom of staple channel with hacksaw blade.

1/32

3/16

End plate

1¼

¼ x 2½-in. stove bolts

2

6

6

Slots for height adjustment

¾-in. plywood base clamped to drill press table.

Fence

View through stapler

Plunger

Staples

3/16 x ¾ x 6

Steel end plate

3/16 x ½ x 6

¼

Hardwood sandwich with staple channel.

Louver

sample with a pencil or crayon so you can see how close the planer cuts to the center line. The object is for the louver edges to end up about ¼ in. thick, while the center is a full ⅜ in. thick when viewed from the end. Adjust the planer height until it planes to the center line. Now, run all the louver stock through, flip the louvers over (without changing ends) and run the other side through. Double the angle either by adding another 3° angled strip on top of the first one, or replacing the first strip with a 6° strip. Using the samples again, readjust the planer height to cut to the middle of the louver. Reverse ends on all the pieces and run the remaining two sides through as you did the first two. It's easy to get confused and run the wrong side through, so work out a system of stacking to enable you to remember which sides haven't been planed. After beveling, you can round the edges on the shaper or router table with a ¼-in. round-over bit.

Cut the louvers to length, usually ⅞ in. longer than the distance between the stiles. This allows for a ½-in. long round tenon at each end.

I cut the tenons on the radial-arm saw with the jig shown in figure 4. The louver fits snugly into the circular cutouts in the plywood uprights. So it doesn't wobble in the cutouts, I sandwich the louver between two triangular guides. I mount a wobble dado blade on the saw and adjust the blade height so that the louver, in a horizontal position, just slides under the blade. A stop that hits the end of the louver in its center (where the tenon will be) is clamped to the fence. This stop determines the length of the tenon. With the saw carriage locked in place and the saw running, insert the louver sandwich through the jig holes. Push it through horizontally under the blade until the end touches the stop block, then rotate it to cut the tenon.

The operator is a strip of round or half-round stock about ½-in. in diameter that moves the louvers in unison. Each louver is connected to it by two interlocking staples, one in the louver and one in the operator. I use U-shaped galvanized staples about ³⁄₁₆ in. wide and ⅝ in. long. Each shutter needs two operators, one for the louvers above the center rail, one for those below.

For small jobs in softwood, or for minor repair work, you can break up a row of staples with a knife or heat, then hammer them in with a tack hammer. However, if there are many to do, it can be very time consuming and if the wood is even moderately hard the staples tend to bend. To cope with these problems I designed a stapling jig that uses the drill press to press the staples into the louvers (see figure 5). It works just like a regular staple gun. It's basically a hardwood sandwich with a space in the center just wide enough and high enough for a row of staples to slide into. I lined the bottom of the staple channel with an old hacksaw blade to keep the staples from digging into the wood. I scavanged the spring-loaded follower from an old Arrow hand stapler. I ground the sides of the spring-loaded follower's rod down to fit through the row of staples, removed the clip at the end and reattached the spring with a lump of solder at the end of the rod to keep it from coming off. Unlike air staplers, my jig allows me to control the depth of penetration. By using the same blocks that I used to drill the louver holes, I can also space the interlocking operator staples perfectly. Accurate spacing here is essential for smooth operation.

To staple the louvers you'll need to make a fence to support the louver at 90° to the drill press table. Unplug the drill press, chuck up the jig's plunger (ground from a spade bit) and set up a stop on the fence that quickly centers the louvers under the stapler. Adjust the height of the stapler until it's about ¼ in. from the louver. Lower the quill to press in the staple. Adjust the drill-

After gluing the frame joints, Erickson inserts the louver tenons into their holes in one stile, then tightens the clamps enough to slip the other ends in the opposite stile. With both ends in place, he draws the clamps up tight. Louvered shutters were standard features on Southern antebellum houses. The shutters at left were made in the 1840s. Only the bottom louvers are movable.

press depth stop so the staple protrudes about ³⁄₁₆ in. from the edge of the louver and staple all the louvers.

Replace the fence with one the same height as the thickness of the operator and center the operator's width under the stapler. Position the stapler above the operator so there's room enough to slip a louver under the stapler. Reset the depth stop on the press. On the long fence, line up the same set of blocks that you used to drill the louver holes and use a similar stop setup to locate the staples at the ends of the operator. Place the operator end against the stop block, and insert a louver under the stapler at right angles to the operator. Press in a staple that interlocks the louver staple. If you don't want to line up each louver by eye, set a stop and butt one end of the louver against it. If your operator is round, draw a pencil line down its length to keep the staples in a straight line.

Before assembling the frame, drill or rout a slot in the edges of the top and middle rails for the ends of the operators (see figure 1). I use Weldwood plastic resin glue for the frame joints because it's water resistant and sets up slowly. Spread the glue and pull the joints together with pipe or bar clamps until all of the joints are within an inch or so of being tight. Insert the louvers in one stile. Tighten the clamps until the opposite ends of the louvers almost touch the other stile, and insert these ends in the holes. Now pull the frame tight. Watch for any sign of binding that might indicate that a louver isn't in it's hole. When the glue is dry, drill and peg the tenons, cut off the horns and cut the rabbet where the shutters overlap. As a final touch, I run a decorative bead on the overlapping edge. □

Ben Erickson is a professional woodworker in Eutaw, Ala.

Mosaic door followup—*With regard to James Ranne-feld's article (see pp. 64-65), it seems to me that if wide, solid wood pieces are glued to a plywood core and subjected to great environmental changes, the glueline will eventually fail, unless the glue is applied only to the center portion of each piece to allow for free expansion. The author doesn't state clearly how to cope with the possibility of this happening. If only the center portion is glued, shouldn't the sectional drawing show splines between the stile and the mosaic elements also?* —*John Briggs, Midvale, Utah*
JAMES A. RANNEFELD REPLIES: In my article I allowed that solid wood will expand and contract across the grain, and thus suggested that the mosaic pieces should be relatively small (under 12 in. wide) and connected by a network of splines. The size of each piece can vary, depending on the wood species (e.g., mahogany is very stable, oak very unstable), and on the quality of the wood finish, the degree to which it impedes the transfer of moisture between air and wood.

Each mosaic piece should be glued as widely and uniformly as practical to prevent individual pieces from warping and cupping, further straining and degrading the glue bond. We don't spline the mosaic elements to the rails and stiles because if the pieces are properly glued and cross-splined, it is impossible for any of them to dislodge.

Curved handrail—*I'm making a winding staircase and need help with the curved railing. What's the best way to bend 2½-in. thick stock? How do I profile the curved rail on the shaper?* —*Hap Davis, Calgary, Alta.*
GARY BOUDREAUX REPLIES: Forget about bending 2½-in. thick stock. Laminate your railing. I've had good luck laminating handrails as shown in the drawing. Make the outer layers as you would any molding; laminate them to flat inner pieces no thicker than ¼-in. These inner laminations should be wider than the finished railing and planed to shape after glue-up.

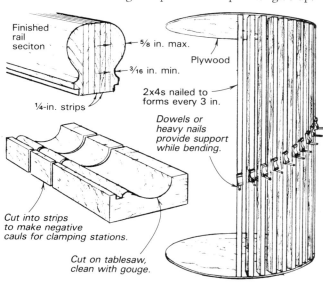

Finished rail seciton

⅝ in. max.

³⁄₁₆ in. min.

Plywood

¼-in. strips

2x4s nailed to forms every 3 in.

Dowels or heavy nails provide support while bending.

Cut into strips to make negative cauls for clamping stations.

Cut on tablesaw, clean with gouge.

For bending and clamping, you need to make a negative caul of the molding out of a soft wood like pine. Cut this caul into short pieces to support the rail and to give it backing at its clamping stations. Depending on your staircase design, you may be able to bend the railing around the outside stringer. If not, you'll have to build a bending form from plywood and 2x4s as shown, the same diameter and height as the staircase. The railing will follow the same rise and run as the stair treads, so lay out the clamping stations accordingly. I

find it helpful to do a dry run. When everything is laid out properly, apply a slow-setting glue like yellow glue to the laminations, then drive a finishing nail through the entire stack, right in the middle of its length. This will help keep the laminations from sliding out of alignment. With at least one other person to help, start clamping in the middle and work out toward each end, bending and clamping as you go.

The only problem I've had with this system is the need for so many clamps (two every 3 in). The thin lower edge of the railing wants to flare out, so use plenty of clamps to avoid gaps in the laminations.

Transparent glaze—*I have a large quantity of molding that's been finished with Deft clear lacquer. For a number of reasons, it can't be stripped and refinished. Is there some sort of transparent finish that I can apply over the lacquer to darken the molding to a brown fruitwood color?*
—*R. Winkleblock, Arroyo Grande, Calif.*
BEAU BELAJONAS REPLIES: A glaze will enable you to control the amount of color and transparency. First, you need to mix up a glaze medium from 1 part varnish, 1 part mineral spirits or turpentine and ⅛ part boiled linseed oil. To make a brown fruitwood, I'd use raw sienna and burnt umber, which can be bought as universal colored pigments, oil colors or Japan colors. Add a bit of raw sienna and a touch of burnt umber to your glaze medium, keeping track of proportions. Start with small amounts—you can always add more.

Mix up a sample and test it on a small section of your molding. Let stand for five minutes, then gently rub with the grain. If it isn't dark enough, add more pigment. Once you've reached the right consistency, make up a bigger batch. Brush it on, let it stand for five minutes, then gently rub it off. Try to rub in one direction. If the glaze pulls too much or seems to drag, add a little linseed oil. Let dry overnight.

The next day, after the glaze is dry, I like to give it a coat of satin varnish tinted with a bit of burnt umber. This evens the glaze and gives the finish more depth.

Truing up a level—*I have a 4-ft. wooden level with fixed vials that seems to be about ¼ in. out of plumb. How can I true it?* —*Bruce Dichter, Minneapolis, Minn.*
KAREN TYNE REPLIES: First, test your level by placing it against a vertical surface, say, a wall or a door jamb. Test one edge of the level first, then flip it around and try the other edge. An accurate level will yield the same bubble reading off both edges, whether the surface is plumb or not. Repeat this test on a horizontal surface.

Wooden levels usually become inaccurate for two reasons: the wood warps, or the vials get knocked out of alignment. Sight down the level to check for warpage. It doesn't matter if the face of the wood is bowed, but if the edges are crowned, straighten them with a hand plane or a jointer. If your level is edged with brass strips, you may be able to remove them to plane the edges. If not, sand the brass flat with a long sanding block, or have a machine shop take a light cut with a grinder, making sure the edges are kept parallel.

Some skewed vials can be pried out and reset, but it's often easier to knock them out with a hammer and buy replacement vials and glass windows (crystals) from the level's manufacturer. To install, set the end of each vial in a dollop of painters' crack filler (add a little vinegar to retard curing), adjusting the vials in the unhardened filler until they test accurately from both edges, plumb and level. Let the filler dry overnight, then seal with a coat of white latex paint. The crystals fit into a small groove and can be mounted in a bead of putty or semi-hardening caulking compound.

Among the differences that arise when the scale is changed from cabinets to houses is the problem of moving timbers around the shop. Levin's solution is a four-sided truss of 2x4s pierced by the axle and wheels from a garden cart.

Working with Heavy Timbers
Woods, tools, layout and joinery of the housewright's trade

by Ed Levin

Traditional frame carpentry is something most wood-workers know little about, although its principles can be applied to any project where wood is joined to wood on a large scale. Timber framing, already in decline by the time this country was colonized, was superseded early in this century by the 2x4 balloon frame and its derivatives. The ancient art is only now coming back, albeit on a small scale. Modern timber-framing practice suffers dearly from this break with continuous tradition, to the extent that many self-taught practitioners—myself included—have to expend considerable energy rediscovering the craft. The methods I will describe are merely one man's solution to some of the problems of working with large, heavy timbers. Why timber frame? What is it in these days of balloon framing with prepackaged popsicle-stick studs that makes someone wrest whole living trees from the forest and laboriously shape them into a dwelling place? I have no simple answer. Timber framing is slow, difficult and expensive. It's also strong, durable, beautiful and righteous.

The frame — Timber framing can serve the structural needs of almost any kind of building—from traditional Japanese houses to modern fancies, as well as the classic colonial American house and barn. The frame shown in the diagram on the next page is of a typical late 18th-century New England house—still the most popular style among timber framers.

Sills sit over the masonry foundation and engage the first floor joists and the feet of all exterior posts. The sills are the first timbers laid down in a building, and often the first to be replaced—being close to the ground and in contact with masonry makes them prone to rot. The sills should be large enough to keep the ends of posts and joists clear of the masonry. Typical sizes are 6x6, 6x8 and 8x8.

Major horizontal timbers above the sills are called girts and plates (the plate is usually the beam that supports the roof rafters). Their dimensions vary, but girts should be as deep or deeper than the joists they hold, and no wider than the posts they tenon into. Diagonal sway bracing stiffens the frame against wind, impact, resonant vibration, earthquake and internal moving loads—an extreme case of the latter would be holding a dance on an upper story. Summer beams break up long floor spans into manageable lengths. Because the summer beam has a long unsupported span and is heavily loaded, it is often the largest timber in the frame.

There are two kinds of roofs in the traditional frame. The common rafter roof has rafters on 3-ft. to 5-ft. centers with sheathing laid across the rafters. In the principal-rafter-and-purlin roof, rafters are spaced farther apart (7 ft. to 9 ft.) with purlins framed into them at 3-ft. to 4-ft. intervals and roof boards running with the rafters. Some typical dimensions for common rafters: 3x6, 3x7, 4x6, 4x7 and 4x8; for principal rafters: 6x6, 6x7 and 6x8; and for purlins: 3x4, 3x5 and 4x4. Collar ties often join rafters near the center of their spans. Tie is a misnomer as it is not in tension but in compression, and keeps rafters from sagging at midspan. Finally, roofs with a purlin system sometimes have a true ridgepole. This is a member closer in size to the rafters than to the purlins, into which the tops of the rafters are tenoned.

Wood — Strong, beautiful and durable oak is the premier framing material in the Anglo-American tradition. However,

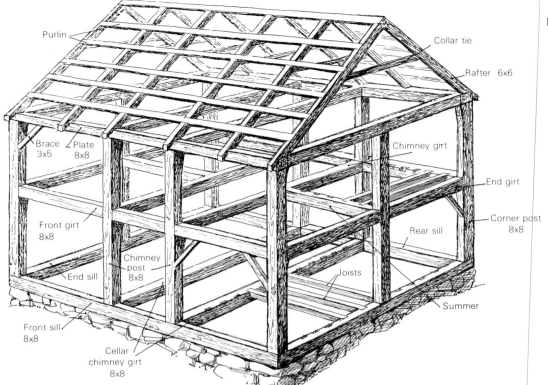

Purlin

Collar tie

Rafter 6x6

Brace
3x5

Plate
8x8

Chimney girt

End girt

Front girt
8x8

Corner post
8x8

Rear sill

Chimney
post
8x8

End sill

Joists

Front sill
8x8

Summer

Cellar
chimney girt
8x8

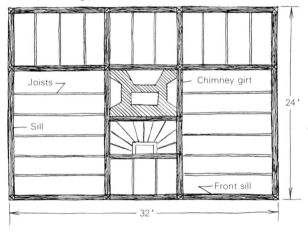

First floor framing plan

Joists

Chimney girt

Sill

24'

Front sill

32'

Framing diagram (above) and first floor plan (left) of a typical two-story house in New England of the late 18th century. The contemporary frame in the photo follows the same scheme, except that its second story posts are reduced to a knee wall. This permits almost as much usable space, with considerably less timber.

oak is unyielding, heavy and slow to dry, and the availability of other suitable species caused Americans to diversify timber usage. The Northeast abounds in old frames of spruce, maple, pine, beech, hemlock, chestnut, fir, and even basswood, butternut and poplar, although current usage in New England favors oak, pine, spruce and hemlock.

Choice of a framing material depends on taste, availability and price. Hardwoods are stronger, cut cleaner and finish well, but are expensive and prone to greater shrinkage. Softwoods are lighter and cheaper and they work more easily, but they are weaker and don't cut as cleanly. Softwoods with high moisture content (pine and hemlock) are weaker when used green, and care must be taken that timbers do not sag while drying. I prefer oak (red oak in my vicinity) in houses and good clear spruce in utility buildings.

Hand hewing was the method of converting logs to timbers before machine sawing took over, and remained common into the early 20th century. The shift to sawn timber was gradual, happening earlier in cities and later in rural areas. In many places the transition to sawn beams never took place, since timber framing was supplanted by balloon framing.

The bulk of mortise-and-tenon timber construction going on today uses native lumber sawn at local mills. But dressed Douglas fir and southern pine beams are available in a vast array of sizes and lengths (it's not difficult to procure a 40 ft. long fir 12 in. by 16 in.). At the other extreme, hand hewing continues among a select group of owner-builders. Many local mills can't handle logs longer than 16 ft. so using a broadaxe or chainsaw mill may be your only alternative to imported fir for long girts, plates and rafters.

From *Fine Woodworking* magazine (July 1979) 17:43-53

Should you frame with green wood or dry? Nowadays, most framers use unseasoned timber. The schedules of both builders and homeowners don't permit waiting for beams to dry. With a drying rate of roughly a year to the inch, it can take a decade for a large oak timber to air dry. I know of no place where you can purchase dry beams. Historically, there is evidence both ways. Because it is next to impossible to hew dry wood, beams were probably shaped while green and then seasoned before the joiner started his work. Rapid seasoning and shrinkage of timber can cause checking, but coating the ends of the beams with paint, varnish, paraffin or a commercial end sealer guards against this.

Whether you work green or dry, shrinkage is inevitable. Even air-dried timber (of say 15% moisture content) is going to move when placed in an enclosed, heated space where low relative humidity in winter may cause an equilibrium moisture content of 6% or less. So, to prevent disastrous cracking during that first winter, maintain humidity with a humidifier or by placing shallow pans of water on heaters or woodstoves. All the same, as the new frame settles into the drier interior environment, shrinkage will cause additional checking, usually accompanied by loud and eerie cracks and groans. The timber framer's primary concern is not checking however, but rather the effect of shrinkage on the joinery.

Tools of the trade

Measuring and marking tools — The power-return tape is hardly a specialized tool, but it is unbeatable for locating joints in the length of the timber. Try to use the same tape throughout the framing. I recommend the 25-ft. long, 1-in. wide variety. The steel (nowadays aluminum) rafter square takes over after the tape for marking lines across and around timbers, as well as for laying out roof angles. It can also be used to mark mortises and tenons and many other joints.

Use a knife for marking across the grain and a scribe for marking along the grain, following the edge of square, bevel or template. I prefer knives and scribes to pencils. Even when they're adequately sharpened, pencils break easily on rough timber. Cut and scribed lines can also be split cleanly—you can set the edge of your chisel right *in* the line when chopping or paring a joint. When crosscutting with a power saw, the grain will not chip up beside a cut line. This not only makes for neater work, but it also signals when you are cutting off the line because the saw starts to raise up flecks of wood. I use an ordinary utility knife for marking, and make scribes by grinding points on hardened 16d twist nails.

The combination square is better than the traditional try square for timber work. It is used to check for square inside mortises and notched or lapped joints, and on the shoulders of tenons. It also doubles as a depth gauge and as a handy straightedge to check surface flatness.

We use marking gauges to lay out mortises and tenons and in all applications calling for a straight line parallel to an edge. Ordinary gauges work well up to about 4 in. from the edge. Beyond this you need something larger. The homemade gauges in the photo are really just heavy-duty panel gauges with a couple of modifications. The stem (sliding part) of the gauge is wedge-shaped and fits tightly in a wedge-shaped mortise, eliminating annoying slop. The stem carries three spurs and scribes three parallel lines, one for each edge of the mortise plus a centerline. For points I use hardened (Sheetrock) screws that have been chucked in an electric

drill and pointed while spinning against a grinding wheel. The screw thread allows you to adjust the heights of the spurs to get all three to mark evenly on erratic surfaces.

Templates are handy for laying out frequently repeated joints. Aluminum templates hold up best, but are tedious to make. Wood templates are easier, but move with the weather, get nicked and rounded over by the knife and scribe. Newsboard (heavy cardboard) templates are quickest and hold up well, but the difficulty of assembling two pieces rigidly at right angles restricts its use to flat templates.

Aside from layout for hewing, the chalk line is used primarily in those few cases when a timber must be laid out from a centerline rather than an edge. Of greater utility is an unchalked line in a reel, to check beams and assemblies for straightness, and also to measure the crown in bowed pieces.

The race knife or timber scribe was used by the carpenter to inscribe identifying marks on timbers to ensure proper assembly of a frame. It consists of a handle with one or more hook-shaped blades sharpened like gouges, which were drawn across the beam and scooped out a small trough in their wake. Such specialized marking tools have largely been supplanted by their distant relative, the lumber crayon.

Cutting tools — We rely mostly on 4-pt. crosscut saws and ripsaws with the standard tooth pattern. These cut well and are easy to sharpen, although it's hard to find saws with such coarse teeth. A pruning or docking saw can serve as a crosscut, and, for a ripsaw, either refile a docking saw or have a reliable saw doctor retooth a good saw for you. Its edge should be straight or slightly bellied to counter the tendency to leave a high spot in the center when sawing down to a line.

A mallet is for striking chisels when chopping joints, also for driving pegs and pounding joints home. We use 3-lb. mallets, with a cylindrical iron head filled with renewable rawhide inserts. Wooden mallets don't stand up to steel-hooped chisels.

A variety of chisels is useful, starting with the slick: a big 3-in. to 4-in. wide paring chisel with a long handle offset to clear the work. The slick is used to surface large areas, and is pushed (never struck). Framing chisels are standard. We cut mostly 2-in. and 1½-in. mortises, and employ 2-in., 1½-in. and 1¼-in. chisels. A chisel of slightly smaller than nominal dimensions is useful when chopping the ends of mortises, lest the tool become inextricably wedged in the joint. If you're like me and rely on the flatness of the backs (unbeveled side) of chisels, you'll probably have to resort to imported tools.

The corner chisel is currently out of favor in my shop—when using it you are cutting two surfaces at once and so need twice the concentration. They're also a nuisance to sharpen. I find a sharp framing chisel perfectly adequate.

A large (1-in., 1½-in.) bevel-edged chisel is useful for cleaning up in acute angles (inside dovetails) along with a small (¼-in., ⅜-in.) cabinetmaker's chisel for getting into even more restricted areas. I should mention that green oak corrodes steel almost instantaneously. Never leave a chisel in a mortise, and oil your tools after use. A hatchet is invaluable for roughing-out if you work by hand.

The plane is the unsung hero among timber-framing tools. A bench-rabbet plane (Stanley #10, Record #010, also known as a coachmaker's rabbet or jack rabbet) is a versatile tool for cleaning up and flattening out surfaces in timber work. We use a plane to knock off discontinuities around knots and

Measuring and marking tools include (clockwise) a power-return tape, combination square, marking gauges, steel rafter square, templates and scribes.

Cutting tools include a boring machine, chisels, planes and mallets. The large mallet (called a commander, beetle or persuader) weighs 30 lb., and is used to drive parts of the framework together. The drawbore, or drift pin (forefront) is used to align drawbored holes in mortises and tenons prior to inserting a wooden pin.

checks, to level crowned surfaces before marking out, as well as to dress housings and finish cheeks (and sometimes shoulders) of tenons.

A drawknife is used to remove bark from waney corners and, with a spokeshave, to cut decorative chamfers on beams.

The pre-19th-century tool used for boring out waste before chopping mortises was the *T*-auger. The modern carpenter has recourse to a ½-in. electric drill or drill press. Historically sandwiched in between, the boring machine had a brief but glorious career. The machine is placed on the timber and sat on by the workman. The coffee-grinder handles give tremendous leverage, and when the desired depth is reached (in-

dicated by a scale on the side of the machine or by a built-in depth stop) a set of gears is engaged to retract the bit and most of the chips. Boring machines are also used to drill peg holes. They are a joy to use, a good alternative to electricity.

If you do your drilling electrically, use a powerful (6 amps or more), slow-spinning reversible ½-in. (or larger) electric drill with long handles, and take care when you run into knots or other dense places in the wood that the bit continues to spin rather than the drill. Locating large (2-in.) bits is a problem. The shank of 2-in. Scotch pattern augers can be cut short and chucked. Multispur and other brad-point bits can be used in a drill press, although bits without a twist may have trouble clearing chips in green wood. If you use a drill press, you want to have either the machine or the beam on wheels, and both should be leveled up.

Both drill and drill press have handicaps: With a portable drill, the bit must be squared to the timber surface and held square while drilling. The immobility of a drill press (wheels notwithstanding) makes locating bits over centers tedious.

The circular saw is the most useful power tool in timber framing. Try to find a saw that will cut at least halfway through the stock you are using. This is invaluable for long rip cuts (for scarf joints, flared posts, etc.).

The power plane is for surfacing timbers. Far and away the best machine on the market is a Japanese import (Makita), which planes a 6⅛-in. swath and (when sharp) leaves a glassy surface. You can contact Makita at 12950 E. Alondra Blvd., Cerritos, Calif. 90701, for distributors.

Layout — Layout is the art and science of setting out joints on timber surfaces, and accurate layout is the foundation of workmanlike timber framing. If you can't lay out a joint correctly, then it doesn't matter how carefully it is cut. But if you can, then in nine out of ten cases the cutting will follow almost automatically. The principles of layout in timber joinery are basically the same as those in furniture joinery, with one important difference. The cabinetmaker can overcome most of the spatial orientation problems that are the bane of accurate layout simply by trueing up the stock before marking it out. This is out of the question when working with heavy timber. So, unless you have exceptional skill with adze or broadaxe, or know of a mill which can provide beams that are uniformly straight in length, flat in width, free of twist, square, cut exactly to nominal size and free of defects, you will have to learn to cope somehow with the irregularities in the timber. Even if you have a timber sizer, a massive four-sided thickness planer capable of dressing beams to dimension, you will still have to deal with dimensional instability, knots, checks and twisting. Here are some of the anomalies that make timber layout difficult:

Bow (or sweep) in length—This is probably due to stresses locked into the tree during its growth. When the slabs that reinforce the tree against internal bending stress are removed, the remaining timber, sufficiently weakened, bends or bows.

Crown in width (the same as cup in boards)—Shrinkage in boxed-heart timbers usually causes initially flat surfaces of beams to become convex.

Twist—Again due to internal tensions in the wood. In some species timbers twist as they come off the saw, while in others they may twist as the timber dries.

Taper in length—This may be uniform from end to end or irregular, and is probably due to a milling fault.

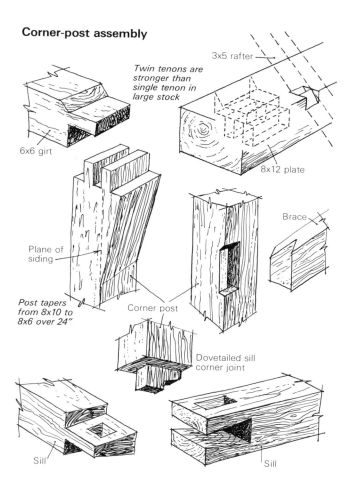

Twin tenons are stronger than single tenon in large stock

3x5 rafter

6x6 girt

8x12 plate

Brace

Plane of siding

Corner post

Post tapers from 8x10 to 8x6 over 24"

Dovetailed sill corner joint

Sill

Sill

The corner post of a barn for sheep (above) is taken apart in the diagram at right. Author used the tapered post to support an unusually wide plate, in order to increase eave overhang from the steeply sloping gambrel rafters.

Faults—Wane, knots, checks, shakes, seams (ingrowths of bark), pitch pockets or decay may not affect the shape of the beam, but they will affect its structural adequacy.

Dimension—The size of roughsawn beams rarely corresponds exactly to nominal dimensions. Variations of ¼ in. to ⅜ in. are not unusual.

Square—Most timbers are sawn out of square. Departures from square of ⅛ in. to ¼ in. are not uncommon—in fact, it is unusual to find a timber in which all four angles are within 1/16 in. of square.

Many of these obstacles to precise layout can be overcome by careful selection of wood for a given job. Some pointers:

Measure beams in length carefully, and avoid locating defects in joints. Checks and shakes should be kept away from the ends of beams where shear stress is greatest. Serious faults should be avoided altogether.

Concentrate knots in the upward (or compression) side of beams and joists, and avoid using bowed timber in posts. Traditional wisdom prescribes laying out bowed beams from a chalk centerline. The bow, however, puts the middle portion of the beam off in left field, causing problems with joints in that area (too much wood on one side, not enough on the other). Better to cut such pieces up into shorter lengths, or discard them. Best of all, use them crown-up as joists or girts, where some upward camber is desirable to offset eventual deflection under load.

A small amount of twist is okay in timbers whose surfaces are not functional (such as interior posts). Use winding sticks plus chisel and/or plane cross grain to bring the surfaces of

different joints into alignment. Pieces of small cross section (especially joists) with a slight twist will flex and straighten out when driven home. Serious twist, however, is an almost impossible problem. Some badly twisted beams may be usable for framing when cut into shorter lengths, otherwise cut them up for cribbing or blocking.

After you have given the timbers their job assignments, you can cope with the layout. The fundamental differences in layout methods are not so much in how layout is performed, but rather in how you prepare the stock. One approach is essentially to ignore irregularities and to mark the beams as if they were cut perfectly or had already been trued up. Accommodate imperfections during a trial assembly by trimming or kerfing the joints where necessary. Each joint must then be numbered so that it may be reassembled correctly.

The opposite of this approach, and the one I prefer, is mass production, using standardized dimensions and interchangeable parts. Some preliminary work must be done on parts of a timber *before* it is laid out to ensure uniformity of size and shape, but preassembly and numbering are unnecessary. For each particular set of joints, create a model timber, that is, an imaginary true beam that will fit entirely within any of the actual timbers you have to work with. I usually establish a dressed dimension of ¼ in. less than nominal. For instance, I find that a nominal 6x8 measures at least 5¾ in. by 7¾ in. and no more than 6¼ in. by 8¼ in. 99% of the time. Thus, I dress 8-in. beams down to 7¾ in. at joints (and make accommodation for pieces up to 8¼ in.).

Once the working size is determined, you need only dress

Layout example

1. Upon close examination, a nominal 8x8 timber rarely measures 8 in. on a side. The faces usually are not flat, nor is it square in cross section.

 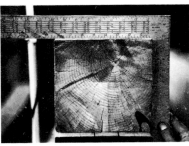

8

2. At the start of a framing job, survey the timbers and choose a working dimension that will fit inside all the real beams—for example, 7¾ in. by 7¾ in.

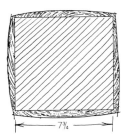

7¾

3. To avoid laborious surfacing without resorting to cut-and-try for each joint, dress all the timbers to working size, but only in the area of each joint. For many joints, this means merely planing a shallow flat.

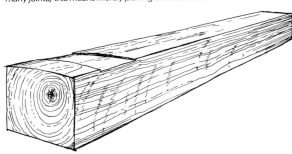

4. However, where a major beam joins a post, it is good practice to house it fully within the post, lest all the weight be borne by the tenon alone. For example, an 8x8 corner post is to be mortised on two sides, to accept the tenons on front and end girts.

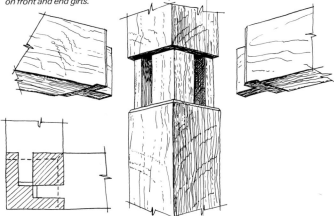

5. Find the corner closest to 90°. This will become the outside corner of the building and the sides meeting here will be designated as face side and edge. If no corner is 90°, choose the one that is closest but greater.

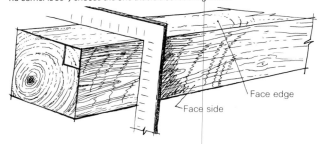

Face edge
Face side

6. Measure to locate the top of the finished post. Because there is no square end to measure from, make a small hand-saw kerf at the zero point in the arris (corner) where face side and edge meet, and set the end of the tape in the kerf. Square across and gauge the depth of the housing from the face side or edge. If the face side and edge are crowned, plane them flat in the area of the joint.

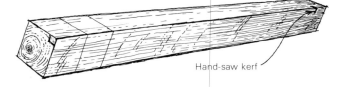

Hand-saw kerf

the timber down to size *right at the location of the joint.* By setting joints in shallow housings or gains you avoid the impossible and unnecessary task of trueing up the entire beam. In timber framing, the surface of the beam doesn't play an active role except in floors and outside walls, where the timber surface should be more or less correct to accommodate finish flooring and sheathing.

As in furniture joinery, choose a face edge and side, and mark the timber in relation to these surfaces. Floor and roof beams are ordinarily laid out from their top sides to provide an even surface for nailing floor and roof boards. Likewise, timbers set in outside walls should be gauged from the outside for a smooth surface for sheathing. In other locations, the face side or edge can be chosen arbitrarily, although it's wise to lay out all members in a given bent or wall of a building from the same side.

Beams are laid out from arris to arris (corner to corner). Because most timbers are sawn from the heart of the tree, the differential between radial and tangential shrinkage causes the surfaces of beams to become convex during seasoning.

Therefore, it is necessary to flatten the surface in joint areas with a plane before laying out a joint.

Knots (and checks) in the surface of a timber often cause a slight ripple on the face of the sawn beam, which can throw the steel square off. Check beams for straightness in length before squaring across and plane off any bumps. Always square from the face edge and side of the piece in question.

Corrective surgery is required only on two, or at most three, sides of any timber. First of all, in all applications (within the limits set by knots, bow, etc.) the carpenter should select as the face edge and side of any timber the two most nearly perpendicular adjacent surfaces. This is especially important in corner posts. When the face side/edge angle is square, only the joints in the two off-sides need be housed. When this happy situation does not occur, then one face surface (side or edge) must be selected as primary, and the other squared to it. Thus a corollary principle: If a face edge/side angle of 90° does not occur in the timber, select an angle of greater than 90° and dress down to square. Angles of less than 90° should not be used because they cannot be corrected without causing

7. *The housing in which the beam fits will be between ¾″ and 1″ deep, depending on the actual size of the post. Set a gauge at 7″, and from the face side mark the surface of the housing for the mortise opposite.*

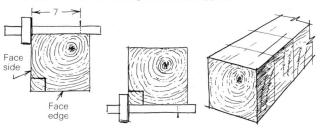

If the reference corner is not 90°, use the framing square to determine how much compensation is necessary and set the marking gauge accordingly.

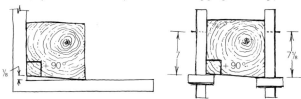

8. *Use a crosscut saw or a circular saw to cut shy of the line and make a series of parallel cuts at intervals a little wider than your chisel. Only the end cuts are necessary, but the others ensure against sloping grain and make it easier to chop out waste. Be careful if you use a circular saw: When the housing depth is gauged from the side opposite the mortise, the surface on which the saw rides may not be parallel with the plane of the housing. Check housing depth on both sides and set the saw for the shallower. Then chisel out the waste from the edges inward, to avoid splitting below the line on the far side. Pare or plane cross-grain down to the line, from the edges into the middle.*

9. *Rotate the beam and from the face edge lay out and cut the gain for the opposite mortise. Now add mortise and tenon (next page).*

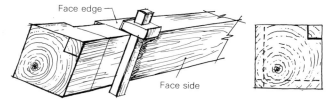

10. *Notice that in this situation the depth of the tenon must be reduced to 7¾″, and the resulting shoulder on both the tenon and the housing must be chamfered for a neat fit.*
When two beams intersect in the same post, their inside vertical shoulders must also be chamfered to avoid interference. (See fig. 4)

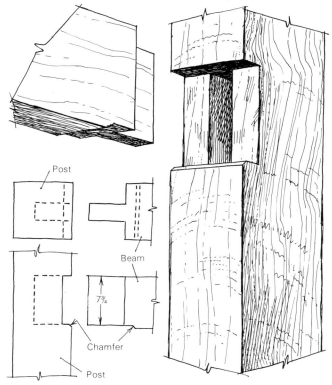

discontinuities (at the corner where face edge and side meet) that make accurate measurement impossible. In beams (joists, girts, plates, etc.) this primary surface is normally the top, while in exterior wall posts it is the outside.

In practice in our shop, pieces 4 in. by 6 in. or smaller are usually run through a thickness planer and then worked up with stationary tools as much as possible. The bulk of beams 6 in. by 6 in. and larger makes it easier to use portable tools. It depends on personal preference and your equipment. The basic rule is obvious: When it's easier to move the tool than the wood, portable tools are called for. When you get to the point where pieces are light and holding them down becomes a problem, then stationary tools are helpful.

Of course, in a hand-tool shop this is a moot point. My sympathies lie in both directions. My earliest work was done entirely by hand, with the exception of a chain saw to fell the trees and a tractor to drag them out of the woods. I peeled, hewed, sawed, drilled and chiseled with the traditional tools of the housewright, 1800s vintage. And while sawn beams and power saws have supplanted tradition, all of our mortises

(as well as most peg holes) are still drilled out with the boring machine and chiseled by hand.

To those who see this layout scheme as excessively laborious, I would point out some mitigating conditions. First of all, joinery in any building is concentrated in posts. And it is always prudent framing practice to house beams into posts in any case, lest all of the weight carried by a girder rest on its tenon alone. Housings also restrain timbers from twisting. In addition, trimming male members (tenons, lap tongues) to size is a minor matter. Finally, recall that the standardizing of parts eliminates the need for trial assembly.

Cutting the mortise and tenon
Consider a tenoned girt joining a mortised post. In plan view (next page, top right), you can see that two boxed-heart pieces of equivalent species and moisture content tend to move together—as the tenon shrinks (or swells) so does the mortise. If the joint is cut well, the cheeks of the tenon remain snug in the mortise.

Things don't look so good in section. The tenon shrinks in

height, but the mortise, being long grain, does not, which leaves a gap. The shoulder also tends to pull away as the post shrinks. The remedy for this situation is drawboring and pegging the joint, which causes the post to shrink toward the beam instead of away from it. Drawboring also slightly offsets the loss of rigidity, but the real answer to that is integral diagonal bracing of the whole frame. The tenon only withdraws when it is on a beam. When the tenon is at either end of a post or rafter, gravity prevails. Shrinkage also causes slop in the lap joints used for joists. Using dovetail joinery is one way to counteract this problem. As the male dovetail shrinks in width, the female dovetail shrinks at right angles across it. The net result is, the two shrink together. If the joint is properly proportioned, this action compensates for the shrinkage almost perfectly. Even if the joint does happen to become loose, the male dovetail can only withdraw slightly before it tightens up again.

I will illustrate cutting the basic joint between post and girt, and then describe other joints that can be made with similar procedures.

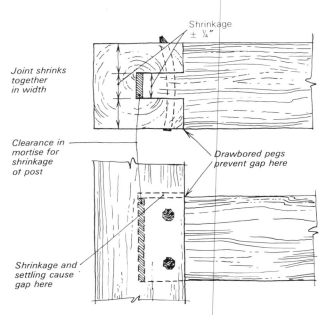

1. Here, an 8x8 oak post is mortised for a central tenon 2 in. thick and 4 in. long on the end of a 8x8 girt. The girt is housed ¾ in. into the post, and secured with two 1-in. octagonal pegs. For photographic purposes, we planed the timber clean. Normally, we cut the joints in rough timber and plane just before raising.

2. Gauge the mortise from the face edge (or side). Mark the centers for drilling out waste (and mark for the peg holes at the same time). Our mortise gauges have three spurs—one for the centerline—so it's merely a matter of measuring lengthwise and ticking off the centers. I deepen these marks with an automatic center-punch so the worm on the auger drops right on. The wedge-shaped worm on a boring-machine auger tends to close up checks, shifting the bit sideways so where there is a surface check within the mortise, adjust the drilling center to compensate. Once you've started the drill you're committed.

3. Bits should equal or be slightly smaller than the width of the mortise. I drill out as much waste as possible, and bore as many holes as will fit just touching or slightly overlapping. Make sure the bit is square to the surface of the housing. The end holes should always be flush with the end of the mortise, regardless of the spacing in between. Boring machines often have a depth scale engraved on their sides, but it's better to make a stop. When all the holes are bored to the same depth (about 4¼ in. here), the mortise will have a clean, flat bottom, leaving no uncertainty as to clearance for the tenon.

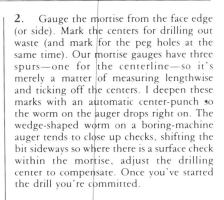

4. I usually bore the end holes first. Then, I hopscotch around so as to drill holes

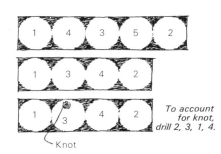

To account for knot, drill 2, 3, 1, 4.

Knot

neither or both of whose neighbors have already been bored, possible in mortises with odd numbers of holes. This is easier on the machinery and least conducive to the bit slowly falling into an adjacent hole. Knots are the greatest cause of this problem, and are best not included within the joint in the first place. Where unavoidable, anticipate how the knot will affect the bit and switch around the drilling order. In the drawing, uneven resistance to the drill caused by the knot in hole number 3 might push the bit into the end hole. Drill number 3 first, leaving solid wood instead of empty space to resist displacement.

5. Chop and then pare out the sides of the mortise (left). Then chop the ends (right), checking with a combination square. For the final passes, the chisel can be set right in the layout lines. In a 2-in. mortise, I usually use a 2-in. chisel for the sides and a 1½-in. of 1¼-in. chisel for the ends. A 2-in. chisel in a 2-in. mortise is liable to get caught in end grain. After the mortise is completed, drill the peg holes, making sure the drill runs parallel to the surface of the housing.

6. Locate the tenon in the length of the girt and, working from the face edge and side, square around for both the end and the shoulders. You will have two parallel lines 4 in. apart running around the beam. Squaring around the timber is like surveying land — you want to end up where you began. If the last line doesn't link up, something is wrong. Cut the waste off the end of the beam by sawing around all four sides rather than straight across. With a hand saw, this means starting a kerf all around and then cutting from corner to corner. With a circular saw, set it to cut halfway through the smaller dimension and work around in one direction, cutting on three sides. If the blade won't reach this far, cut all four sides and finish with a hand saw. These procedures minimize error. Most circular saws don't hold an angle in heavy work, so check frequently for square. If the angle setting has a plastic knob, replace it with a nut and tighten with a wrench.

Cut on the wrong side of the line. This enhances visibility when using a circular saw and adds clearance for the end of the tenon. Clearance allows for shrinkage of the post—a green oak 8x8 may shrink as much as 7/16 in. along a side. Allow at least ¼ in. between the tenon and the bottom of the mortise. In joints with opposed in-line tenons, the combined length of the tenons should be ½ in. less than the distance between shoulders. If you plan to use a circular saw to cut the tenon cheeks, chisel and plane the end of the beam flat and square.

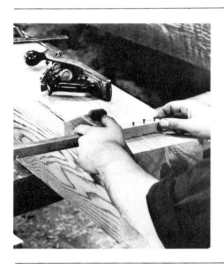

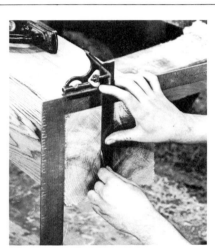

7. The layout may now be completed. Because girts are floor beams, the primary reference surface is usually the top and the secondary one the outside. Flatten these face surfaces with the plane. If they are square to one another, the tenon may be marked with the gauge at the same setting as for the mortise. If the angle is slightly greater than 90°, dress the side down to square and then gauge. In the unhappy event that the angle is less (or substantially greater) than 90°, gauge the top surface and square down across the end (right). Then gauge the bottom of the tenon with the gauge, resetting so that it lines up with the marks on the end of the beam.

8. When using hand tools, saw the shoulders first. I use a 7-point crosscut saw. In the absence of large knots and if the grain is straight or slopes uphill toward the shoulder, the cheeks can be chopped out with a mallet and chisel (or hatchet). Leave 1/32 in. to 1/16 in. to pare or plane away. If the grain surprises you and starts to run downhill, chop the cheeks carefully across the grain, always working into the center. Where there are knots or difficult grain, saw the cheeks with a coarse ripsaw. Again, it's wise to leave a little bit to clean up with chisel, slick or rabbet plane.

9. When using a circular saw, the order is reversed. First saw the cheeks close to but not on the line. As you can see from the picture, the saw table rides on the end of the timber. When sawing the shoulders, at least one cheek is liable to be out of line with the surface of the timber, so check the depth of cut on both sides and saw shallow rather than deep. The shoe of the saw must ride on the inboard side of the shoulder because waste will move at the end of the cut.

10. After the waste is removed, finish the cheeks by paring or planing. Check cheeks and shoulders for flatness and square, and correct where necessary. If you are not planning to preassemble your framework, mark and drill offset peg holes. In assembly, the shoulders of the tenon will be pulled home as the pegs are driven in.

There are several common variations on the mortise and tenon. For a through mortise, mark both sides and drill and chisel halfway from each side.

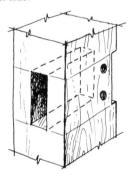

Diagonal braces are usually anchored with the chase mortise and brace tenon. When making the tenon with power tools, saw the end of the brace at 45°, then saw the single cheek, saw the shoulder, saw the square end, and finally drill the peg hole. With hand tools, saw the shoulder before chopping cheek.

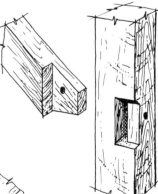

The tenon can go into an ordinary square mortise, since the sloping top of the tenon is not a bearing surface. Or, you can cut a chase mortise by drilling one less hole and chopping back at 45° or more to the beam surface, always checking for clearance.

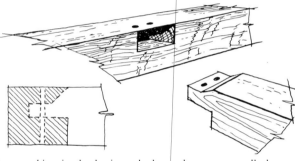

When working in the horizontal plane, the tenon usually has an undersquinted (sloping) entrant shoulder. Gauge from the flattened upper surface of the summer beam or girt. Cut the mortise in the usual way, then scribe or gauge a depth line on its inside surface. Saw down to this line at either end and at several intermediate points, using a hand saw. Chop out the waste, pare and check with a sliding bevel. You'll have to adjust the location of the peg holes to allow for the housing.

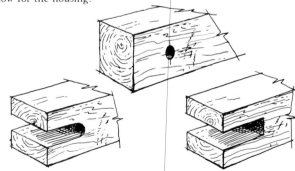

The tenon is unchanged when the mortise is open except for the location of the single peg. Lay out the mortise as if it were a tenon, then drill one full-width hole at the closed end (drill halfway from either side). Saw the sides of the mortise as if they were tenon cheeks, except the kerf is on the other side of the line. Paring is difficult and planing impossible inside an open mortise, so saw right up to the line. Knock out the waste and chop the end square, again working from both sides.

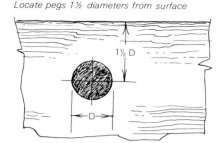

Locate pegs 1½ diameters from surface

Holes in tenon are offset...   *...so pegs will draw joint tight.*

Pegs — Wooden pins or trunnels (treenails) are the primary fastening devices in timber construction. Wood for pegs should be strong and decay resistant. I like white oak pins in softwood frames and locust pegs in oak frames. Green pegs are easy to work and limber enough to snake through a drawbored joint. The peg seasons with the bend dried in, preventing withdrawal. I use dry wood which swells as it takes on moisture from the green framework, locking into place. Pins can be square, hexagonal, octagonal or round, either parallel-sided or tapered. Hexagonal or octagonal pegs drive more easily than square with less distortion of the wood, yet their corners still bite in the walls of the hole. Round pegs should be dry and 1/32 in. or 1/16 in. oversize. Tapered pegs start easily in drawbored holes, but fit tightly when pounded home. Untapered pegs should be pointed to ease entry. If a peg is too blunt it will catch and damage itself and the joint.

Peg size is expressed as the diameter of the hole bored, and ranges between ¾ in. and 1 in. for light and heavy house framing, 1⅜ in. for ship planking and 2 in. for covered-bridge framing. There are many procedures for making wooden pins. Here are several:

Split and shave blocks of wood with a froe and work up the rough pegs with drawknife and spokeshave. Shaved pins can be of any shape and may be tapered or parallel-sided. Shaving works well in straight grain, but is trying and tedious in wavy wood, which is best worked up by turning or sawing.

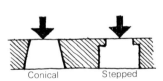

Conical   Stepped

Peg-forming holes drilled through steel plate

Drive split or sawn blanks through progressively smaller holes in a steel plate. The holes are all relieved on their bottom sides. Another type of peg-former is a hollow iron tube sharpened on its upper end and fixed above a hole in the bench. Rough-hewn blanks are driven through the tube.

Straight or tapered round pegs can be turned on a lathe. Or you can produce round pegs with a witchet or rounding plane. Flat-sided pegs can be machined from sawn lumber. Cut boards into square strips with a table saw and knock the corners off with the saw or jointer. When shaving or sawing, the blank should be left two to four pegs long and cut to length and pointed after shaping. Pegs should be long enough for the pointed part to protrude from the joint.

Drawboring — Drawboring is the technique of offsetting peg holes in mortised-and-tenoned pieces so the joint will be pulled home as the peg is driven in. You can do this by drilling the hole in the mortised piece, assembling the joint and marking the tenon through the hole. Or offset the holes by

careful measurement and layout. Either way, make sure that the hole in the tenon is offset *toward* the shoulder.

Amounts of offset vary with size and species of timber and peg, type of joint and carpenter. Best is to make up some sample joints and try out different amounts. For reference, here are some of our latest recipes using 1-in. pegs.

The basic rule of thumb for locating pegs is to center them 1½ peg diameters away from the mortised surface.

Use a single, centered peg in 4-in. wide mortises. For 6-in. to 10-in. wide joints, divide the width of the tenon by four and use two pegs at the ¼ and ¾ points as measured from the face side or edge (for an 8-in. joint pins would be set at 2 in. and 6 in.). In very wide tenons three pegs can be used. In the other direction, center holes 1½ in. from the edge of the mortised piece and offset around 3/16 in. in the tenon.

To resist tension, peg holes in chase mortises should be set where they have as much wood behind the pegs as possible.

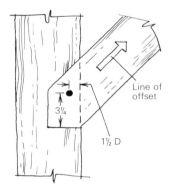

Line of offset

For 3x5 braces with 4-in. deep tenons this is about 3¼ in. from the square end of the tenon. Keep centers 1½ in. in from the edge of mortises and offset about ⅛ in., but at 45° to the shoulder of the tenon— along the line of the brace. In open mortises a 1-in. pin should be set 1½ in. from both the shoulder of the tenon and the closed end of the mortise. Offset ⅛ in. or less along a line perpendicular to the miter angle between the two pieces (in rafters this miter angle is a plumb line).

Before pounding in pegs, check alignment by looking through the peg holes. If you don't see mostly daylight, the joint must be tightened. Knock it home or clamp up if the persuader does not avail. The traditional tool for pulling joints together is the drift or drawbore pin—a long tapered rod of metal that is tapped into the peg hole and then withdrawn. If none of these methods closes the joint, the peg hole can be partially or totally redrilled in place.

Use a mallet rather than a hammer when you are pounding in a peg, since steel may mushroom or split the end. You can use a little wax or oil on the surface of the pins to ease their entry, but if one does start to mushroom, tighten a hose clamp around its end. This will hold the fibers together while you pound the peg in. □

Ed Levin, of Canaan, N.H., has been a housewright for more than a decade.

Scribed mortise-and-tenon joinery in this 29-ft. trussed log bridge make all its parts securely interdependent.

Trussed Log Bridge
Scribed joints for structural strength

by Monroe Robinson

I hadn't thought of log work as being within the realm of fine woodworking until I saw the work of a master, Lee Cole, several years ago. After watching Cole work on a few jobs, I was ready to start a log project that had been offered to me eight years earlier: a 29-ft. trussed log bridge spanning a creek on a wilderness homestead at Lake Clark, some 140 air miles southeast of Anchorage, Alaska. The bridge was needed to connect the buildings that the owner had built on both sides of the creek. It needed to be strong and wide enough to support the front-end loader used on the homestead and to aesthetically complement the log buildings and the wilderness environment. It also required a rock foundation because the creek floods annually.

The project was started in the spring of 1978 when the creek flowed at its lowest. Two of us chipped through gravel and poured a concrete footing in water 18 in. below the water level in the creek. Before the spring breakup we built stone walls up above the high-water level of the creek. After we got the main logs, we finished up the walls about 8 ft. high and constructed a shelf on the top of each wall for the bridge to sit on. These had to be slightly different heights above the water line to accommodate the taper of the logs. All the rock, gravel and sand that we used we collected from the lake shore. Only the cement and reinforcing steel were flown to the site.

We obtained a permit to cut white spruce from federally managed land on Lake Clark, then selected, felled and peeled about two dozen logs. We skidded them into the lake, lashed together a raft with chain and towed it three miles across the lake, right to the homestead. We sawed some of the logs, which were 10 in. to 16 in. in diameter, into 4-in. thick decking boards using an Alaska chain-saw mill. We squared up the sides of the boards but left the natural taper of the logs to get maximum decking.

The three main logs (one chord for each side of the bridge and one in the center) were moved into place on rollers and oriented bow-side down to increase the bow during drying, since the objective was to have a bridge that would be level or just slightly higher at the center. The decking was temporarily laid upon these logs, and the remainder of the logs put on a rack. All the wood was allowed to dry for a year.

The following summer we removed the decking and turned the main logs over to have them bow-side up. We sawed a flat along the tops, making each log bow exactly ¾ in. Next we re-rounded the logs with a drawknife, leaving only a 2-in. wide flat along the top of each log for attaching the decking. A small flat leaves less area where water can collect.

The log joints in the bridge differ from the joints in a log house. In a house one log is set above its eventual resting place, scribed to match the contours of the log beneath it, rolled over, notched out to the scribed line and then rolled back into place. If the joint doesn't close up tightly, a log can always be notched a little more without affecting those already in place. When the fit is tight enough the builder goes on to the next log.

With a bridge, all the logs on each side are dependent on one another. None can be shortened, rotated or angled differently to help make one joint fit without affecting the fit of the other joints. As the drawing shows, the bridge has mortise-and-tenon joints at both ends of the brace logs and at the lower ends of the outer diagonal web logs. All-thread bolts run through the length of the brace and vertical web logs, and the joints between all the logs are scribed. These make construction rather more complicated than stacking the walls of a house. No part of the structure is really in place until all the parts fit.

Before any joints are cut, the centerline of each log must be determined. This establishes the path of the bore in those logs to be connected by all-thread and helps in laying out the joints and positioning the logs in relation to one another. Since the true centerline is concealed within the log, I projected it onto the outer surface. First measure across the end of the log from any four directions, marking a line at the center of each measure. With these four lines, a point can be picked that most closely represents the center of that end. Now using a carpenter's level, mark a plumb and a horizontal line through the centerpoint extending to the edges. Do the same on the other end of the log. Then snap four chalk lines along the length of the log connecting the lines on the log ends. These chalk and end lines can now be aligned with a carpenter's level to position the log precisely as desired—vertically, horizontally, or at any angle or rotation.

Next the vertical web logs and the braces are bored along

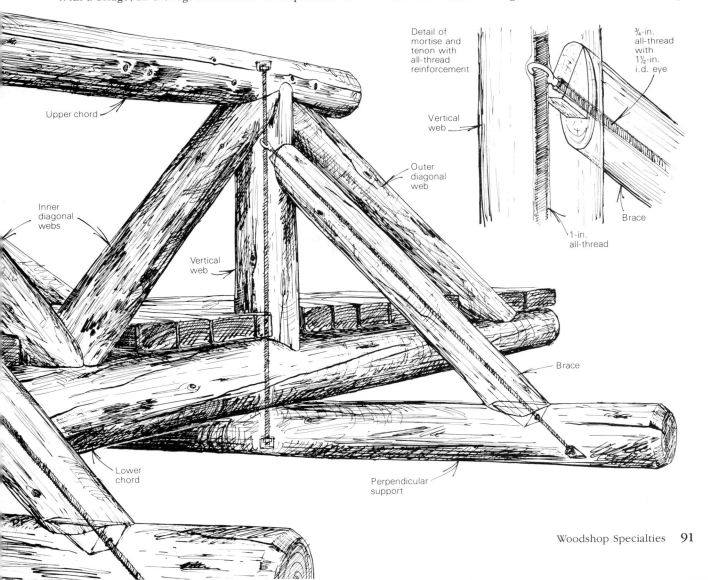

Detail of mortise and tenon with all-thread reinforcement

Vertical web

Outer diagonal web

Upper chord

Inner diagonal webs

Vertical web

¾-in. all-thread with 1½-in. i.d. eye

Brace

1-in. all-thread

Brace

Lower chord

Perpendicular support

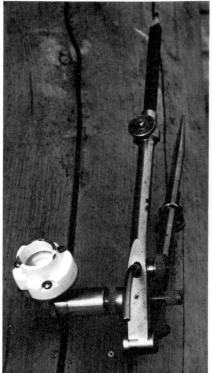

Author uses a ship auger with extensions to bore for the all-thread that secures the vertical web and brace logs, photo right. A pair of Starrett No. 85 dividers with a custom-made, adjustable target-bubble level, below, scribes the contour of one log onto the end of an adjoining log. The level helps keep the points of the divider plumb while scribing. Below right, Robinson has oriented the vertical web log horizontally to scribe its contour to the end of a brace log.

their length to receive the all-thread. We used a ship auger with several extensions (photo, top) to drill 1½-in. holes for the 1-in. all-thread in the vertical webs, and 1¹⁄₁₆-in. holes in the braces for ¾-in. all-thread. To assure that the hole ran the center of the log, I drilled half the length of the log from each end, meeting in the center. Ream out the juncture by drilling past it. It's best to drill these holes in the rough logs before cutting any joints, so that if a log has to be scrapped because a hole went astray, you won't have put wasted work into it.

Now the ends of each log must be scribed to match the contours of the adjoining logs, and in the case of the braces and lower ends of the outside diagonal web logs, tenons must be cut. To scribe the contour of one log onto another, I used a pair of Starrett No. 85 dividers with an adjustable target-bubble level, which I had custom made (photo, above). You can get one from C. Norman Brown, S.R.A. Box 4008Q, Anchorage, Alaska 99507, or make one yourself with compasses and a bubble level. With the bubble adjusted so the tip of the steel point can be kept plumb to the tip of the pencil, an exact transfer of the contour of a horizontal log can be scribed to the end of an adjoining log, whether that log is plumb or diagonal. It requires positioning the log to be scribed within a few inches directly over the horizontal log.

We scribed the bottom ends of the vertical and diagonal logs first, positioning them exactly above the spot where they would sit on the lower chord or on the perpendicular log, and at the proper angle. Waste from the decking provided braces for the log while scribing. The contour of the horizontal log is scribed on the end of the adjoining log, and the waste is removed using chain saw, ax and gouges. In the case of the

From *Fine Woodworking* magazine (March 1982) 33:78-81

Gouges are used to finish shaping the scribed shoulder of a brace log, above. The hole, which will receive the all-thread, was bored the entire length of the log before the tenon was cut. Below, a finished joint.

outer diagonal webs and braces, stock for tenons must be left. To lay out the tenon, we measured 1 in. on either side of the centerline for the cheeks, and 1½ in. on the other side of the centerpoint from the acute angle of the log's end for the edge of the tenon; the tenon has three shoulders. We used a handsaw to saw down the cheeks, and removed the waste with gouges and chisels (photo, top).

The mortise for this tenon is located using the chalkline on the horizontal piece (measuring 1 in. on either side of it) and the scratch from the steel tip of the dividers when the pencil end scribed the contour onto the adjoining log. This scratch marks the farther end of the mortise; the other end can be judged by eye. The photo above shows the relationship between the mortise and tenon.

The joints connecting the top ends of all the diagonal logs

to the vertical web logs are oriented perpendicular to the joints at the bottom end of these logs. Therefore the scribing technique using the bubble-level dividers cannot be used here; the bubble level only tells you when the divider points are plumb. Instead, I used two different methods to scribe these joints. For the joints between the outer diagonal web logs and the vertical web log and also for the joint between the lower ends of the inner diagonal web logs, I positioned the logs to be matched close together and held the divider points in line with one another, horizontally rather than plumb, without using the level. I set the dividers to mark ½ in. short of the final scribe, then notched out the waste and moved the logs closer for a more accurate rescribing and final fit.

For the other upper joints (between both the brace and inner diagonal web log and the vertical web log) I laid the vertical web log horizontal and then, using a carpenter's level, positioned the upper end of each diagonal log plumb above it at the proper angle. Then it could be scribed using the bubble-level-divider technique described earlier. I could have used this technique for the joint between the outer diagonal web log and the vertical web log, but the former is 10 ft. long and unwieldy to set up.

Before assembly all the joints and drilled holes were given numerous coats of creosote and a solution of pentachlorophenol in fuel oil. The all-threads were coated with grease, and the mortises were filled with enough grease to prevent water from being trapped if it ran in along a crack. The decking and exposed surfaces of the logs were treated with a mixture of 47½% fuel oil, 47½% creosote and 5% pentachlorophenol. Reading later about the health hazards of pentachlorophenol makes me leery about using it again.

To assemble, first the perpendicular support logs were positioned under the lower chord logs using temporary staging built on the creek bed. Then the vertical web logs were positioned, and the holes already bored in their length were used to guide the bit down through the lower chord log and the perpendicular support log. The braces were positioned, and the holes bored in their length were used to guide the bit down through the perpendicular support log and up into the vertical web log to meet the hole in its length. The brace was removed and gouges were used to enlarge the hole in the vertical web log to accommodate a 1½-in. i.d. eye that was coupled to the ¾-in. all-thread running through the brace. The eye was positioned in the mortise and the 1-in. all-thread passed through it, from the top of the vertical web log through the lower chord and perpendicular support logs, where it received a washer and nut for later tightening. The lower end of the all-thread running through the brace also received a nut that was tightened later. Next the outer diagonals were placed, then the inner diagonals. Mortise-and-tenon joints are unnecessary at the bottom of these inner diagonals because they wedge one another in place against the vertical web logs. Mortise-and-tenon joints at the tops of both inner and outer diagonals aren't needed either, because the upper chord log positions the others. The upper chord log was bored for the 1-in. all-thread and all nuts were tightened.

Within a year after construction the bow in the bridge had settled into levelness. □

Monroe Robinson is a woodcarver in Chugiak, Alaska, who also does architectural commissions. Photos by the author, except where noted.

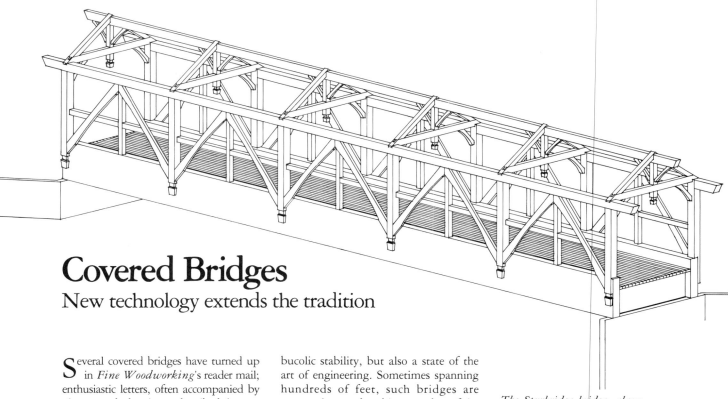

Covered Bridges
New technology extends the tradition

Several covered bridges have turned up in *Fine Woodworking*'s reader mail; enthusiastic letters, often accompanied by photos and drawings, described how a commission to refurbish some venerable wooden trestle, or to erect one anew, had led to a labor of love. Wooden bridges, covered for shelter from the seasons, embody not only our notions of bucolic stability, but also a state of the art of engineering. Sometimes spanning hundreds of feet, such bridges are among the woodworking wonders of the 19th century. The four bridges shown here are exemplary of those being built and rebuilt today, often employing innovative construction features combined with sound, old timber-frame techniques.

The Sturbridge bridge, above, combines modern gluelam girders, which span the stream, with a traditional timber-frame superstructure. The two main girders are connected at intervals by plywood boxes that support the roadbed. Below, the bridge is halfway home.

Gary Childress

From *Fine Woodworking* magazine (May 1984) 46:44-47

Joining timbers and gluelams

When Sanford Homes Inc. asked our design team to construct a covered pedestrian bridge for Sturbridge Village, their development in Englewood, Colo., we jumped at the chance. Our experience is in modern, cost-effective timber-frame houses, and our commitment is toward owner- and community-involved building, so here was a new opportunity to combine tradition, technology and education. We decided on a combination beam/truss bridge, a replica of a 19th-century design, but with modern gluelam members. And we would set aside time throughout construction to accommodate tours from the local schools, an idea that proved popular enough to fill at least part of most afternoons.

The Sturbridge bridge is 75 ft. long and contains more than 15,000 bd. ft. of timber. The lower chords are two 48-in. thick beams glued up from 2x10 fir by the Georgia Pacific Co., which custom-laminates such beams to meet the stringent specifications of state engineering inspectors. The beams are lag-bolted to eleven 10-ft. long plywood box joists, which support the roadbed of the bridge. The face of one of these can be seen at the right end of the bridge, just under the road planking, in the drawing on the facing page. Atop this substructure we erected six bents of 10x10 and 6x8 fir, trussed together with 4x10 braces, all the joints pinned mortise-and-tenon. The roof itself, along with the siding, is boarded with red cedar.

Historically, covered bridges were assembled on the bank and pulled across the river by a team of oxen, hence the term "bridge pull." We proceeded similarly, but instead of oxen we used a 140-ton crane. This required careful selection of the bridge-building site in relation to the bridge's abutments. The crane's reach was such that the bridge had to be approached from the side, lifted, and rotated into position. The photo on the facing page shows the structure moving toward its abutments.

In contrast to the stark relief of 14,000-ft. Rocky Mountain peaks, the covered bridge over this 20-ft. stream-bed offers pedestrians a small sense of security. More than bridging the stream-bed, the project spans old and new technologies, and has become a focal point of the community it serves.

—*Stewart Elliott,*
Dovetail Limited, Boulder, Colo.

Split-ring framing

Our client, Ed Rush, was looking for a steel I-beam bridge, covered by a wooden shed, to span the 50-ft. creek that borders his property in Lebanon, Mo. We offered a contemporary alternative: a multiple king-post truss bridge of wood joined not with mortise-and-tenon and trunnel, but with modern timber-fastening hardware.

Wooden covered bridges, while relatively common in the United States during the early 1800s, gave way by 1900 to all-metal truss bridges. Inadequate wood preservation made the wooden joints—particularly compression joints—susceptible to rot and early failure. A more dramatic danger was the shower of sparks from wood- and coal-fired locomotives, which caused the immolation of hundreds of covered bridges.

Our solution? Prohibit steam locomotives from our bridge, and use split-ring timber fasteners (from TECO,

Photos: Dan Chiles

Chiles' multiple king-post bridge.

5530 Wisconsin Ave., Chevy Chase, Md. 20815), which would eliminate traditional water-collecting joints. Our materials list included 10,000 bd. ft. of lumber, consisting mainly of 3x10 white oak for the trusses, pressure-treated 3x8 red oak for the deck, and 1x8 mixed oak for the siding. For roofing we used

Fifty-foot sides were assembled flat, hoisted into place, then connected top and bottom.

TECO

oak shakes handsplit by a local farmer. We estimated our labor (by consulting historical accounts from experienced builders, and taking into consideration electric drills and gasoline chainsaws) to be five man-months.

Early bridge builders sometimes erected temporary pier bridges on which they assembled the permanent timber trusses. We decided that it would be easier to build the two wall trusses on land and then rent a crane to lift them into place. Our first step was to build a large fixture on the site: 55 ft. long, flat to within ⅛ in., and capable of supporting more than 10 tons of green oak. Four-by-four oak stakes braced with 2x6s made up the platform that fit our needs.

The steel rings of the TECO system fortify bolt joints in overlapping timbers. Each ring is sandwiched between two timbers (half its thickness embedded in one timber, half in the other), and it resists shear forces many times the load limit of the bolt alone. Installation entails positioning the timbers, boring the bolt holes, and then disassembling to cut the circular grooves that receive the rings (photo, above left). The timbers

To reinforce bolted lap joints, Chiles inserted split-ring fasteners between the timbers of his bridge. The TECO cutterhead has four grooving bits, and either a center bit, as shown, or a center pilot that follows a hole drilled during mockup assembly. In 3½-in. thick timbers, the 4-in. dia. rings (also available in 2½-in. diameter) can sustain shear loads in excess of 5,000 lb.

are then reassembled, with care not to leave out any of the rings, and cinched together with ¾-in. carriage bolts, some as long as 22 in. When the first wall truss was completed, we built the other one on top of it, making layout easier.

The crane cost $50 an hour, so by the time it arrived one fall Saturday morning, we'd rehearsed our bridge-pulling procedures well. The crane lifted one wall truss, which we braced, then the other into place on the piers, whereupon we connected them with 4x10 oak joists. Next we hoisted 4x8 ceiling beams atop the truss walls, to form a third truss, which strengthened the whole bridge. Atop the ceiling went a roof structure of conventional frame design made of 2x6 rafters and 1x4 battens. We decked the inside, roofed and sided the outside, and our covered bridge was ready to face its first winter.

After three and a half years, the bridge has weathered to a silver gray without benefit of any wood finishes. It looks as if it's been part of the landscape for many years.   —Mike Chiles,
Chiles Power Supply, Inc.,
Springfield, Mo.

Restoring a Long-truss bridge

Shown at right is a photo of the partially reassembled Stoats Mill bridge, which I helped save here in Ripley, W.Va. When Mill Creek watershed site 13 was to flood the area where the old bridge once stood, the U.S. Soil Conservation Service contracted me to move the 105-ft. bridge nine miles to Cedar Lakes Park, restore its deteriorated trusses, and re-erect it across the small lake.

The truss design was patented in 1830 by Col. Stephen H. Long of the U.S. Army Corps of Engineers and it carries his name. The Long truss is unique because it deflects little at midspan, and wear at the joints is minimized by pre-stressing the braces and counterbraces. The Long truss can also be retuned by adjusting an integral wedge system in the joints to compensate for shrinkage and wear.

As we took the joints apart, we discovered that the Stoats Mill bridge had been prefab—all its parts were coded and numbered for assembly. The bridge was originally built in 1887 by local residents, who copied the plan from a nearby bridge instead of paying the pat-

ent holder the usual $1-per-linear-foot royalties. Ironically, although they copied the external design faithfully, they left out the wedges that made Long's design so sturdy. We wrote away for a copy of the original patent, and made the missing parts, installing them as we reassembled the structure.

We set the bridge trusses on abutments of hewn stone taken from other bridge sites, without disturbing the mossy faces of these 2-ton stones. Although we replaced several of the bridge's 8x10 pine members that had rotted due to neglect, we saved every piece we could in order to keep the structure's historic fiber intact. Much of our refurbishing should have been part of the bridge's regular maintenance. I'm encouraged that the state of West Virginia is now working at restoring all of its remaining 16 covered bridges.

The Stoats Mill bridge is particularly graceful for its camber, rising 9 in. at midspan. After rebuilding the bridge, we parked a 4-ton truck and two cars at the center of its deck, and there was less than ¼ in. of deflection at midspan.
                    —Bob Parsons,
Parsons Builders, Ripley, W.Va.

Arched timbers in Oregon

Oregon once had an estimated 450 covered bridges, of which about 50 still survive—at least one in every county except Multnomah. So when the small Multnomah community of Happy Valley needed a bridge, they opted for wood, hoping that they would be able to afford it. We came up with a covered bridge that took advantage of standard prefab parts such as church arches and laminated bridge girders manufactured by Weyerhaeuser. By searching the catalogs for standard parts that could be fit together in unusual ways, we were able to come up with a custom design without incurring the extra cost of custom setups. Accommodating a two-lane highway that carries 1200 vehicles a day, the 65-ft. bridge cost the county a little under $100,000, which is less than they would have had to pay for a steel or concrete bridge. A county leader hailed it as "a bargain and an amenity." We're pretty well pleased with it, too. *—Marshall Turner, Western Wood Structures, Tualatin, Ore.*

Multnomah County's (Ore.) covered bridge, of prefab arched gluelam fir with cedar.

Fly Rods from Split Bamboo
With a hand plane and lots of gadgets

by L. U. Beitz

The anonymous craftsman who in 1859 tried fastening a split-bamboo tip to the butt of a hickory fishing rod started a revolution in rod technology and craftsmanship. Charles F. Murphy of Newark, N.J., soon became the first builder to make a complete six-sided split bamboo rod of Calcutta cane. Previous rods were turned and shaved from the springiest woods available: lancewood, greenheart, ash, hickory. They were heavy by any standard, up to 15 or 20 ounces, and positively limp compared with bamboo.

A typical flyfishing rod before bamboo was about 12 ft. long, consisting of two or three sections connected by thread wrappings or metal ferrules. The rod would have been turned round to about ¾-in. diameter just above the handgrip, and would have tapered smoothly to about ⅛ in. at the tip. When they discovered bamboo, last century's makers reproduced the shape of the rods they already knew. To do this, they split and planed Calcutta cane into triangular sections, tapering in length, then they glued the strips into a hexagonal shape. People tried turning the rods on the lathe to round them, but quickly discovered that turned rods lacked strength—the cane is weakest toward its pith, and every precious fraction of its outside surface must be conserved. You can't sand away protruding edges when you make fly rods. If you do, the rod will be stronger in one direction than in the other, resulting in an erratic action. For the tip of a fly rod, a four-foot sliver of bamboo has to be beveled to a perfect equilateral triangle, and tapered from ⅛ in. to ½2 in. Then five other pieces have to match it exactly—all this using a material that, ounce for ounce, resembles wood less than it does steel (see Bamboo, p. 100).

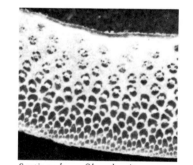

Section shows fiber density.

A fishing rod is basically a spring used to store energy. In spinning or baitcasting rods, the energy is transmitted to a relatively heavy lure that then pulls the light line from the reel. In flyfishing, however, it is the weighty line itself that is cast (almost like snapping a whip), and the nearly weightless fly goes along for the ride. A good caster is able to put as much energy into a long cast as he would into driving a railroad spike—just about all he has. Sometimes that's what it takes to get the fly to the wily trout. A thick rod suffers too much from air resistance. A weak rod can't store enough energy for decent casts—it merely breaks. The test of strength-for-weight makes bamboo the finest natural material for fly rods. Its only competition comes from man-made materials (fiberglass and graphite) that closely imitate its structure—long, stiff fibers in a binding matrix.

Rodmakers since Murphy's day have refined their techniques and their concepts of what a good fly rod should be. The old rods were long: 12 ft. to 15 ft. was not uncommon. Length, in a wooden rod, compensated for weakness—if you couldn't make a long cast, the rod got you halfway there anyway. The early bamboo rods were nearly as heavy as wooden ones. They were way overbuilt, but fishermen took generations to get used to a weak-looking rod. Toward the end of the century, progressive makers (Hardy in England, Leonard in America) introduced lighter and shorter rods at every opportunity. Then Tonkin cane replaced the weaker Calcutta cane. By the mid-forties, fifties, and sixties, master rodcrafters and designers such as Everett Garrison, "Pinky" Gillum, Lyle Dickerson, George H. Halstead and Jim Payne, were making the finest rods ever produced in the world. Their rods are now collector's items, selling for four figures. About a dozen companies are still engaged in bamboo rodcrafting. Although their output is excellent in quality, many people have had a hand in the making of each rod. Some of these production rods are priced in the $500-$600 range. Today, a few dedicated builders carry on the tradition of the hand-split, hand-planed, precisely balanced split-bamboo fly rod. In this article I'll describe the building of such a rod. I've included the taper specifications of a rod by Garrison, from which I made the 7½-footer shown along the bottom of these pages. At the end there's a source list for the materials and equipment you need to try these methods yourself.

Selecting and splitting the cane—Let's start building a two-piece (butt and tip), 7½-ft. fly rod, plus an extra tip. Alternate use of two tips prolongs the life of the rod, and if one tip is damaged while fishing, the angler isn't cast adrift.

The Tonkin cane pole, or culm, runs a standard 12-ft. length, with a diameter of 1¾ in. to 2½ in. Its nodes—humpy rings around the circumference—are closer together toward the bottom, about 10 in. apart, spreading to near 16 in. at the top. It is from the thin-walled top that we plot out the

Author's 7½ ft. split-bamboo fly rod shown actual size, with ebony ferrule plug.

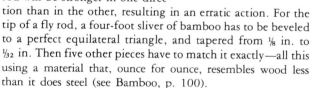

From *Fine Woodworking* magazine (May 1982) 34:68-73

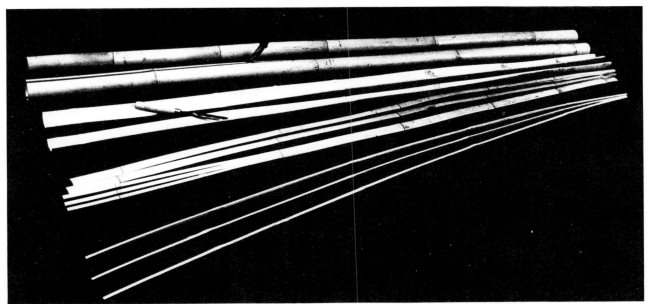

The long fibers in Tonkin cane allow it to be split into many narrow strips that retain lightness, strength and resiliency.

Fig. 1: Strip arrangement

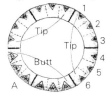

A. To arrange the strips that will become the finished rod, split the culm into at least 18 pieces (dotted lines), choosing pieces for each butt and tip section from adjacent parts of the culm. Tapered triangular strips will be planed from the dense outer part of the culm.

B. Strips will be alternated for balanced action in the glued-up rod.
C. Stagger the brittle nodes to avoid weak spots, then trim rough sections to length before filing and planing.

sections of a 7½-ft. rod. The stouter end can be used for making an 8-ft. or 8½-ft. fly rod; these use thicker strips.

Saw the 12-ft. culm into two 6-ft. lengths. Put aside the thicker piece and place the other piece on the bench to be split up. We'll aim to split strips the full length of the piece, and it's not hard to do—the fibers run very straight.

Study the culm carefully, planning to avoid scuffs, scars, water stains and other imperfections. A few minor water blemishes are bound to show up, since only one culm in a thousand is absolutely perfect in all respects. Look for an overall light-straw color. Greenish culms, or deep yellow ones should be allowed to season several months longer.

Now using a stout knife split the culm down its length into halves, starting at the thicker end. Be careful—bamboo edges can be glass-sharp. Along the U-shaped split half, at each node, is a solid interior wall or dam which must be cut out with a gouge before further splitting. After you've leveled the inside of the culm, split each half into three preliminary pieces, each about 1 in. wide. Then split each of these 1-in. pieces into three or four strips—you'll need at least 18 good strips for the three rod sections. These strips are considerably wider than they will be after planing. Because the culm structure varies slightly in density around its circumference,

number each strip so you can make each rod section from adjacent parts of the culm, as shown in figure 1A. To even out irregularities and keep the rod's action uniform, strips that were adjacent in the culm should be placed opposite each other within each rod section (figure 1B).

Next, stagger the nodes. Lay the six strips that will comprise the tip section of the rod in their proper sequence on the bench. The first strip stays put. Move the next strip about 2 in. along the length of the first. Shift the following strip another 2 in., and so on (figure 1C). This will stagger the nodes in a helix along the finished rod. Check the positions of the nodes along the entire length of the tip. If any are too close together, move the strips a little to balance them out.

Now mark and cut all the wood to length. Cut the 12 strips for the two tip sections to 47 in. long, the butt strips to 46½ in. These lengths allow 1 in. to be cut off each end after the strips have been glued together.

Filing and straightening the nodes—The 18 split strips are considerably oversize at this stage. Before proceeding with the planing, we must remove the bumps at the nodes. To flatten the nodes, place each one in a metal vise and file it down level with the enamel on the outer surface of the cane. The upper

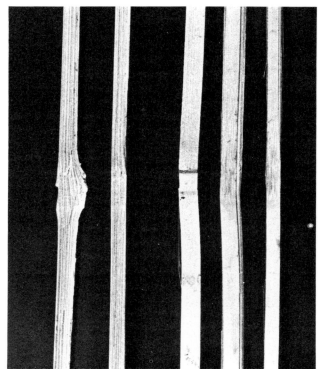

Tonkin cane will split along the grain, producing wavy strips. On the left is the side view of a node as split from the culm. The second piece has been leveled inside and out. To maintain fiber continuity, split the culm (third piece, enamel face), file the nodes level with the surface of the enamel (fourth piece), then heat-bend the strips over an alcohol lamp until they are straight (far right).

Bamboo

Bamboo is technically a grass—and the fastest growing plant in the world. Researchers have clocked some of the Orient's 1250 species at a growth rate of nearly 4 ft. a day. The type used for fly rods *(Arundinaria amabilis)* is cultivated on high, windy bluffs where a less hardy plant would fail. It grows hollow, its ¼-in. walls reinforced by solid plugs every foot or so at the nodes. The 3-in. diameter stems break through the ground and shoot up to 40 ft. tall in just two months. After this initial spurt, the walls toughen over the next 5 or 6 years until they are densely packed with long, resilient fibers. If you break a piece of high quality bamboo, the fibers will stand out in a bundle of 6-in. lances. Poor quality bamboo breaks leaving fibers only half-an-inch long. The growing conditions are part of the difference, and nowhere are they better than in a 25-sq. mile area around Tonkin, China. Tonkin cane is currently available after a 50-year hiatus in trade with China. While synthetics such as fiberglass and graphite fiber may match its lightness, stiffness and strength, they can't match the beauty and traditional appeal of Tonkin cane.

surface is now level (as shown in the photo, left), but the strips are not yet straight. Straightening the nodes is not easy, but it's critical—we want the longest fibers possible in the finished rod. If you leave a little crook or bump in the node area, the plane will rip the fibers there, undercutting the cane, which will weaken the finished fly rod.

We straighten the strips over an alcohol lamp, wearing gloves. At each node, hold the concave underside of the strip over a low flame until it becomes pliable. Then you can bend it straight. Easy does it. Too much pressure or too little heat will crack some of the fibers in the strip. The flame may scorch the underside, but these areas will be planed away.

Preliminary planing and removal of enamel—Each strip must now be planed to a tapered triangle. We use two planing forms. The first, shop-made from hard maple, has a 90° V-notch, oriented 30° to one side, 60° to the other. This V will hold a rectangular strip with its enamel side down, so a 60° angle can be planed on one of the inner sides. Don't plane the enamel face. It is the strongest part of the cane and it must be conserved. When you've planed one side of the strips to 60°, they're ready for another planing form, this one with a 60° V-notch. You can make a 60° wooden form. The easy way to do this is to joint two 1-in. by 2-in. maple boards (5 ft. long, more or less) and then bevel them to

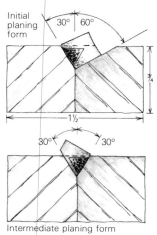

the correct angle on the jointer. Place these beveled edges together to form a V-groove. Then taper the edges of the boards until the groove has the correct size and degree of taper. The width of the faces on each strip should conform to column C in the rod-taper chart (p. 103). Fasten the boards together, and you will have a non-adjustable form—good for a rod or two. This form is so easy to make that you might as well make a few of them in graduated sizes, saving the most precise form for those last few strokes with scraper or plane.

Instead of a series of wooden forms, I now move over to the same adjustable machinist-made form that I use for final planing. I set it wide enough to give the strips good support. Place a strip, enamel face down, snugly in the 60° V-notch and plane a 60° angle on its other inner side. Then turn the strip in the form and lodge it with the enamel surface up. We want to remove as little as possible from the enamel face, but we have to true it so it registers in the form. Using a scraper (since the plane would remove too much material) take two or three passes to remove the thin layer of enamel, making the surface true and flat and bringing out the nice grain beneath. There will be no further scraping or planing on this surface.

Binding and heat-tempering—When you've planed the sides of each of the 18 strips down to approximately 50% larger than the rod designer's specified tapers, they're ready for a heat treatment to dry and toughen the cane's fibers.

The six-strip sets for each of the three rod sections (one butt, two tips) are nestled into shape, then tightly wrapped with cotton twine by a binding machine—this will keep them from warping when they're in the tempering oven. The binding machine operates by means of a stout linen cord wound into a double loop over the hex section, as shown in figure 2. A weight suspended from a pulley provides the proper tension, a couple of pounds. Turning the crank moves the rod section along a cradle. Cotton cord, feeding off its spool through a tension device, wraps around the hex in a spiral for the full length of the section. When you reverse the linen loop you get a snug criss-cross wrap.

After the three sections have been bound, they're heat-treated in an oven to temper the bamboo and increase its resilience. My oven is a length of heavy-gauge aluminum pipe with a perforated propane-fueled gas pipe underneath. The three rod sections are placed inside and rotated by a small rotisserie motor. The sections cook for two hours at about 350°F. Then they're turned end-for-end for another two hours. The once-tight binding is now quite loose, because the cane has shrunk from moisture loss.

Final planing—With the binding removed, the 18 strips are ready for final planing. My final planing form, made of twin steel bars, as shown in the photo on the following page, has screws set every 5 in. One-eighth turn of a screw opens or closes the notch 0.001 in. A 30° angle on the inside edge of each bar forms the required 60° V-notch. The angles are machined on both top and bottom of the form—one for thin tips, the other for hefty butt sections.

I start with the screws of the form adjusted larger than the final taper specifications. I gradually plane the sections, still oversize, to their required taper, alternating the two inner faces. I prefer to begin with a Stanley No. 60 low-angle plane set to take a 0.004 in. or 0.005 in. shaving. Measure the shavings with a micrometer—you want to know how much bamboo you're removing with each pass. Keep the plane level with each sweep to maintain a perfect triangle. Flip the stock between every couple of passes.

You will note that the strips are becoming quite flexible when they are bent in one plane (perpendicular to the enamel face), yet are much stiffer when bent sideways. The hexagonal glue-up will maximize this directional stiffness.

The strips will still be considerably oversize. What we are aiming for is not the final size but the correct taper, so we can take full-length passes. When the taper is right to within 0.010 in., go to a precise plane such as the Stanley No. 9½. This tool, like the low-angle plane, must be razor sharp. Taking off shavings of 0.002 in. with each pass, work each strip down. It's a slow process. Check each strip frequently with a micrometer, as you plane the bamboo down closer and closer

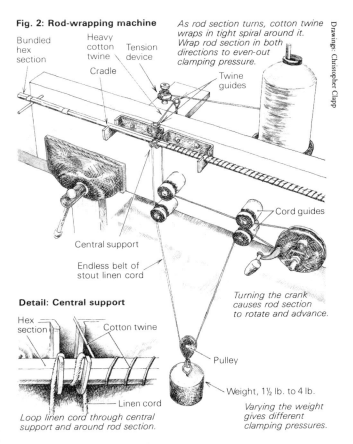

As rod section turns, cotton twine wraps in tight spiral around it. Wrap rod section in both directions to even-out clamping pressure.

Drawings: Christopher Clapp

Bundled hex section

Heavy cotton twine

Tension device

Cradle

Twine guides

Central support

Endless belt of stout linen cord

Cord guides

Turning the crank causes rod section to rotate and advance.

Detail: Central support

Hex section

Cotton twine

Pulley

Weight, 1½ lb. to 4 lb.

Linen cord

Loop linen cord through central support and around rod section.

Varying the weight gives different clamping pressures.

toward the perfect taper. Perfection is when each strip conforms precisely to the design at every 5 in. along its length.

Gluing—Now bundle the thin strips together in proper order, and bind the sections with masking tape every 10 or 12

Tape

inches. Using a razor blade, cut each tape so the hex can be opened up and spread apart on the bench. Saturate the exposed edges with strong waterproof and heat-resistant glue, using a wide bristle brush. I use Nelson's Urac 185 or Elmer's resorcinol glue. A 7½-ft. rod with an extra tip will show more than 60 linear ft. of glue line. The Urac formula is honey-colored and thus invisible. The Elmer's will leave a purplish threadline joint.

With glue applied to all surfaces, fold the strips back into their hex shape (the tape indexes them) and wipe off excess glue. Then re-bind the section with the wrapping machine and wipe off as much squeezed-out glue as you can. Before hanging the section up to dry, hand-twist out any curves to minimize the final straightening procedure later on.

Filing and sanding—After the glued sections have cured for two or three days, cut and pull off the glue-hardened binding

A machine shop made this adjustable steel planing form. The top side is for rod tips, the bottom for butts. Turning the screws adjusts the form to 0.001-in. tolerances at 5-in. intervals along its length.

Heat from an alcohol lamp softens the bamboo fibers and allows rod straightening. Keep the rod moving to avoid scorching it.

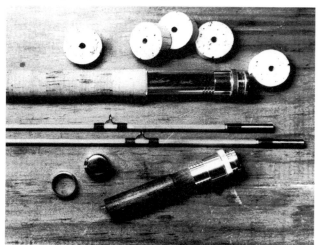

Cork rings, reel seat, mesquite insert, and butt cap, together with a finished rod grip that has been turned to shape.

cord. With a smooth file, clean off the bumps and humps of remaining glue. But remove only glue residue, don't disturb any of the cane surface. Take care to file flat and not to round any edges off the hex. The butt is fairly easy to file, but filing can be mighty tricky on the last 15 in. of each tip, where the diameter goes down to 0.063 in.

Now run a sanding block with 400-grit sandpaper over each surface. Finish up with 600 grit. When I have completed this painstaking business of filing and sanding one of my rods, I usually knock off for a day or two and go fishing.

Final straightening, fitting of hardware and reel seat— Now sight down each of the flats for any bow, curve or twist. Over the alcohol burner, heat the cane where it requires corrections, moving the section actively to keep from scorching it. When cane and glue become pliable, crooks and curves can be eased straight. This trick also works to straighten older rods that have gone out of shape.

To mount the nickel-silver ferrules that will connect the rod sections, round off the edges at the end of the hex in the lathe. Removing too much bamboo will result in a weak point in the rod, so don't use too small a ferrule size. You want a pretty tight slip-on fit. Glue the ferrule on with a five-minute epoxy, which sets with slight expansion. Handgrips are made from cork rings that can be bought with various sized holes through their centers. Boil the rings to soften them, slide them up the butt section, and glue them together. When they have dried, turn them down on the lathe to shape. Then fit the reel seat and its wooden sleeve insert (I use mesquite).

Wrapping of guides, varnishing— Well, you now have a handcrafted split-bamboo rod blank. All that's needed for completion is to wrap on the line guides, install a tip-top guide on each tip and varnish the cane. Most commercial rods use strong but bulky nylon for wrapping, but a fine split-

L.U. BEITZ # 012

This adjustable guide-wrapping tool keeps the thread at the proper tension. Turning the rod produces a silk-smooth wrapping that secures the guide. The wrapping will be varnished for protection.

bamboo rod calls for traditional pure silk. A rod-wrapping tool, which works like a simplified, finger-powered version of the binding machine, keeps the correct tension on the thread by means of a clutch or by the pressure of a spring against the spool. The rod section is turned against this tension until each guide is snugly wrapped in place. For the sake of tradition, I've added decorative intermediate windings between the guides on this rod—they are not necessary for strength.

After you have wrapped the guides along the rod section, at appropriate intervals which you can judge from the full-size photograph, treat the silk with a coat or two of color preserver to prevent its darkening when it's varnished. Then clean the bamboo thoroughly. It is traditional to write the maker's name, the rod length and the weight line for which it was designed on the flats of the shaft near the grip. Use permanent India ink; the rod may last a hundred years.

Varnishing is another meticulous job and must be done in a warm, dust-free room. I use tung-oil varnish and red-sable brushes. While the varnish is drying, I make a ferrule plug to keep the female ferrule free of dust or dirt when the rod is not in use. I use ebony, but any hardwood will do. Turn a 2-in. long, ⅜-in. sq. piece to about 1/32 in. less than the male ferrule, leaving a larger decorative knob on one end. Then glue on a ½-in. wide cork ring to the part that will fit into the female ferrule. When it's dry, turn the cork to the exact size of the ferrule, and cut off the excess wood.

In between coats of varnish (three or four coats applied over a span of some six or eight dry days) you can sew a cloth sack partitioned to fit the rod sections. An aluminum tube for storage and travel will protect your work. □

Les Beitz makes split-bamboo fly rods in Austin, Texas, researching and working from rod specifications that were developed by the craft's most notable designers. He spends about 95 hours working on each $600 rod (1982 price).

Forms, tapers and materials

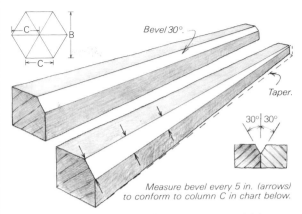

Measure bevel every 5 in. (arrows) to conform to column C in chart below.

To make the tapered planing form, square-up and joint two hardwood pieces. Bevel a corner of each piece to 30° for its full length. Then taper one face of each piece, so the bevel will match column C in the rod-taper chart. Fasten the pieces together to form a tapered V-notch. Several graduated sizes can be made for planing the rough bamboo to final size.

Rod taper specifications:

Below are the measurements for the fly rod that appears full size along the bottom of these pages. It is a medium Garrison pattern, designed for a No. 5 line. The intermediate silk windings between the guides on the L.U. Beitz rod are decorative and optional.
—Column A measures inches from the tip to the butt.
—Column B is diameter of the rod from face to face.
—Column C is the width of the bevel in the form.
—Ferrule size is ¹³⁄₆₄ in., and the guide spacing may be judged from the photograph.

	Tip Section			Butt Section	
A	B	C	A	B	C
0	0.063	0.036	50	0.206	0.119
5	0.078	0.045	55	0.220	0.127
10	0.100	0.058	60	0.233	0.134
15	0.117	0.068	65	0.247	0.143
20	0.131	0.076	70	0.260	0.150
25	0.144	0.083	75	0.275	0.159
30	0.156	0.090	80	0.306	0.177
35	0.168	0.097	83	0.309	0.178
40	0.181	0.104	90	0.317	0.183
45	0.194	0.112		No. 4½ top guide	

Sources:

☐ **Tonkin cane culms:** Harold Demarest, Box 238, Bloomingdale, NJ 07403.

☐ **Steel planing form and binding apparatus:** Hoagy B. Carmichael, 59 Davids Hill Road, Bedford Hills, NY 10507. Carmichael can also supply his book (see below).

☐ **Reel seats, ferrules, aluminum tubes:** Rodon Manufacturing Co., Inc., 123 Sylvan, Newark, NJ 07104.

☐ **Guides, tip-tops:** Perfection Tip Company, 4550 Jackson Street, Denver, CO 80216.

☐ **Silk thread, cork rings, color preserver:** E. Hille, The Anglers Supply House, P.O. Box 996, Williamsport, PA 17701.

☐ **For further reading** about rodcrafting and Everett Garrison's influence, see Hoagy B. Carmichael's *A Master's Guide to Building a Fly Rod* (see above). For the views of an innovative fisherman/rod-designer with tournament flycasting in mind, read Charles Ritz's *A Fly Fisher's Life*, 1979, Max Reinhardt, London (out of print, but worth a search).

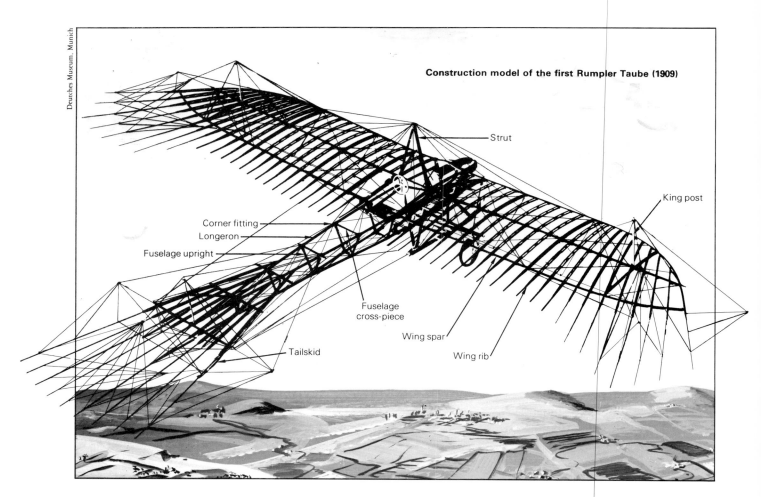

Deutches Museum, Munich

Construction model of the first Rumpler Taube (1909)

Strut

King post

Corner fitting

Longeron

Fuselage upright

Fuselage cross-piece

Wing spar

Wing rib

Tailskid

Flying Woodwork
Light, strong wood got first aviators aloft

by Leonard E. Opdycke

Icarus, the first flyer on record, built his machine from wax and feathers—a disastrous construction. Since his attempt, builders of flying machines have relied on stronger stuff. The materials may vary, but all airplanes have certain features in common. All have wings, commonly one (monoplane), two (biplane) or three (triplane). Almost no biplanes and triplanes are being built today, except as reproductions. Most airplanes have one to three hulls, called fuselages, although no multifuselage design is currently being built. Only the so-called "flying wings" have no fuselages, and none of these are being built today. All except the flying wings have some sort of tail surface, commonly a fixed horizontal surface or stabilizer, combined with one or two moving horizontal surfaces or elevators, and a fixed vertical surface, or fin, combined with a moving vertical surface, or rudder. Landing gear is also common to all planes, consisting of some combination of wheels, or wheels and skids. The airframe has to be braced internally and externally against stresses in all directions.

In general, the airplane is suspended from its wings and dragged by its propeller. As a result, all parts must be braced against the direction of the drag.

Initially, bamboo and wood were used for airframes, with steel or aluminum fittings at the connections. Bamboo could serve as spars or struts only, so it was accompanied from the beginning by wood planks, beams or sheets. Bamboo worked fairly well for small spars if it was braced with struts and wire. The joints in the cane were weak, and were often bound with tape and glue; sometimes the partitions were reamed out and wood dowels inserted to stiffen the cane. Metal fittings had to be used for joining bamboo to wood struts or to other bamboo, and for anchoring the wire bracing; these fittings were often cast aluminum. Struts, usually upright in the airstream,

Leonard Opdycke is editor of the journal World War I Aeroplanes *(15 Crescent Rd., Poughkeepsie, N.Y. 12601). He is currently building a reproduction of a 1914 Bristol Scout.*

From *Fine Woodworking* magazine (March 1979) 15:68-71

were soon made of wood, usually spruce, instead of bamboo, because the wood could be carved to a streamlined shape. After a while the spars, growing thicker and requiring more complex sections, were also made of wood.

By 1912 or so, aircraft structure had pretty much stabilized, although even then there were experiments in all-steel and plywood monocoque structures. But the average airframe used wood primarily in compression, in rectangular bays diagonally braced with piano wire or cable, sometimes with tie-rods. The corner fittings were made of stamped steel plates, and the whole bay was tightened with turnbuckles. Wings were made with two main spars divided in the horizontal plane into the same cross-braced rectangular bays and separated in the two vertical planes with pairs of struts and more diagonal cross-bracing. The whole airframe, then, was a series of more-or-less parallel wooden girders (spars and longerons—the main fuselage beams) separated by wooden cross-members in compression (fuselage uprights and cross-pieces, wing struts and ribs), the whole thing held in compression with miles of wire and wire-tighteners and dozens of steel fittings everywhere. Monoplanes with thin wing sections required one or more king posts both above and below for the many anchoring wires and, sometimes, the wing-warping wires as well. Only when the wings became thick enough to allow internal vertical diagonal bracing did the outside wires finally disappear.

Early efforts attempted to lighten the wood in the airframe in several ways. The first was to vary the type of wood used, depending on stress and location. A frequent solution was to use ash for the forward longerons on the fuselage where the engine would be mounted on steel plates or bulkheads, where the weight was generally needed to overcome tail-heaviness, and where the landing gear and wing attachments were located, along with their bracing wire attachments. Both the longerons and cross-pieces in the rear were spruce. Ash was also used for packing-blocks and small beams requiring special strength, like the tailskid or the seat mountings.

Tapering spars and longerons where possible was another method used to lighten wood in small airplanes. The longerons began in front at about 1³⁄₁₆ in. square and tapered to only ¾ in. square at the tail. Since the uprights were all in compression, simple stress analysis showed that the point of greatest strain was in the middle, so the uprights could frequently be tapered down at each end where they fitted into the corner-plates.

Another method was to rout out the faces or sometimes the corners of the wood spars or struts. Such routing became sculpturesque, leaving rectangular or flat sections for the attachment of fittings, and scooping deep into the faces of spars or longerons. As the routing became more elaborate and the wood pieces became larger, it was easier to build up special sections through lamination or other forms of assembly. Toward the end of World War I it became increasingly common to combine lamination and special fabrication processes with bending and molding, especially of plywood, resulting in some handsome streamlined outer forms. One of the continuing problems with this process was the inadequacy, or rather the irregularity, of the gluing. Hide glues were generally used, and they were not dependably water-resistant. There are, however, reports of glued joints being as solid today as they were in 1918.

The last generally used lightening method was to cut out

holes where design analysis allowed, usually in steel fittings and sections of plywood, the latter appearing in wing ribs and fuselage bulkheads. The cutouts in the steel engine-mounting plates could be reinforced with flanges either pressed out or welded on, and the webbed ribs were strengthened with varying forms of spruce capstripping.

Attempts to strengthen this standard wire-braced structure with panels of plywood nailed and glued across the fuselage bays were unsuccessful, because the wood and the metal expanded and contracted unevenly, and such multimedia frames could pull themselves apart. Airframe design then went in several directions. The first was a combination of welded or bolted steel tube, usually in the front of the fuselage, bolted to a standard wood and wire rear end. The second was the development of modern all-steel welded tube structures. The third was an all-wood frame, often in the form of a Warren truss with diagonal wood struts for bracing. The corners were held together with plywood gussets that were nailed and glued on. Sometimes the wood frame was covered with planking. Fuselages could be planked with thin strips riveted together like a clinker-built boat, or with long tapered strips edge-butted and screwed and glued to the

Wooden fuselage of late World War I Rumpler 7D1 fighter plane under construction.

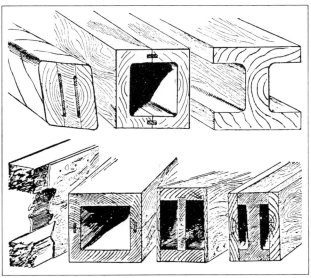

Types of wing spars often used in wooden aircraft: composite wood and steel, wrapped with tape (top left), box spar (top center) and I-beam (top right). Spars in the bottom row are of built-up wood, commonly used with European aircraft.

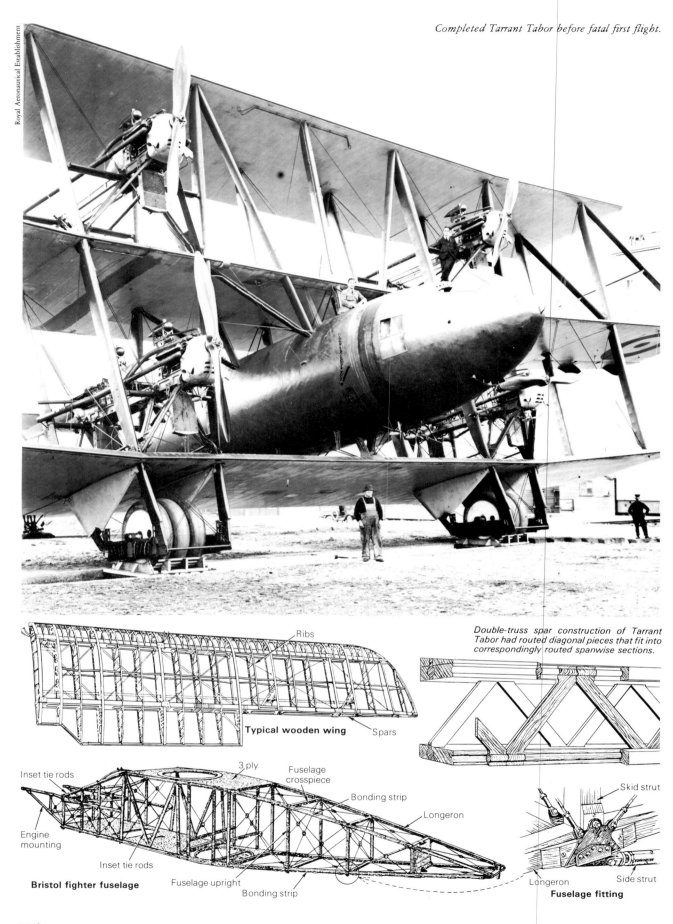

Completed Tarrant Tabor before fatal first flight.

Ribs

Typical wooden wing

Spars

Double-truss spar construction of Tarrant Tabor had routed diagonal pieces that fit into correspondingly routed spanwise sections.

3 ply

Inset tie rods

Fuselage crosspiece

Bonding strip

Longeron

Skid strut

Engine mounting

Inset tie rods

Bristol fighter fuselage

Fuselage upright

Bonding strip

Longeron

Side strut

Fuselage fitting

frame. They could also be planked with small rectangular sections of plywood edge-butted or scarfed and screwed and glued to the frame, or with long tapered sheets of thin plywood wrapped diagonally in several layers and glued to each other, or with big concave panels of plywood layers that had been molded and glued under pressure.

Wood plays very little part in aircraft structure today, except for home and reproduction builders, who usually use one or more of the methods listed above. There is one current general-aviation aircraft builder, Bellanca, that still uses wooden wings: These are now made with plastic-impregnated molded plywood, which results in smooth, strong and virtually weatherproof rivet-free surfaces. The most famous wooden aircraft of modern time, Howard Hughes' great Hercules (the "Spruce Goose") lies in perfect condition in its temperature and humidity-controlled hangar in Long Beach, Calif. It was designed to avoid the use of critically short materials and to make use of factories and craftsmen not already in the aircraft business. It flew once. At one point it was to be scrapped, and several museums had plans to exhibit sawn-off sections of the huge 320-ft. one-piece wooden wing.

Long before the Hercules was thought of, aircraft engineers were beginning to struggle with the problems of larger sizes and weights. One of the most remarkable attempts was begun in April 1918, at the Royal Aircraft Establishment at Farnborough, England, where the Air Board had granted permission and support to W.G. Tarrant, a building contractor, to design and construct two enormous wooden six-engined triplanes, using his method for constructing wing spars and fuselage bulkheads. Most of the first aircraft was built in his own works, and then assembled in the great shed at Farnborough. One of the features of the design was the enormous monocoque streamlined wooden fuselage, free of all diagonal bracing and cross-wires, suited both for bombing and military transport work, and also post-war airline work. Another feature was the girder design that appeared everywhere in the structure. This design required only small lengths of wood, more easily obtained, dried and inspected than the longer lengths commonly used.

The wings, spanning 131 ft. 3 in., required some special design work. The normal spar construction of the period for small aircraft was a single length of spruce, tapered at the tip and sometimes routed between the ribs. Frequently, due to the difficulty in getting long lengths of aircraft-grade spruce, the spar would be laminated of two or three thinner pieces, which could themselves be made of shorter lengths scarf-jointed. Larger or heavier machines used box spars with two span-length beams, often themselves laminated. The two beams were joined vertically with two sheets of ply, sometimes cut with the grain at 45° to the span. Such box beams had to be carefully varnished inside, leaving clean sections for gluing; they could not later be inspected for water damage, and sometimes became unsafe. It was such a beam in the wooden wing of a Fokker Trimotor that failed, killing Knute Rockne, and brought about the end of wooden wings in American transport aircraft. But in the big Tarrant Tabor, the box spars were so big that vertical ply webbing would have buckled, or would have been too heavy. So Tarrant designed the elaborate double-truss shown in the diagram at left, using the specially routed small diagonal pieces laid into the correspondingly routed spanwise sections. The enormous wing struts were built up as long hollow boxes of Oregon pine,

Royal Aeronautical Establishment

Rear end of Tabor fuselage under construction.

square in section, and streamlined with long thin sheets of molded plywood fairing on each side.

The fuselage, measuring 73 ft. 3 in. long, was built on a series of wooden girders made in ring form, similar to the wing spars. The rings were held together with full-length longitudinal fuselage spars; neither the rings nor the spars had to be cut away where they intersected. The fuselage was covered in four molded quarters, each quarter being assembled on its own separate mold first, and then scarfed and glued to its neighbor on the Tabor frame. The four skins were made of two diagonally wrapped layers of 1½-in. wide wooden strips, each from 1 mm to 3 mm thick, depending on their location.

The weight of the three wings, together with their struts, was 8,900 lb.; the fuselage frame without the landing gear weighed 4,050 lb. The completed aircraft ready to fly weighed 44,672 pounds, certainly the largest and heaviest aircraft of its time.

The rest of the Tabor's story is very sad. On the day of its first flight the two pilots in the nose taxied out onto the field, ran the engines, did a straight tail-up run, then opened up the top two engines fully and the giant triplane went over on its nose, crushing the front end of the fuselage. Both pilots were killed. The project was abandoned and the second Tabor was not completed. The Tabor, perhaps like the Hughes Hercules, was an attempt to carry woodworking beyond what was practical at the time. The growing expense of aircraft-grade woods, the fabrication time and the difficulties with weatherproofing, even with modern glues and finishes, make it less and less likely that the wooden airplane will ever return in quantity. But for the individual craftsman or restorer, wood is still the exciting and living material that it was for the Wright brothers in 1903.   □

Making It Big
Constructing and carving large sculptures

by Federico Armijo

Quite by chance in 1972, after completing a commission to design and make sculptured door handles and benches for a shopping mall in Phoenix, Ariz., I got a phone call from the developer asking if I would be interested in creating a large-scale sculpture for the Sears Court in the same mall. I was elated. I'd always wanted to do a large-scale piece, and here was my opportunity. Two months later my studio completed the 20-ft. high oak sculpture. It weighed six tons and required a crew of seven people to build.

Though the following is a description of how I planned and built another of my commissioned pieces, the sculpture for the Broadway Court in Phoenix, the basic design and construction techniques I'll talk about can be adapted to handle almost any large-scale project requiring long, heavy laminations. For example, variations of the clamping form I'll describe later could be used to make laminated beams for curvilinear roof structures or other architectural components. A good source of general information about large laminated beams is Chapter 10 of the *Wood Handbook,* published by Forest Products Laboratory, U.S. Dept. of Agriculture. Write to the U.S. Government Printing Office, Washington, D.C. 20402, and ask for stock #0100-03200.

The Broadway Court sculpture is 30 ft. high, weighs two tons and is made of Philippine mahogany. Its design began with several meetings with the developer and the architect; the conversations centered around aesthetics, materials, costs and scheduling. Then I visited the site. Architectural drawings are helpful, but if you're going to comprehend the possibilities of the space, there's no substitute for seeing where the sculpture is supposed to go.

Designing a large-scale sculpture demands care and continual sensitivity to the relationship between the materials used and the composition of the piece. One mistake in judgment or planning, given the huge size and weight of such a sculpture, can turn into a serious financial loss or, even worse, injury to a workman or a bystander. Many things therefore must be considered—milling and fabricating the laminations, mobility of component pieces, transportation and setup of machinery, insurance and costing. And all of these factors must be kept in mind while you are still designing the piece.

The first step in the actual design is to construct a scale model from a series of

Paul De Gruccio

Large-scale sculpture demands careful planning and close cooperation between builder, client, structural engineer and installation crew. Above, Armijo's oak sculpture for the Sears Court in Phoenix is 20 ft. high and weighs close to six tons. Right, 30-ft. sculpture of laminated 8/4 Philippine mahogany at the Broadway Court Mall in Phoenix leans 5° and is supported by an I-beam that runs through the central spine and is anchored in a concrete footing below. The cement base was poured after the sculpture was installed.

sketches. Sometimes, if the original idea is strong enough, I bypass the sketching process and compose directly on the band saw, working with suitable-sized scraps of wood. The modelmaking phase is slow, often taking a week or more to fully develop a pleasing design. Experience has shown me that for a formal presentation to a prospective client, it's best to have prepared two or three different models.

Because selling a design to a client involves a lot of subjective considerations on both sides of the bargaining table, you should have several "design packages" in your presentation, each of them within a different price range. Don't underestimate the importance of your presentation, and try to have a ready answer for every question you might be asked about design, materials costs and time schedules. Winning your client's confidence is necessary to getting his contract.

Once I'd gotten the contract for the Broadway Court sculpture and the model had been approved, I hired a structural engineer to study the model and to determine the minimal required sectional properties for static and dynamic stresses. His job was made more complicated because the sculpture leans 5° from vertical in one direction. On completing his assignment, he handed me 10 pages of computations, and I was legally bound to follow his specifica-

tions in every detail. After purchasing several thousand board feet of 8/4 Philippine mahogany, we began to laminate the stock for one of the sculpture's 30-ft. long central beams and its adjoining wings or fans. Fortunately the design allowed for uniformly dimensioned plies throughout, though the length and thicknesses of the different laminations varied. So our initial step was to glue up the stock for the plies by edge-joining 4½-in. widths of the 8/4 stock, which we cut alternately into 14-ft. and 16-ft. lengths. The boards were clamped so that the end-grain joints were staggered, and we reinforced these with dowels for added strength. When gluing was complete (we used Titebond throughout), we surfaced each ply to a finished thickness of 1½ in., having oriented the grain during assembly to minimize tear-out as the laminated boards were fed through the planer.

While one part of the crew was making the plies, another group was busy preparing the forms for laminating the curved beams, which when glued together would form the basic shape of the sculpture. We began by making the base of the form from a number of wood pylons (figure 1, detail A). We spaced these 2 ft. apart, then aligned them with a level/transit and bolted them to the concrete floor. Next we bridged the pylons with lengths of 6/4 fir planks, which we bolted onto the tops of the

pylons (figure 1). We double-checked with the transit to make certain the base was absolutely level and perfectly straight. Wedges driven between the floor and pylons let us bring the whole length of the base into a single plane. This required a lot of tedious work, but to build an accurate, workable form requires a true base, else you'll end up with twisted laminations.

With the base complete we built the curved superstructure that would determine the arc of the lamination (figure 2). Fir uprights (2x8s) were cut to appropriate length, depending on the part of the arc they supported, and then nailed to the ends of the pylons and cross-braced with short lengths of 2x4s. On the back side of the form, every other upright was cut to extend 12 in. above the surface of the form. Their purpose was to align the stacked laminations and to provide vertical clamping surfaces. The bed of the form we made from 6/4 fir planks sheathed with ¾-in. plywood to smooth out the junctures and add strength to the curved platform. Figure 2, detail B shows an end elevation of a typical pylon assembly. To finish the form, we covered it with plastic film so that glue squeeze-out from the laminations would not foul its surfaces.

First we laminated the two halves of the central supporting beam, each half consisting of six plies 1½ in. thick, 9 in. wide and 30 ft. long. Each board was

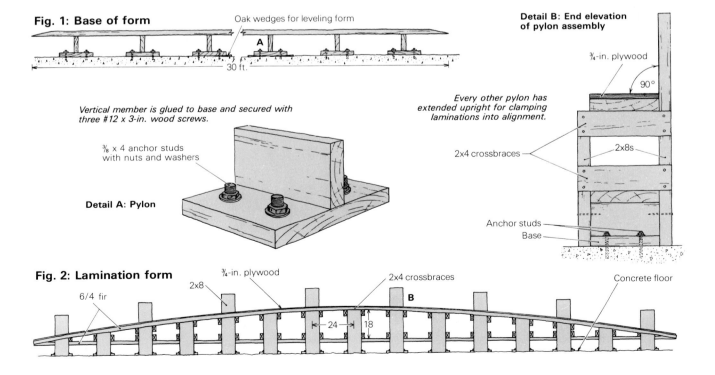

Fig. 1: Base of form

Oak wedges for leveling form

A

30 ft.

Vertical member is glued to base and secured with three #12 x 3-in. wood screws.

⅜ x 4 anchor studs with nuts and washers

Detail A: Pylon

Detail B: End elevation of pylon assembly

¾-in. plywood

90°

Every other pylon has extended upright for clamping laminations into alignment.

2x4 crossbraces

2x8s

Anchor studs

Base

Fig. 2: Lamination form

6/4 fir

2x8

¾-in. plywood

2x4 crossbraces

B

24

18

Concrete floor

scraped free of mill marks left by the planer, which was carefully tuned and adjusted to produce no snipes that would interfere with the strength of the glue lines. Making sure that all gluing surfaces were clean, we oriented the grain the most advantageous way, staggered the butt joints in the plies and stacked the boards on sawhorses in their proper sequence so the first one on would be the last one off.

Gluing up a beam of this size required close cooperation among the three team members to eliminate unnecessary, time-wasting movements and foul-ups that might ruin the lamination. Gallon glue bottles were prepared, and 100 bar clamps were adjusted and placed into positions along the form where they could be gotten to quickly, and the whole procedure was rehearsed to ensure that everyone understood what to do and when to do it. To keep the glue from setting too quickly, we stopped the airflow through the shop. One person poured a substantial bead of glue down the center of each ply, while another spread it evenly. Then all three men placed the ply on the form. Spreading the glue and stacking the plies was done as rapidly as possible, and when all six plies were stacked, we clamped them to the extended uprights (figure 3) using battens to align them before we clamped them down to the curved surface of the form. The clamps holding the plies in alignment against the uprights weren't so tight as to make clamping downward difficult. We also used battens across the width of the plies to provide even clamping pressure. To avoid bubbles and ensure uniform distribution of the glue, we began clamping the beam in the center and proceeded outward to the ends.

The next day we removed all of the clamps and scraped off the excess hardened glue. Then with the help of roller tables to support the curved beam, we ran it through the thickness planer to joint the edges. The second half of the main beam was made in exactly the same way, and when it too was jointed with the planer, the two surfaces mated perfectly. Before gluing the two halves of the main beam together, we slotted the bottom portion of it to receive an I-beam, which became the supporting member of the sculpture.

After bolting it in place we glued the two halves together. Then the six curved laminations for the wings, each two plies thick, were glued to the main beam, three on each side, and staggered to form blanks for curved surfaces. The other half of the sculpture was fabricated in the same way, only it was not as long. These two halves were not to be joined until the entire piece was installed at the site, where they would be connected by a central mass of shaped wood and four 1-in. tempered steel bolts (figure 5).

Being interested in making the wings graceful, slightly concave and convex forms along the length of the sculpture, I devised a sliding jig for my portable circular saw and router (figure 4). Ingenious variations of this basic jig can produce more complex forms, but the simple one I made slid along the length of

Fig. 3: Laminating the beams

Align plies by clamping them with battens against the uprights with light pressure; then, working from the center out, clamp the plies to the form using battens across the top, one for each pair of clamps.

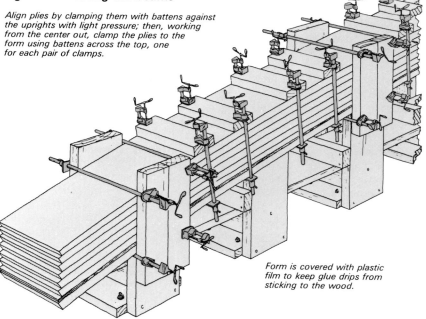

Form is covered with plastic film to keep glue drips from sticking to the wood.

Fig. 4: Jig for saw and router

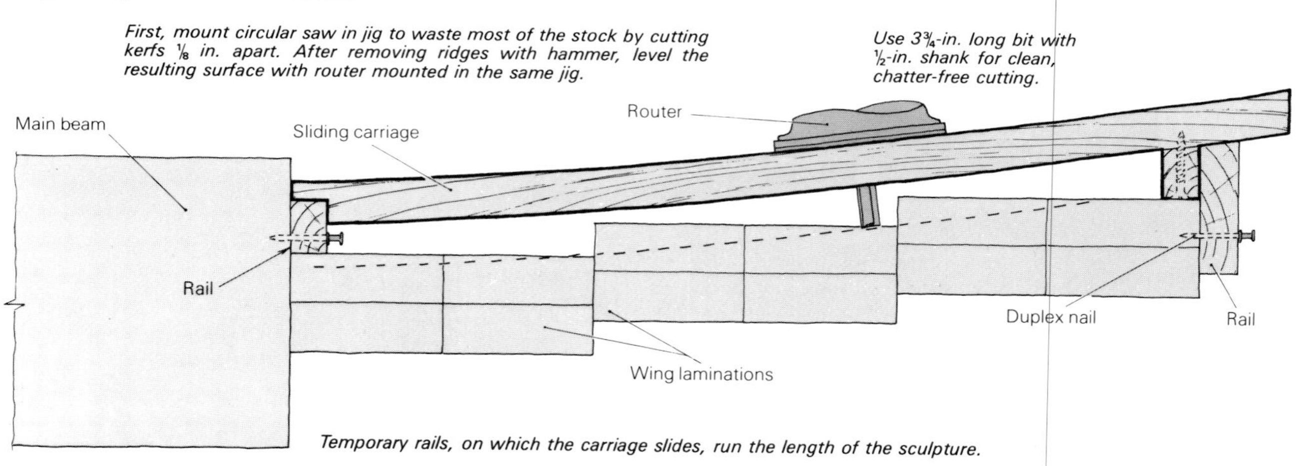

First, mount circular saw in jig to waste most of the stock by cutting kerfs ⅛ in. apart. After removing ridges with hammer, level the resulting surface with router mounted in the same jig.

Use 3¾-in. long bit with ½-in. shank for clean, chatter-free cutting.

Main beam

Sliding carriage

Router

Rail

Wing laminations

Duplex nail

Rail

Temporary rails, on which the carriage slides, run the length of the sculpture.

the sculpture's wings and allowed me to cut a series of kerfs across the grain with the circular saw. Spacing the kerfs about ⅛ in. apart, it was easy to remove the rest of the wood by striking along the grain with a hammer. Next I mounted the router in the jig and leveled the surface using a ½-in. straight-face bit with a ½-in. shank. All four wings of the sculpture were treated in this manner, and we simply turned the jig over to produce the convex surfaces.

Turning the sculpture over was not an easy matter so we finished one side of each half before attempting to invert it. This was done with the use of an overhead chain hoist. To sand the surfaces, we used pneumatic sanders with foam-backed discs, which minimize swirl marks and gouges. In appropriate places we used vibrating sanders, and where necessary we sanded by hand. We started with 80-grit silicon-carbide abrasive and then finished the surfaces with 120-grit paper. Given the size of the piece and the fact that I was going to lacquer it, further sanding and smoothing seemed a waste of time.

First we stained it with Watco "decorator red." Then we stained with "black Danish oil" to get the look of vermilion (padauk), followed by a coat of Thompson water seal. Next came a coat of sanding sealer, followed by two coats of Sherwin-Williams moisture-resistant lacquer, rubbing between the sprayed coats with 400-grit wet/dry paper. With a wool wheel charged with buffing compound, we burnished the entire piece, then applied a final coat of natural Watco oil wiped off with a soft cloth. The sculpture glowed with a subdued luster.

We loaded the sculpture on a flatbed truck with a forklift in the middle of a blizzard. It was no fun at all. But the next day, sculpture and crew arrived intact in Phoenix.

We rolled the two halves of the sculpture into the mall on heavy-duty dollies where the crane operator could pick them up and hoist them into position—using a 12,000-lb.-test nylon strap. Since cranes and their operators charge by the hour, I had met earlier with the operator, and we had rehearsed the whole installation process using a model of the sculpture. So the actual installation went quite smoothly. Figure 5 shows how the sculpture was mounted on its concrete footing.

For a project like this, I can't overemphasize the importance of communication and collaboration. It took the combined efforts of more than 50 people to see it through to the end. And from beginning to end, every aspect of the project was insured. Workmen's compensation protected the craftsmen in the shop from accidental injury; a general liability policy covered non-employees in the shop on business, and a product liability policy protected me against possible loss from an injury caused by a defect in the sculpture. I also required certificates of liability from the transportation company and from the crane company, and all of these policies and certificates became part of the contract file. If you decide to build a large-scale sculpture, be prepared to spend as much time in your office pushing paper as you do in your shop working wood. □

Federico Armijo, of Albuquerque, New Mexico, makes sculpture, furniture and doors in wood, metal and stone.

Fig. 5: Sectional elevation of sculpture

First half of sculpture

Second half

A——————A

1-in. tempered bolt

Wood plug

I-beam

Concrete base was poured after sculpture was installed.

3,000-lb. concrete base

Concrete footing

85°

¾-in. anchor bolts

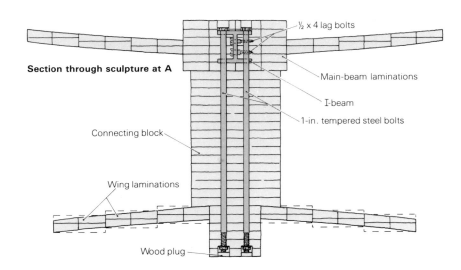

Section through sculpture at A

½ x 4 lag bolts

Main-beam laminations

I-beam

1-in. tempered steel bolts

Connecting block

Wing laminations

Wood plug

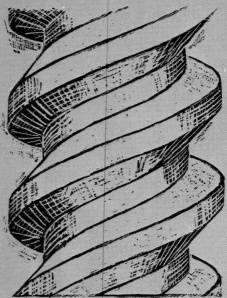

Finding no dies large or coarse enough, Lewis McClure, left, hand-carved the wooden screw for his replica of the Gutenberg printing press.

GUTENBERG REVIVED

This working replica of Johann Gutenberg's wooden press sprang from Whitney Seymour's lifelong fascination with printing. Seymour, an attorney and avocational publisher, asked his woodworker neighbor Lewis McClure to build the press. Working from old picture postcards, McClure drew up plans, had them confirmed by a German museum that owns another replica, and documented the entire project in a book entitled *The McClure Press*, published by Seymour's Lime Rock Press in Salisbury, Conn.

McClure had to overcome the same technical obstacles that dogged pressmakers in the 1450s—fabricating the heavy wooden screw that presses paper against the inked type. Finding no modern taps and dies up to the task, McClure followed the example of Gutenberg's contemporaries: he laid out the screw on a fat dowel, then painstakingly carved it by hand, using dense bubinga so the threads would survive the stress the screw would be subjected to in use. "I spent about a third of the two years it took to make the press working on the screw and the nut it runs in," says McClure. "The rest was child's play."

McClure's 32-page book gives construction details for a ⅝-scale reproduction of the original. His replica is on display in Salisbury's Scoville Library, which is, appropriately, the oldest public library in the United States.

From *Fine Woodworking* magazine (January 1985) 50:116

Framing Pictures
Choosing and making suitable moldings

by Jim Cummins

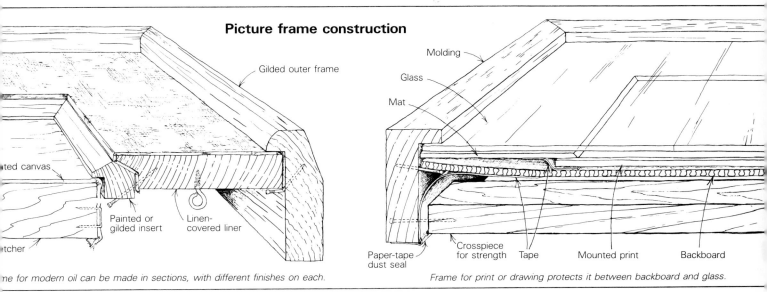

Picture frame construction

Gilded outer frame

...ted canvas

Painted or gilded insert

Linen-covered liner

...tcher

...ne for modern oil can be made in sections, with different finishes on each.

Molding

Glass

Mat

Paper-tape dust seal

Crosspiece for strength

Tape

Mounted print

Backboard

Frame for print or drawing protects it between backboard and glass.

Illustrations: E. Marino III

Department-store frames, mass-produced, rarely succeed at matching up with works of art that are made one at a time, nor do they readily suit rooms and tastes that are personal and distinctive. Custom-made frames, on the other hand, seem extravagantly priced, and there's no guarantee of satisfaction there, either. You and the framer can pick a molding that suits the picture just fine, but in your home it may not look quite right. The next time you need a frame, you might try making your own. You can end up with something you're satisfied with, save money, and perhaps develop an interesting sideline. After all, none of the separate operations involved in framing a picture is very difficult.

Frames are commonplace because they're necessary. Once we realize what's required of a frame, we are on the way to making one, because a frame's functions determine both its construction and its visual design.

Function and design—Design in framing is related to function—not only physical function, but also the visual and emotional function the frame plays as it affects the picture, the room, and the viewer. Consider four functions as you choose a frame: protection, enrichment, focus and transition.

Protection: A watercolor cannot be cleaned, so it is sealed up behind glass in its frame. Pastels need protection not only from dirt, but also from physical contact, because they smudge easily. Needlepoints can go either way; while cleaning them may mean restretching them, glass does interfere with the appreciation of their texture. An oil painting should be cleaned every 20 or 30 years and is protected by its removable coat of varnish. Glass in this case is not only unnec-

essary, its hardness and reflection would diminish the texture and lucidity of the painting. Hence oils are left unglazed. The frame may still protect an oil by preventing the wooden stretcher the canvas is mounted on from warping or by actually holding together multiple panels (as in the case of some Renaissance paintings). In the same way, the frame protects a flimsy piece of paper by providing a stiff mat to which the paper is attached. The strength and size of the frame depend somewhat on the weight of the picture, although in the case of a large poster—in its pure form a piece of artwork originally meant to be pasted to a wall without a frame at all—the frame may be made with hidden supports that allow its visible part to be minimal.

Enrichment: Stone-age cave paintings have no formal edge, the cave itself is the frame for the art. Egyptian or Greek murals were framed by the rooms in which they were done. Picture frames, as we think of them today, began in the Renaissance: the artist scooped out a board to paint on, leaving the edge full for stiffness—frame and painting were one piece. Painting was then regarded as more of a craft or a science than an art, and the frame was within the artist's sphere of work. The workmanship in the gilding, inlay, carving and design of the frame reflected his general competence, and encouraged a good price for the art. Eventually, artists left the framing to others; by the time of the High Renaissance, it wasn't unusual for the frame carver and gilder to make as much money as the painter himself. The artist, however, probably designed the frame. Money aside, a frame still reflects on the art in it. Paintings rich in color and subject matter, suggesting opulent times, require complementary frames;

rustic frames suit rustic subjects. Most drawings look best with a mat and narrow frame, but a Picasso line drawing, just a few strokes, can have all the richness of an oil, and be able to balance an ornate gold frame without losing its character. *Focus:* Since the style of a painting, its color, texture and period, should be balanced by the frame's design, the frame, in effect, makes the painting into a larger object. The frame's continuity provides a visual field that defines the subject matter and directs the eye into it. The regularity of the frame first draws the eye to it, then sends it into the picture. A frame therefore should attract the eye—with gold leaf or fancy carving, for example, or a mat under glass. The proportions are important. Visual effects that are too much the same, such as a 2-in. frame with a 2-in. mat, trap the eye. Too colorful a mat or too bright a finish will do the same, which is why some frames are made to look faded and old. Many modern works of art are designed to catch the eye without much of a frame. A broad, uninterrupted wall may be all that a strong oil painting needs to be seen at its best. The frame merely covers unsightly staples, tacks and ragged canvas at the picture's edges. Lack of focus is the reason that lumberyard moldings don't work well for frames. They are designed to shoot the eye along, to make it wing outward in order to enlarge rooms and break up flat, blank walls. This is the opposite of what a frame should do.

Transition: While a painting is an object with merit of its own, a framed painting doesn't do well without reference to the room in which it hangs. This is why paintings in museums often look absurdly overframed. Their period frames need period rooms. The frame's color, reflection, richness or simplicity, even its width, must relate to and be seen along with its surroundings. A room without a framed painting is no worse off than a framed painting without its room.

Measurements—If we look at a basic frame we can start to tie the abstract and the practical together. Look at a frame from the back, and note the different ways it can be measured.

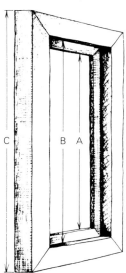

A is "sight size," what you'd see from the front. B is "glass size" or "rabbet size," the size to which the mat, glass and backing are cut. We normally call a frame by its rabbet size, although the rabbet is cut $\frac{1}{16}$ in. or so larger than the mat and glass, to allow a comfortable fit for standard-size glass. If the frame is too tight, the mat and backing will soon buckle, and the glass may break or force open the corners of the frame. Frames for oil paintings are usually made $\frac{1}{4}$ in. oversize, room for pegging out the stretcher that keeps the canvas free from ripples and sags. C is "overall size," but the term can be misleading because the length of the molding needed for a frame is the sight size plus double the width of the molding. An 8x10 frame (rabbet size) made from a 2-in. wide molding needs sides that measure about 12 in. and 14 in., so instead of 3 ft. of molding, you actually need almost $4\frac{1}{2}$ ft. because of the waste at the miters.

Cutting miters—Professional framers have specialized machines for making miters. These include guillotine choppers that cut a 90° notch, making two miters at once, Lion trimmers that neatly slice one miter at a time, 45° cutoff saws radial-arm saws, and industrial pneumatic and hydraulic monsters weighing tons. But you can cut a perfect miter on a tablesaw, if you forgo speed and automatic accuracy.

First, check that the sawblade is parallel to the miter-gauge groove in the table. A blade that is not parallel will seem to work fine when the gauge is on one side, but on the other side it will force the molding away during the cut, changing the angle. And vice versa. This is one reason for making sample cuts and checking that two pieces meet to form a 90° angle. If the molding is forced away from a nominal 45° on one side, then the other side (the side that will cut the true angle) must be fudged to compensate. Worse, moldings of different widths and profiles will be pushed different amounts along the gauge fence, so no single gauge setting will work for all shapes if the blade itself isn't parallel to the table grooves. Carbide blades, with their wide teeth, allow a little latitude if the cut can be completed before the molding contacts the side of the blade. Set the blade high, and push the molding only as far as necessary to complete the cut.

Check that the miter gauge is a good fit in the groove. Sometimes the grooves themselves are different sizes. I've had to peen the slide to fit one groove, and file the other groove wider. If the gauge wobbles, you can't expect an accurate cut. If the gauge binds, even a little bit, you can't tell if the work is binding—a potential disaster. Once your gauge runs smoothly, you can improve it further by adding a backup fence that's L-shaped in cross-section. It will support both the back and the bottom of the molding as it is being cut. Make the backup fence long, then cut off its ends at 45°, with the gauge sliding in its grooves. The fence ends now mark the

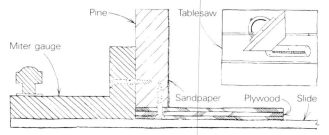

line of cut. Glue fine sandpaper or non-slip tape to the fence so the molding won't slide while you're cutting it.

Never trust the angle indicator on the gauge, since any error will be multiplied by the number of cuts in the frame. Instead, make a template for setting the gauge. Either scribe lines on the saw table (use a sharp pencil or a machinist's scratch awl) or take a piece of 8-in. wide plywood long enough to contact the full miter-gauge fence, and lay out a square and its diagonal on one end. With the gauge set to 45°, nibble toward the diagonal line, adjusting the gauge until the cut is exactly on the line. This is a perfect 45° cut—from now on you can use it to set the miter gauge. With the saw turned off, raise the blade as far as it will go. Place the template against the miter fence and slide it over to the sawblade. Rotate the miter gauge until the diagonal evenly meets both the front and the back of the blade, then lock it. Flip the template over to reset the gauge for the opposite cut.

Instead of resetting the miter gauge every time you make a

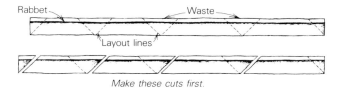

Rabbet —   — Waste —

Layout lines

Make these cuts first.

corner, saw all the right-hand miters at once. If you are taking more than one piece from a length of molding, mark it to make sure the miters go in the right direction and that you are leaving enough for waste. It's easy to come up short, and embarrassingly easy to cut a miter that goes the wrong way. Remember that every cut will leave the piece larger on the side away from the rabbet. Locate and draw the first miter on the back of the molding, and make a clear mark inside the rabbet where the miter line meets it. Then write the rabbet size to be cut on the back of the wood. This helps avoid cutting three 24-in. pieces and one 30-in. piece for a 24x30 frame—another familiar pitfall. Carefully lay out the rest of the rabbet marks and sketch in the miter marks as you go. When you saw the molding, cut on the marks in the rabbet— the drawn miter lines are just reminders.

Some moldings won't sit flat on the saw table, and special pains must be taken to keep them from rocking during the cut. Make blocks and wedges as needed. Extra-deep moldings (like some shown in the box on page 119) may be too high for your saw. Cut these flat on the table, with the blade tilted to 45°, and the miter gauge set to 90°, as shown in the drawing below. Always use a sharp, fine-tooth blade. Dull blades will only force the molding away, while coarse ones won't leave a good gluing surface.

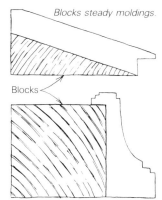

Blocks steady moldings.

Blocks

Joining frames—In spite of perhaps a dozen other methods that can be used, nearly all picture frames are joined with glue and nails. You start by making two Ls, and then join the Ls. In our shop, the process goes like this:

We put one side in a machinists' vise (padded), and hand-hold the other side in position to drill holes for the nails. This allows the corner to tighten to the maximum when we set the nails. We don't use those 90° vises that hold two sides together for gluing and nailing, because the corners will never be tighter than you can set them in the vise. If you make it a habit always to put the long side in the vise and glue the short side to it, you can avoid joining the sides in the wrong

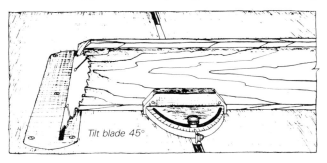

Tilt blade 45°.

order, which results in a diamond shape instead of a rectangle—if you can get the miter together at all. Put glue on both miters to be joined. We use ordinary yellow glue. If you prefer to use white glue, let it thicken first; as it comes from the store it's too thin for miter joints. Apply enough glue so that it squeezes out along the entire glueline when the joint is nailed, then wipe off the excess with a wet rag.

If you are right-handed, support the short side with your left hand, and pick up an electric drill with your right. Drill holes for the nails or brads, not allowing the corner to shift. We use 1x18 brads for small frames, 4d finishing nails for larger frames, and up to 10d where extra length is needed. In soft woods such as pine, use a #56 drill bit for the brads, and a #50 bit for all finishing nails. Angle the holes a little to get the most purchase. A common mistake is to start the nails too close to the corner, which results in no gripping power at the head. Use your three-dimensional imagination to keep wood around the nail. If a 4d nail seems a little short, and a 6d nail might split the wood, just set the 4d nail deeper. On very wide frames, where even a 10d nail is too short, you

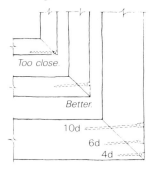

Too close.

Better.

10d

6d

4d

can hold the inside of the miter tight while the glue dries by stapling it from the back in addition to the nails.

Support the weight of the loose side while it's in the vise. At no time should the free side hang by the nails. We rarely nail across corners from both sides, because it's the glue that keeps the corner together, not the nails. If a corner pulls up tight when the first nails go in, that's all that's necessary. Cross-nailing, or using elaborate metal fasteners, can weaken a corner by imposing additional strain and shock. Force applied to pull up a corner just builds stress into the joint, and sooner or later it will crack.

Repeat the process with the other two sides, and then join the two Ls. If the frame is not too heavy, just support the free L as you did the free side. Handle the Ls carefully—you have a good, tight corner when you set the nails, but until the whole frame is joined any shock or twist will open it. We have a tilting vise that lets us support heavy Ls on the table. You can block up the free end; but it's usually easier to hold things than to set up blocks or to tilt the vise. Helpers are rarely any help.

Join a complete frame at once, don't let the Ls sit around and take the wrong set. If you finish joining the frame before any of the glue has dried, the stresses will even out, the frame will be stronger, and it will dry square. Clean the glue from the rabbet, or it may break the glass when the picture is being fitted into the frame.

Glass—Glass comes in several varieties. Ordinary window glass weighs about 19 oz. per sq. ft. Picture glass is 15 oz. to 17 oz. per sq. ft.—more expensive, slightly clearer, and usually available only in frame shops. The trend is to use window glass for most frame jobs. Non-glare glass has been surface-treated to reduce reflection, and is best used in direct contact with the art—any separation, as caused for instance by a double mat, will blur the image. Allowing glass to contact artwork is chancy because moisture condensation can cause

Photos: Karen Sahulka

Predrilling nail holes guards against splitting, ensures good starts in the right direction for maximum purchase. One side of the frame is held in a machinists' vise, the other is steadied from underneath by hand, the forearm resting on something solid.

Cabinet joints evolve to meet changing requirements for strength. In picture framing, the nailed miter continues to hold its own.

Free side of the frame must be hand-supported at all times until the corner comes out of the vise. Nails pull the miter as tight as it will go—tighter than a corner vise can be set.

damage. Non-glare glass, incidentally, won't perform miracles in really bad situations—it has an overall "bloom" which you can't see through at all. Try changing the height of the picture or letting it tilt out from the wall. If your frame is very large, your local hardware store may stock the size only in double-strength window glass—too heavy for framing. You would be better off using Plexiglas.

Matting—Artists' supply stores sell matboard, differentiated from cheaper illustration board by its surface finish and light-colored paper core. Standard matboard sizes are 30 in. or 32 in. by 40 in., and 40 in. by 60 in., with a smaller color range in the larger size. Until recently, colored matboard was made by gluing cover sheets to a pulp center that contained acids left over from the paper-making process. These acids would gradually seep out through the cut bevel, and nearby portions of the art would turn brown. Museums and collectors don't like that at all. Instead, they use board made from 100% cotton fiber (rag), and processed without acid residues. A new type of matboard, called Alpha-mat, is chemically buffered to have a long, acid-free life, and comes in over fifty colors.

Sometimes artwork is simply laid on top of a matboard (to show the edges of the paper), but usually, after a color has been chosen to suit the artwork and its surroundings, an opening with a beveled edge is cut in the board. This bevel can be cut by hand or by machine. In our shop, we use utility knives (with a new blade for each mat) and a metal straightedge. Lay out and cut matboard from the back. Make neat corners by overshooting the mark—a slight overcut won't be obvious. The mat border is usually from 1 in. to 4 in. wide. A stiff backboard (usually corrugated cardboard or acid-free Fome-Cor) protects the back of the art and keeps it flat in the frame. The art can be attached to it using small hinges or straps of acid-free paper and paste at the top edge, so it hangs and can expand or contract in the frame. Don't use masking tape—it will soon dry out, turn brown and stain through to the front of the paper.

Mounting—Posters, eye-catching outdoor advertising, were designed to be pasted to walls without frames at all, so they don't require fancy mats. But posters are typical of many lightweight papers that need mounting (pasting to a heavier board) to keep them from wrinkling badly. Valuable works of art should never be mounted—collectors and museums insist on maintaining the paper in its original condition. But for most of us, wrinkles interfere with our enjoyment of what we hang on our walls. There are many modern mounting systems using special-purpose adhesives and boards that will stiffen artwork without damaging it. A frameshop can advise you whether or not to try a particular mounting job yourself. If you want to try, it's a lot like veneering and just as difficult to fix when something goes wrong. Use wheat paste, dampen the print, countermount a similar paper on the back of the board to equalize tensions, weight the art down while it dries, and make sure it's really dry before removing the weights.

Stretching—Often, instead of gluing something down, you can stretch it. Oil paintings on canvas are usually stapled to stretcher bars. If you are stretching an oil, make sure the stretcher is square, then staple pieces of cardboard to the back corners to keep it square while you work. It is more important to keep the tension even than to try to get the painting

A mat cutter's grip presses the backs of the fingers against the surface to hold the bevel angle. Practice canting the knife until the blade travels straight, pulled by the entire body, not the arm. Once the grip is mastered, a straightedge can be used for peace of mind. Blades are cheap—use a new one for every mat.

super-tight. Stretch needlepoints and crewels around heavy cardboard or ¼-in. plywood. If you stretch a crewel over art-ists' stretchers, put matboard behind the fabric, otherwise the wood may show through the stretched-open weave.

Fitting and hanging—Putting the picture into its frame is called fitting. The sandwich of glass, mat and backboard is usually held in by the pressure of small brads in the rabbet.

Twist.

Go through twice.

Oils can be toenailed into their frames. Weight adds up—if regular screw eyes don't seem strong enough, try mirror hangers, or fasten a sturdy crosspiece behind the frame. Double the picture wire if you can't find any heavy enough. Most pictures that fall off walls do so either because the hanger failed in the wall or because the frame was split when the screw eyes were being in-stalled. Drill a hole before you force the screw eye—splits only get worse.

Set the screw eyes about a quarter of the way down from the top of the frame. The lower they are, the more the picture will tilt from the wall. Wind the wire twice through the screw eye (so it won't slip), and don't make the wire too tight—a tight wire has only about half the strength of a loose one.

Wherever you hang the picture you have framed, make sure that there is enough light to see it, and enough room to stand back and enjoy it. Having done all this work on the frame, I'm afraid that you will never be able to see it the way others will. To them it should be almost invisible. "Is that a new painting?" is the best thing visitors can say about your framing. "What an interesting frame . . ." means that you haven't quite got it right. □

Jim Cummins, associate editor at FWW, *has owned the Vasco Pini Frame Shop in Woodstock, N.Y., for nearly 20 years.*

A tablesawn molding

The tablesaw is a versatile machine, even if you don't want to invest in a molding-head cutter. You can make most of the moldings shown in the box on p. 119 with a regular 10-in. blade. You can also make good copies of many other designs that strike your fancy. One customer recently brought in a painting from the 1920s, still in the frame in which it had won a national award. I copied the frame as shown in the photos on the next page.

I used sugar pine because it machines and finishes well. Harder woods can be used, but work should go slower, espe-cially when making coves. Wood must be dry, or you're wasting your time—miter joints open up quickly if the wood moves much, often within a week of when the heat comes on in the fall. A 60-tooth carbide combination blade leaves a surface I hardly need to sand. This blade can't be hurried, but you shouldn't let it burn the work either. Ripping with a coarser blade would be much faster, but I'd rather make the cuts right than sand and fuss with the molding later.

I don't like to do careful ripping like this on pieces that are more than 6 ft. long. There isn't enough control. In making this frame, one long side and one short side added up to about 4 ft. in length, so I worked with two 4½-ft. pieces. For a large frame, I make all the sides separately. I joint the stock square on two sides and then cut it to width and depth on the tablesaw. I make one extra piece, to see the results of each saw setting before risking the frame itself. This piece can be saved and used as a template for saw settings when you want to duplicate the molding. I make the piece about 2 ft. long to start, even though the final template can be as short as an inch or two. For the time being, the extra length allows you to cut off the ends as you go along if you don't like the way a test cut starts. Instead of measuring angles and doing a lot of mathematics, I usually sketch the profile on the end of the test piece and then set the blade and the fence to cut just shy of the line.

I make cove cuts with a shopmade adjustable-angle fence, which is shown at the bottom right on the following page. To get the idea of how it works, lay a board at an angle across the saw table, with the blade up about an inch and the saw turned off. Imagine that this board is the fence; sight along it and change the angle. Notice how the blade's profile changes from a circular cross-section (with the board at right angles to the blade) to a deep, narrow elliptical shape when the blade and board are almost parallel. If you run the work across the blade at any one of these angles, the shape you see is the shape of the cove you get. A smaller blade will give you a tighter curve, and tilting the arbor will make one side of the curve steeper. You can make molding without making the adjustable fence, by clamping the board to the table, but ad-justments are tedious and difficult to duplicate.

Start with the cove on the outside edge. A cove cannot be made taking a heavy cut. Once you have adjusted the blade height and locked the fence angle to conform to the drawing on your test piece, you must lower the blade until it barely clears the table. Then take away only about ⅛ in. or less on each pass until the cove reaches the depth you want. The test piece will quickly tell you if you are trying to do too much at once: if the stock rides up, or won't feed without pressure, or if the blade is being forced to bend, you must retreat, lower the blade, and try again. Your last cut should be especially slow and fine, to minimize sanding.

The straight cuts are all made with the regular rip fence. Notice that we leave good bearing surfaces for later cuts as we go along. This makes the work safer and more accurate.

Watch out that you don't trap narrow cutoffs between the blade and the fence—I've had them shoot out of the saw and stick into the wall behind me.

Save your scraps, you can build up other molding shapes from them later. Cut the rabbet last, then watch how a light sanding brings the profile to the line.

1. *Cove starts with a shallow cut using the angled fence shown at bottom right.*

2. *Five passes bring cove to its full depth.*

3. *Three straight passes begin to define the decorative rises.*

4. *Next pass takes salvageable waste.*

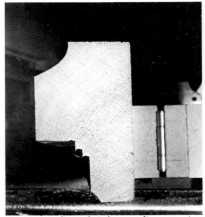

5. *Cove on lip, of tighter radius, requires two passes over a 6½-in. blade.*

6. *Angled top is removed with one cut.*

7. *Starting a decorative step on the outside. A second pass will deepen it.*

8. *Adding one more rise to the face.*

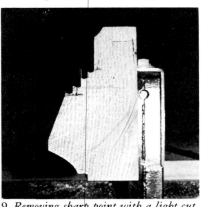

9. *Removing sharp point with a light cut.*

10. *Two cuts clear the rabbet—molding needs only light sanding to soften rises.*

Adjustable-angle fence allows a range of coves to be easily set and duplicated on the tablesaw using regular sawblades.

Moldings you can make

Many moldings can be copied on the tablesaw in a straightforward way. For those that can't, even intricate curves can be achieved without a molding-head cutter by chewing close with lots of linear cuts, and then fine-shaping with gouges and sandpaper. One advantage of making your own molding is that you can adjust the size to suit the job. You could frame anything, from a wedding announcement to the shotgun that inspired the marriage, by varying the proportions of these basic molding shapes, combining them and rearranging them. Wider moldings are frequently carved, finished with stain or gold-leafed. Interiors of boxes, and many liners, can be covered with fabric. —J.C.

When all else fails, chew down near the line, finish with ingenuity.

Modern shapes

Simple shapes suit modern pictures. These moldings can be scaled up or down, as the size of the picture dictates. Finished with stains, leafed, or just oiled, they can be used with mats and glass, or as outer frames for the liners at right when framing oils.

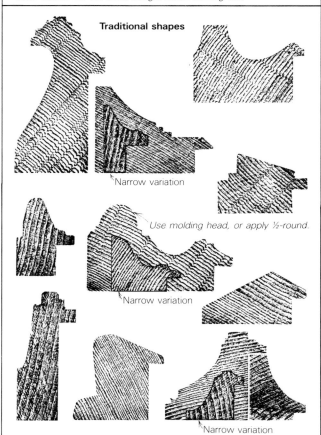

Traditional shapes

Narrow variation

Use molding head, or apply ½-round.

Narrow variation

Narrow variation

These profiles are typical of traditional frames for oils. Scaled down, they suit traditional prints. Sizes can vary from 1 in. to 4 in.; the angles steepen and the shapes simplify as the size becomes smaller.

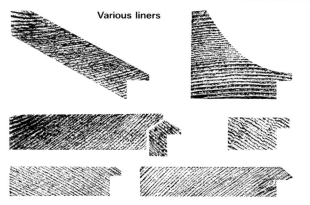

Various liners

Liners vary in width, are usually fabric-covered, and can take the place of mats for oil paintings. Use narrow liners (¾ in. or 1 in.) with wide frames as a visual separator; use liners up to 3½ in. wide with narrow frames. Liner and frame should not be the same width—it's a visual trap that distracts from the picture.

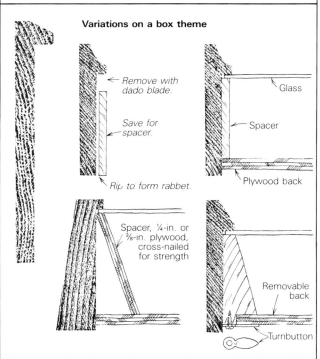

Variations on a box theme

← Remove with dado blade.

Save for spacer.

Rip to form rabbet.

Glass

Spacer

Plywood back

Spacer, ¼-in. or ⅜-in. plywood, cross-nailed for strength

Removable back

Turnbutton

Deep boxes like these can be used to frame arrowheads, medals, memorabilia. Boxes are enriching—a plate on a stand looks pretty good; framed in an octagonal box it looks like a treasure.

Index

FINE WOODWORKING
Editorial Staff, 1975-1986

Paul Bertorelli
Mary Blaylock
Dick Burrows
Jim Cummins
Katie de Koster
Ruth Dobsevage
Tage Frid
Roger Holmes
Cindy Howard
John Kelsey
Linda Kirk
Nancy-Lou Knapp
John Lively
Rick Mastelli
Nina Perry
Jim Richey
Paul Roman
David Sloan
Nancy Stabile
Laura Tringali
Linda D. Whipkey

FINE WOODWORKING
Art Staff, 1975-1986

Roger Barnes
Kathleen Creston
Deborah Fillion
Lee Hov
Betsy Levine
Lisa Long
E. Marino III
Karen Pease
Roland Wolf

FINE WOODWORKING
Production Staff, 1975-1986

Claudia Applegate
Barbara Bahr
Jennifer Bennett
Pat Byers
Mark Coleman
Deborah Cooper
Kathleen Davis
David DeFeo
Michelle Fryman
Mary Galpin
Dinah George
Barbara Hannah
Annette Hilty
Margot Knorr
Jenny Long
Johnette Luxeder
Gary Mancini
Laura Martin
Mary Eileen McCarthy
JoAnn Muir
Cynthia Lee Nyitray
Kathryn Olsen
Mary Ann Snieckus
Barbara Snyder

If you enjoyed this book, you're going to love our magazine.

A year's subscription to *Fine Woodworking* brings you the kind of practical, hands-on information you found in this book and much more. In issue after issue, you'll find projects that teach new skills, demonstrations of tools and techniques, new design ideas, old-world traditions, shop tests, coverage of current woodworking events, and breathtaking examples of the woodworker's art for inspiration.

To subscribe, just fill out one of the attached subscription cards, or call us toll-free at 1-800-888-8286. As always, **we guarantee your satisfaction.**

Subscribe Today!

6 issues for just $25

The Taunton Press
63 S. Main Street, Box 5506, Newtown, CT 06470-5506

NO POSTAGE
NECESSARY
IF MAILED
IN THE
UNITED STATES

BUSINESS REPLY MAIL
FIRST CLASS PERMIT No. 19 NEWTOWN, CT

POSTAGE WILL BE PAID BY ADDRESSEE

The Taunton Press

63 South Main Street
P.O. Box 5506
Newtown, CT 06470-9971

NO POSTAGE
NECESSARY
IF MAILED
IN THE
UNITED STATES

BUSINESS REPLY MAIL
FIRST CLASS PERMIT No. 19 NEWTOWN, CT

POSTAGE WILL BE PAID BY ADDRESSEE

The Taunton Press

63 South Main Street
P.O. Box 5506
Newtown, CT 06470-9971

NO POSTAGE
NECESSARY
IF MAILED
IN THE
UNITED STATES

BUSINESS REPLY MAIL
FIRST CLASS PERMIT No. 19 NEWTOWN, CT

POSTAGE WILL BE PAID BY ADDRESSEE

The Taunton Press

63 South Main Street
P.O. Box 5506
Newtown, CT 06470-9971